Emotional
Infidelity

Emotional Infidelity

How to

Affair-Proof

Your Marriage

and Ten Other

Secrets to a

Great Relationship

M. Gary Neuman

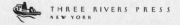
THREE RIVERS PRESS
NEW YORK

AUTHOR'S NOTE

The anecdotes and case summaries are drawn from my experience as a therapist, yet no individual is recognizable. Through the use of composites and substitutions I have protected the identities of those who have shared with me both professionally and socially. Any resemblance between the characters in this book and any persons, living or dead, is purely coincidental. The techniques to which I refer in this book have been used in my practice as a therapist for several years and with scores of clients.

Grateful acknowledgment is made to Warner Bros. Publications for use of the following material:

Lyrics from "You Needed Me" By Randy Goodrum. © 1978 (Renewed) Chappel & Co. and Ironside Music. All Rights Administered by Chappel & Co.; lyrics from "They Can't Take That Away from Me," Music and Lyrics by George Gershwin and Ira Gershwin. © 1936, 1937 (Renewed) George Gershwin Music and Ira Gershwin Music. All Rights Administered by WB Music Corp.; lyrics from "Those Were the Days," by Lee Adams and Charles Strouse. © 1971 (Renewed) EMI World Trax Music. All Rights Reserved. Used By Permission. Warner Bros. Publications U.S. Inc., Miami, FL 33014.

Published by Three Rivers Press, New York, New York.

Member of the Crown Publishing Group, a division of Random House, Inc.

www.randomhouse.com

THREE RIVERS PRESS and the Tugboat design are registered trademarks of Random House, Inc.

Originally published in hardcover by Crown Publishers in 2001.

Printed in the United States of America

Design by Elina D. Nudelman

Library of Congress Cataloging-in-Publication Data
Neuman, M. Gary
    Emotional infidelity ; how to affair-proof your marriage and ten other secrets to a great relationship
    M. Gary Neuman.—1st. ed.
        1. Marriage. 2. Married people—Psychology. I. Title.
        HQ734.N48   2001
    306.81—dc21   2001028956

ISBN 0-609-81000-6

10 9 8 7 6 5 4 3 2 1

First Paperback Edition

For my better half and soulmate, Michal.
Thank you for your love, wisdom, warmth, and magic.

There is that moment
When I am at peace
When I clearly see the love in my childhood
When I face the sadness of life and the loss of loved ones
When I am one with the wind and leaves
When I am rooted, deeply rooted
When I don't fear
When I don't hurt
When I smile eternally
When I know I can never be alone again, even after the moment

There is that moment
That I am with you, my dearest Michal.
Thank you for a lifetime full of moments.

When I refer to my writing or work, I often slip and accidentally say things like, "We felt" or "We discovered." It's not that I speak in the royal "we," but that I know that although only my name is listed as author, there have been so many who have contributed to this work through helping me develop as a person and writer as well as assisting directly with this work.

My dearest Michal, I could not recognize myself without you. I thank you not only for your unconditional love, intoxicating passion, enlightening life lessons, exceptional mothering of our children, and warm energy to help others, but for allowing yourself to be one with me—to look beyond you or me and work to find an "us" that travels wherever we decide to go together, forever. I am proud to be your partner. I love you with everything I am. Thank you.

I've always felt it peculiar to thank one's parents; how could what they've done for you be summed up in words? Yet I must thank you, Mom and Dad, for a lifetime of love and support. Growing up in this world has been a joyous experience that has allowed me to search for who I am. You offered me consistent love, warmth, and undying energy while respecting me enough to allow me to find my way, always letting me know you'd be there for me at every step. I am eternally grateful and will hopefully carry on your trait of giving and loving others.

My in-laws, Stuart and Rochelle, Mom and Dad, have shown me love in so many ways. You've given of your time and energy and have offered support and help in everything I do. The looks on your faces always tell me how much you care and I love spending time with you. You're always on call, whether to read through hundreds of pages of material within two days or to celebrate our happiest moments together. Thanks for always laughing so heartily at my jokes, even when I know they're not very good.

I have been blessed again and again with wonderful children. To Yehuda, Esther, Mikey, Pacey, and Danny, thank you for your love. You are so young yet so loving, warm, and wise. Thank you for your excitement over my work and the pride you take in what I do. Thanks for understanding when I'm overtired. I love you so much. I like you so much. You have enriched my life and my marriage to Mom. Your smiles are contagious, your curiosity is enlightening, your hugs offer peace, and your love makes me feel like the most special person on earth. I love you.

My editor, Betsy Rapoport, you have meant more to me professionally than you know. You believed in me, worked with me to develop this book, and have offered me a respect that has filled me with confidence and greater hope for helping others. Thank you for your positive outlook, upbeat nature, quick humor, and great discussions about my work, which have helped me better express myself. Even though we will never "do coffee," I deeply appreciate your help and friendship. Thank you for the energy you put into this book. You've made me look good once again.

I have yet to call my brother Craig any time of the day or night and ever have him say to me that he cannot talk right then. You're so kind and you don't even know it. Thank you for your brotherly love and advice. You give so much, take so little, and make it all look so easy. Thank you, Jeff, for always being a phone call away and letting me know that you care so very much. It means a great deal to me. And to Steve and Rich, who take such pride in my work and have opened so many personal doors for me in the past, and to my ever supportive brother-in-law David Smith, thank you for being so happy for me when things go right and letting me know you care when life gets confusing. Thanks to you guys for making me always feel like I'm part of the team.

My sister-in-law is the sister I never had, Jill Simons-Smith. You've done it again. From reviewing this book to traveling to the ends of the earth to speak on my behalf, you are always there to help and show that you care. Thanks, Sis.

Tina Constable, Katherine Beitner, and Rhoda Dunn, my P.R. friends at Crown. Thank you for your energy, excitement, and constant hard work to help me get my message out. Your creativity and professionalism is much appreciated.

Stephanie Higgs, who dealt with countless details large and small, and copyeditor, Mary Anne Stewart, who made great suggestions for the book and made it more pleasant to read, thanks to you, and to the many others at Crown Publishing Group that continue to work so hard to help me help others.

Greg Aunapu, although I'm sure you are surprised to show up in these acknowledgments, I thank you for that lunch we shared together when you said to me, "Stop talking about it already and just write it!" Thank you for reviewing my original proposal for this work as well as your friendship.

Jon Gordon, as always, thanks for your ever-supportive friendship, interest in my work, and helpful discussions about Secret #2.

Diane Debrovener, thanks for reviewing my entire manuscript and offering solid, helpful suggestions. I've always appreciated your talent for seeing a large body of work and making it flow as though it was a one-page poem.

Barry and Ami, thank you for your friendship and patient attempt to teach me golf and so many other things.

As always, thank you Bonnie.

Rabbi Tzvi Hersh Weinreb, Ph.D., Rabbi Yochanan Zweig, and Rabbi Joseph Rottenberg, thanks for taking the time to review certain chapters and offering me much appreciated feedback.

A special thanks to each of our very special Golden Couples who took the time and energy to share such personal information because they wanted to help others. Each of you are shining examples of the beauty marriage offers. We will learn a lot from you.

To the One who makes everything possible.

The first bond of society is marriage.

—Cicero

Love is powerful, magical, and hopeful. We wish for it, dream of it, and expect it. When we find it, our lives become saturated with meaning. Our hearts and bodies delight in its dance. We see only sunrises, flowers, and hope.

Then we get married.

It isn't the institution of marriage that's flawed. Rather, it is our culture's perspectives that need mending. Marriage's most fundamental needs have been cast aside for trendier concepts. Those who have found love and have kept their marriages secure and meaningful have a simple secret that the rest don't know, don't understand, and don't even want to consider; it takes a 110 percent effort. *I don't mean to imply that it's painful or painstaking effort. It's an effort of tremendous focus, a loving focus designed to help you nurture and connect with your soulmate.* It's about energy, the very heart and soul of love. Put all you've got into your marriage and you'll have it all, everything you could realistically hope for and even more than you could ever imagine.

I've spent more than fourteen years helping couples in marital therapy and audiences in my marital seminars learn the secrets of changing their focus and working hard to develop great marriages. I've even done the same as I've helped thousands of families in the throes of divorce. Couples have looked at me with desperation, sadness, and utter confusion about how to salvage their marriage. The details varied, but they all voiced similar problems. I bet you share some of them:

+ You have horrible fights that often begin over small issues. You can't discuss any item, large or small, unless you both see eye to eye on it.
+ One of you feels the other is angry and insensitive.
+ You have little or no sex. When you do have sex, it's unfulfilling and often just the wife's way of "appeasing" her husband.
+ You've grown apart. You don't feel like you have much in common anymore and have generally gone your separate ways emotionally.
+ One of you feels controlled by the other.
+ One or both of you are simply no longer attracted to the other. You see yourselves more as casual friends than as lovers.
+ You feel your partner has become a stranger. You no longer truly know each other.
+ You vehemently disagree on childrearing issues.
+ You resent past treatment by your spouse so much that you can't get past it and go on in your marriage.

I've helped countless couples with these issues turn their marriages around and create a successful, loving marriage by using the guidelines and techniques in this book. In these pages, I'll present to you my ten-week plan for a great marriage. However, you won't have to wait ten weeks to see results. Your marriage will change immediately once you start to read this book. Many of the couples I counsel find their marriages changing even one hour after hearing the concepts that follow.

Why am I so confident that you can change your marriage? Because I've seen it happen so many times before. When couples voice their heartfelt marital issues to me, they do so with extreme frustration. They often come to my office or my seminars with no hope. Yet I never share their desperation. In fact, I am filled with hope because, as lost as they seem, one or both of them have the most important ingredient for making a marriage work: *the desire to change.* One or both want it to work even if they have no clue how to accomplish this seemingly impossible task. It is that desire that will turn things around immediately. It is that desire that I cultivate to help every couple develop a plan for a great marriage. Whatever your marriage may be suffering from, the fact that you are reading these words tells me you want better. That's all you need to start the process of focus and working hard at making your marriage a more loving and meaningful one.

I recognize that the concept of marital work may be dangerous to the sale of a book. One of my dear friends warned me that it sounded like I would be asking a lot of people. After all, it's normal for us to want the easy ride. We want to hear how we can have an incredible marriage and raise our kids with little effort, how to make a million dollars while sitting home and eating chocolate cake (and lose weight too). You probably already lead a complicated, energy-sapping life. Now you have to hear some marriage counselor tell you how much more energy you have to put into your marriage?

Yet I have found, and want to share, the answers, as I know that a great marriage takes work. However, I'm not going to ask you to change *who you are* as much as request you to *change your focus*. Changing your attitude and focusing your energy into the right marital experiences will transform your marriage immediately. It has to, because it will change the dynamics of your relationship. Relationships can't stay still when somebody is pushing forward. Believe me when I tell you that just making the commitment to put forth the effort to create a great marriage will change your relationship forever. As you follow the "blueprint" outlined in this book, you'll notice changes immediately that will give you renewed confidence that you and your mate can create a great marriage, one beyond your expectations.

What Is a Great Marriage?

Marriage doesn't belong on a scale that can weigh effort, warmth, or love. It tugs at our deeper selves, offering us a hopeful belief that marriage is more than a union to procreate, create a friendship, or fit into the culture. Its potential reaches beyond what any one of us can explain. The closeness of spirit, the intimacy, the sense that you've known each other forever and then some, that you've somehow been completed as a person, defy simple explanations about love. We may not understand it, nor do we have to. But all of us want to feel it—all of it.

I'm not a dreamer. I understand the reality of life, and much of my book is about helping you have realistic expectations of love. But at the same time, I've had the most meaningful experiences in helping to change so many marriages from bored, loveless, or anger-filled relationships to loving, meaningful ones. I've witnessed the incredible power of love, faith, and hope that can change a marriage within days. There is nothing more wonderful than having two people decide to allow love to take over. It's a magical yet simple step. I've also worked to create my own great marriage, and it continues to be emotionally intoxicating. *I believe that marriage is both magical and achievable—but only if we put in the commitment of great loving energy and focus, not because we simply expect it to happen because we're in love.* When I speak in this book of the positive relationship I have with my own spouse, remember that it came because of years of great emotional energy put into reaching such a goal. And my marriage continues happily with the same focus on love. What I offer you is straight talk about a successful plan I developed from my experience working with struggling couples and from my heart to give you that same dream made reality.

There is no explanation for how love changes us. There is no reason for you to feel better just because your lover held you close without offering any concrete solution to your problem. But you do. There is no reason that life looks more colorful today than ever before just because you have love in your life. But it does. Love is important to every human being. It is the breath of life. It is the reason why life continues to be created.

Don't Be Satisfied with a "Decent" Marriage

I don't believe in "okay," "decent," or "solid" marriages. I'm against them. I believe in the human spirit and its need and ability to offer and receive love. *I believe only in great marriages, and that you should expect and reach for no less.* You may have picked up this book because you have a "poor" marriage, or just a decent one. You may be thinking, "Gary, I'd be happy if I could just get through tomorrow without a fight with my spouse. A great marriage? Now you're talking 'Welcome to Fantasy Island.'" I know the look. It's the one I see in my private practice daily. The couple in front of me wants relief from pain and struggles. They can't even consider what a great marriage might be. It seems too far beyond reach. The problem is that it doesn't work to simply put forth a little more effort with the hopes of changing your marriage from poor to decent. It doesn't work to try to find loopholes and rationalizations for why you shouldn't have to put too much energy into your marriage. It doesn't work to say, "Okay, we just won't talk about this anymore," or "We promise to stop fighting," assuming that once that happens, love will just fall into place. Love will fall all right, but not into any place near you.

Why commit yourself to mediocrity? Why focus only on "fixing what's broken" instead of striving for great? Relationships feed off the energy between two people who are trying to be close. Put in only half-hearted energy, and you'll get only half-hearted results. *It's not about just doing the right thing as much as it's about trying to do as much as you can.* That is why so many marital techniques fail. Changing just a part of your life, doing a little tweaking, or learning how to say something just right isn't going to make the difference. However, showing your spouse how important this relationship is to you by making a significant effort to love more and more does make the difference. By following the blueprint laid out in this book, you and your spouse will learn to develop a great and unique marriage. This plan will work because it will help you focus needed energy into your marriage, and it will send all the right messages about how important love is in your life.

Countless spouses have told me that they are no longer in love. "Can you find the love again after it's gone?" they ask in frustration. And although these suffering spouses can't see it, the answer is yes. I ask these couples to work toward creating a new relationship by following an actual plan. I don't focus only on the "problems" but show them how these problems began. The most well-meaning spouses can lose track of their marriage and become emotionally distant very quickly. I offer them a fresh outlook on an old, tired relationship. For many couples, trying to return to an earlier place in their marriage won't do. For most spouses, the key is to learn a whole new approach to love. After opening themselves to a new marriage, these spouses are absolutely amazed that within a week or two they can begin to see hope again.

For example, there have been many couples in my office who couldn't envision ever having meaningful sex with their spouse again. But it all changes when the relationship becomes one full of focus on respect and sensitivity.

"Can people really change?" these spouses want to know. It's the wrong question. The better question is, "Can my spouse and I change our focus and direction and bring out the best in each other?" To that I respond with a resounding "Yes!" Your marriage doesn't require you and your spouse to become different people, just better focused. I have never asked, nor will I ever ask, anyone to stay in a loveless or miserable marriage. I only suggest you make huge efforts to create a great marriage. You can find love again or discover a love you've never even felt before, if you make the commitment.

Love Won't Conquer All

It's the most dangerous lie that our culture has seemingly accepted: love is easy. We picture the Hollywood screen image of a handsome couple look-

How Much Time Do You Spend on Your Marriage?

Create a pie chart on a piece of paper and then graph the amount of time in your day you spend on different activities such as work (whether in or outside your home), parenting, sleeping, time for self, eating, exercising, and so on. If you're like most, you'll notice that none of the large chunks of time are dedicated to marriage. In fact, that part is probably no more than a sliver compared with the time you spend on other "important" activities.

Now draw a second pie chart outlining how you think your time should be spent. Draw more time for your spouse and marriage and begin to recognize that as a necessary goal to a happy marriage.

ing deeply into each other's eyes while romantic music kindles our dreams. We use these images to support what each of us desperately wants to believe: that love falls into place naturally and effortlessly. When our marriage doesn't turn out quite as we expected, we blame our spouse or look for other "outside" factors. We think, "If we can just stop fighting, if our kids would just be a little older, if my in-laws would just lay off a bit, if we just had more money . . . " It's not the "ifs" that stand in your way. It's your understanding of love and marriage.

Too many people have told me, "If it's this hard, my spouse must not be the right one for me." In every other aspect of life, we understand that we get out of it what we put into it. *If we operated our business the way we run our marriage, most people would be bankrupt.* Don't bankrupt your love. You want a successful business or a close bond with your child—you're told it takes effort. You want a great marriage—you're told "Don't worry, love will conquer all." It's a deeply inconsistent message. Marriage is no different from any other important goal.

Communication Is *Not* the Problem

I'm sure you've heard that people divorce because of communication problems. It's not that simple. As creator of the Sandcastles Program®, an international organization that offers support groups for children and parents experiencing divorce, I've had the opportunity to learn from over a hundred thousand children and parents who have completed the program. I've learned that couples who divorce are often wonderful communicators, people who always desired to love and be loved. They were as hopeful on their wedding day as I was on mine and you were on yours. Communication problems? They communicated so well that each spouse could tell you exactly what the other one would say about them. Very few would say, "I don't know what happened" or "I don't know what he or she wants." They weren't suffering from communication issues. They were suffering from a misunderstanding of some of the most crucial, fundamental messages and rules of marriage. Here are some common mistakes they made:

• They allowed too much emotional energy to be spent with people outside of their marriage.
• They maintained an emotional distance to avoid ever becoming too needy of their spouse.
• They constantly stepped on each other's toes over who was responsible for what.
• They didn't consider how their past might be affecting their marital relationship.
• They didn't make the time for their marriage or lovemaking, so they couldn't grow together.
• They lost focus on their marriage when their children were born.

These divorced couples did so many things that led them astray. Worst of all, many of them didn't think much about it as their marriage slipped away from them little by little. They only paid attention when things were getting bad. Once, they had it all. They were good communicators. They were in love and dreamed of a fantastic marriage. And love still didn't work for them.

These ex-spouses called out to me for help in finding the right path for future love. Like you and me, they wanted to succeed at marriage and were willing to do whatever it took. But they didn't have a *blueprint*. Books and marital advisors pushed them in all different directions. As one forlorn husband told me about his marital counseling experience, "I've never communicated so clearly about being so confused."

How Great Is Your Marriage?

Answer the following fifteen questions, then tabulate your responses to find out how your marriage stacks up.

1. Your spouse has gained ten pounds and says to you, "I've really put on a few pounds lately." You would say:
   A. "You could lose some weight. Since you brought it up, I'll admit that it's kind of a turn-off."
   B. "C'mon, you look great!"
   C. "Actually, I was wondering if you were in some sort of eating Olympics."
   D. "If you'd like, let's find a diet together. We could both use a healthier eating plan."

2. You receive a promotion or some other great news. You would immediately:
   A. Tell your spouse before anyone else.
   B. Tell your friends/colleagues, then celebrate with them.
   C. Tell the person you are hoping to have an affair with.
   D. Tell your mother.

3. A sexy person is flirting with you. You would:
   A. Flirt back, feel great, and say, "I hope we talk soon."
   B. Excuse yourself immediately because you remembered you "have an appointment."
   C. Excuse yourself by saying, "Excuse me, but my spouse just beeped me and we have plans."
   D. Flirt back and then ask this person to join you for coffee.

4. It's 9:30 P.M. on a Wednesday night, and you've just finished putting the kids to bed after a full day's work. You would:
   A. Turn on the television set and "zone out."
   B. Ask your spouse to join you for some quiet time—reading together in bed, taking a walk, or hanging out in the living room.
   C. Make lunches and clean the kitchen with your spouse.
   D. Leave to go to the board meeting for the organization you volunteer for.

5. You've just had a fight with your spouse. The first person you would discuss it with is:
    A. Your sibling.
    B. Your opposite-sex colleague.
    C. Your friend.
    D. Your spouse.

6. When a topic arises that you think your spouse and you will disagree on, you would:
    A. Only discuss it when you think your spouse is in a good mood so you won't blow up at each other.
    B. Act on your opinion and then tell your spouse.
    C. Open the topic up for discussion with your spouse while keeping an open mind.
    D. Avoid discussing it at all costs.

7. On an average week, you spend ____ hour(s) talking, having fun, or spending some enjoyable time *alone* with your spouse.
    A. Over seven.
    B. Between four and seven.
    C. Between one and three.
    D. Less than one.

8. When you think of your sexual relationship with your spouse, you think:
    A. It's loving and getting better. We really connect.
    B. It's boring.
    C. What sex?
    D. It's usually nice, and at times it's special.

9. The last time we were on a vacation alone for two nights or more was:
    A. Before we had kids.
    B. Within the last six months.
    C. Within the last year.
    D. Over a year ago.

10. When you think of your spouse, you primarily think:
    A. We deserve each other's craziness.
    B. He/she tries hard to be a good spouse. I feel we can get over the bumps.
    C. How did I end up with him/her?
    D. He/she is loving and sensitive and has a lot of goodness.

11. Your childhood was:
    A. Some good/some struggle, but you're not sure how it has affected who you are.
    B. Just about perfect.
    C. Some good/some struggle, and you can see some of the ways it has affected who you are.
    D. Some good/some struggle, but you can't think about it.

12. Your spouse would say that you:
    A. Really understand him/her and know what he/she needs to feel loved.
    B. Have little understanding of who he/she is but are willing to learn.
    C. Work diligently to be sensitive to him/her.
    D. Haven't a clue as to what he/she wants from you.

13. Your spouse and you strongly disagree on which school to send your child to. You would:
    A. Fight about it in front of your child and resolve it by one of you just telling the other to do "whatever the heck you want."
    B. Discuss it and find some compromise so that each of your goals are achieved to some degree.
    C. Fight about it in private and make up, then one of you will just give in.
    D. Discuss it and agree to find out more information by talking to other people about it, visiting other schools, and so forth.

14. You feel your spouse isn't doing his/her part in helping with the work at home. You would:
    A. Discuss it, assign each other jobs, and then within the next week fall into the same situation you're in today.
    B. Fight about it and have no resolution.
    C. Don't discuss it because you know it won't help anyway.
    D. Talk it out, design a plan of how each of you will take on certain roles, and basically keep to this plan.

15. You're depressed because your parent died unexpectedly almost two years ago. Your spouse would:
    A. Never criticize you and patiently wait for things to get better.
    B. Threaten to leave you or have an affair within the next few months if you don't snap out of it.

C. Constantly complain about you and tell you he/she doesn't know how much longer he/she can take it.

D. Take you to a therapist and tell you he/she understands and will always be there for you.

Scoring:

	A	B	C	D
1.	1	3	0	2
2.	3	1	0	2
3.	1	2	3	0
4.	0	3	2	1
5.	2	0	1	3
6.	2	1	3	0
7.	3	2	1	0
8.	3	1	0	2
9.	0	3	2	1
10.	1	2	0	3
11.	2	0	3	1
12.	3	1	2	0
13.	0	3	1	2
14.	2	1	0	3
15.	2	0	1	3

Your score: _____

Interpreting Your Score:

40–45 *Great marriage:* You understand each other. You have strong marital skills and are taking the time to use them. You have properly protected yourselves from outside unhealthy intrusions on your loving marriage. Continue doing what has gotten you here. Create realistic goals and plans for your future to ensure that you will continue to focus time and energy on your marriage.

25–39 *Solid marriage:* You are working hard to maintain and develop a great marriage. You have many healthy marital skills but need to provide your marriage with more "alone" time to hone these skills. Use this book to continue to focus on the importance of your marriage. Listen carefully to each other, and discuss each other's feelings. Talk about what makes your marriage special and how you could do even better.

10–24 *Rocky marriage:* You need to learn some new marital skills and discover that your marriage has to come first for it to survive. You are falling into traps causing you to feel lost in your marriage, with no plan to work it out. Don't give up. Focus intently on what your marital commitment must mean, and use this book to help guide you through the various important areas of marital focus. Make a firm decision to start today with a new vision, one full of hope and renewed confidence that with diligent effort and focus will offer you a wonderful marriage.

0–10 *Unsatisfactory marriage:* You are frustrated with your marriage. It's not giving you love and support. In fact, it's draining your energy. You need immediate action, a commitment between you and your spouse to change your relationship around immediately. You'll probably need someone else's help as well, such as a marital therapist or clergyperson. Dive into this book and don't skip any part. Start your relationship from scratch, and try to set your sights on learning new skills and attitudes. Replace the sadness of your marriage with a firm determination to make it work with love.

Everyone wants a happy marriage, but like so many other couples, you may have lost sight of how to create and keep one.

My plan is simple: *focused energy with a blueprint*, the same way you build any other structure. As you open this book, open yourself to a whole new way of looking at marriage. Put away what you think marriage should or should not be. Throw out the images of what marriage means to your neighbors, parents, or friends. Some of what you will read may sound drastic. But I promise that whatever I suggest, it's nothing nearly as drastic as divorce or a loveless marriage. When people hear what I have to say, sometimes they tell me that the real world doesn't work that way. Don't believe it. The fact that over half the marriages in the real world end in divorce doesn't justify your feeling that the antidote is unrealistic. As a marital therapist for more than fourteen years, I've learned that this blueprint works. As a happily married man for more than fourteen years, with five spectacular kids, I *know* this blueprint works. Put aside your preconceived notions and learn the simple secrets that those who are happily married around you have always known.

Make the *commitment* to create a great marriage and, with help from this book, you will find it, whether you have a "good," "decent," or "poor" marriage today. Recently, a friend of mine came to get my feedback about his marital problems. "Since my wife and I decided that I was going to travel all this way to talk to you about our marriage, things have already dramatically improved," he shared. You, too, will see your marriage improve immediately once you begin the steps in this book. And remember, when you have achieved a great marriage, you will be "abnormal." Statistically, you will fall into a severe minority (only about 25 percent) of couples who are happily married. Thus, following the blueprint of this book may sound abnormal. I surely hope so, if an abnormal marriage has come to be defined as one full of love and romance.

This book gives you the tools to unleash your warm, loving energy. The details are up to you and your spouse. Both of you are unique and deserve a unique game plan. This book will help you find your own personal path.

You Need to Fix Yourself, Not Your Spouse

Whenever I finish speaking to a group about marriage, a few people always say to me, "I wish my spouse could hear this. He/she is the one who *really* needs to hear it." These are the same people who constantly shake their heads while I'm speaking. They're thinking, "My spouse, my spouse, my spouse." Instead, they need to be thinking, "Granted, my spouse may play a huge role in this issue, but what can *I* do to change?"

It's normal to shy away from responsibility, especially when it looms large. Your spouse is an easy target to blame. It does take two to tango, and if your spouse isn't "into it," you may shrug and determine it's no use. But the beauty of marriage is that even one person can make enormous changes. This does *not* mean you are the main problem. Rather, because marriage is predicated on loving energy, either spouse can cause change by refocusing that energy in another direction. *If you change the way you relate to your spouse, then you are concretely changing the relationship. Your spouse will respond.*

If your spouse is stuck in negative behaviors, you can turn that around by making changes in yourself. If you want your spouse to be willing to change, change yourself first. For example, your mate may be unconsciously too scared to make him- or herself vulnerable to you and this relationship. You will directly soften that fear by showing how much energy you are committed to putting forth. You're saying, "Come on in, the water's fine. You don't have to worry about opening yourself up emotionally to me only to find that I won't meet you halfway. I'm going first. I want this to work for both of us."

Of course, you do make yourself vulnerable by making changes without an equal commitment from your spouse. But it's a decision you must make for the sake of love and family. And it's a safe risk because the odds are in your favor. When you show your spouse you are willing to place loving energy into this relationship, it becomes contagious. Your behavior can create a safe haven for love, one that helps your spouse feel touched by, and more connected to, you. Most of the time, all someone needs is a little push. You are going to give your spouse a huge push—but not one that says, "Get up off your butt and start loving me." You are going to offer the best motivation for love the world has ever known by saying, "I love you," plain and simple, through your new behavior.

Don't underestimate how you can free up your spouse's loving energy just by making the adjustments asked of you in this book. Sooner than later, your spouse will wonder, "What's going on? I'm starting to like this. I could get used to this loving focus." Your spouse will want to know more about your changes and how to become a part of it all. Then you can include your mate in the loop and begin to read and discuss the issues in this book together. You took a relatively small chance and the returns were dramatic.

You Know More Than You Think

Marriages falter for many reasons. Often spouses end up holding back their love. They never learned what giving really means, or perhaps they have been hurt too much to be able to offer their full selves. By the time couples end up in my office, they're usually in a holding pattern, waiting to see the other one change. They've tried and tried to make things work but feel as though they've been hitting their head against a wall. Their dreams of an idyllic marriage have faded. They're tired and don't believe there's much else to do. I make the following two obviously simple but important points.

1. *If you keep trying the same thing, you're not trying.* Trying the same thing over and over hundreds of times doesn't constitute trying hundreds of times. If something isn't working, by all means try something else. If you've been trying to send the same message to your spouse over and over again, stop it. Be hopeful now, because you can make new attempts in new ways. I'll show you how.

2. *You know exactly what to do—you're just not doing it.* The first time I meet with a couple for marital counseling together, each spouse never hears anything new. They've each heard it again and again and can almost always repeat it verbatim. These people come to me to tell them what to do. What do you say to your teenage children when they're fighting? "Just work it out," right? "If your sister is complaining about your put-downs, stop making them. If your brother doesn't like you broadcasting his personal affairs, stop doing it. If you each need help from one another, just bury the hatchet already and give it." Wise words for your children—far wiser for yourself. Often spouses have drawn an emotional line in the sand that holds them back from doing exactly what they know they need to do. Now it's time to do it. Show your spouse that love is the priority by making changes in the way the two of you relate.

Making your marriage work ain't rocket science. It's focused energy that can't help but make the two of you trust, love, and care more for each other.

Reality Check

Most everyone wonders about everyone else. We wonder if there are other people out there more sensitive, more giving, more financially secure, kinder, less angry than our spouse. We create an image of the neighbor's spouse who has it all together, who requires so much less maintenance than our own spouse. Don't be fooled. There is no perfect person or marriage. Did you ever notice how surprised you are when you find out one of your friends is having marital problems? Or your friend tells you he or she was abused as a child, is using drugs, or is about to claim bankruptcy? You're shocked because you allowed yourself to imagine that a public image is always consistent with a private life. People always put their best foot forward in public. You have no idea what's really going on behind closed doors, nor should you. But never mistake privacy for perfection.

If you're considering divorce, expecting to trade in for a better model, beware. Every model has problems. You have private problems and weaknesses you don't announce to others. Let me let you in on a secret. So does your spouse and every other person. But you can work it out within your marriage.

It's Worth the Effort

"Why should we put in all of this effort?" I've been asked by couples who've suffered from years of marital discontent. It's understandable that you want out quickly if you're in an unhappy marriage. Yet consider the following crucial points.

1. *The rate of divorce increases every time you remarry.* The second time you marry, you are facing a 62 percent chance of divorce—and just when you thought it was safe to go out, you'd be looking at an over 70 percent chance of divorce if you married for a third time. Countless people have told me that they think they can "do better." Unfortunately they weren't discussing their car or the cost of a new computer. They were commenting on their lifemate. We figure we should be getting better as time goes on. Yet we are creatures of habit.

If you have difficulties in your first marriage, it's not all about your poor choice of a spouse. It's about *you.* You fell in love with this person. You worked with this person to create whatever you have or don't have. Running into someone else's arms without a great deal of soul searching won't bring you to new heights. It usually brings you problems quite similar to those you had in your previous marriage. It's better to get rid of the problem and keep your spouse than to get rid of your spouse and keep the problem. Have you ever had the experience of meeting a friend's second spouse and wondering why he or she seems so familiar? Then it dawns on you: the person is just like the previous spouse.

When you're experiencing difficulty in your marriage, find new solutions, not a new mate. Don't throw around simple excuses like, "We were young," or "He/she doesn't get it." Give yourself and your spouse much more credit. It's not easy getting divorced and starting over with someone new, or finding that someone new. Odds are you won't find the "perfect marriage" any more than you did in your first try. It is well worth every effort to make this marriage better and stronger.

2. **Divorce often traumatizes children.** If you had children, you made a decision without realizing it to make this marriage work. After listening to over 100,000 children experiencing divorce who completed my Sandcastles Program®, I've learned that divorce is devastating to kids. Even though I've dedicated much of my professional life to helping these children cope, we must recognize how much better it would be *in every case* for these children's parents to be able to make their marriage a loving one. Notice I didn't say it's better for children if their parents stay married. Don't ask yourself to remain in a miserable marriage. Ask yourself to put forth supreme effort for the sake of your children to make your marriage great.

When your children experience your divorce, it significantly complicates your life and ability to move on to other relationships. There is nothing worse for you as a parent than to see your child in pain and recognize that you are partially at fault for causing this pain. Don't underestimate how much energy it takes to help your child adjust. Don't underestimate the amount of control over your child's upbringing you may lose when your child is with your ex for whatever amount of time. When your children look at you with tears in their eyes and say, "Why can't Daddy/Mommy be here with us?" "Why can't you and Daddy/Mommy try harder?" "I want to be with Mommy/Daddy more," you will wonder in retrospect if there wasn't a better way of dealing with your marital issues. Divorce is a painful process and requires enormous energy and focus on your part. You and your children would be far better off if you put all that energy into making your marriage great.

When your kids are adults and want to know if you really tried to make the marriage work, what will you tell them? Their lives were changed dramatically forever because of a decision made by their parents. Don't they deserve an extreme effort on your part to create a loving marriage?

3. **You are still going to have to learn to work with your spouse even after divorce.** If you have children and want them to be healthy adults, you will find yourself

working together with your spouse on a variety of issues. A friend of mine told me, "I work together more with my ex now than I ever did when we were married." *Work together with your spouse now at creating a loving marriage rather than working together later to create a loving child of divorce.*

4. *Divorce is hell.* You may think now that your divorce would be amicable and everything would go smoothly, but this is rarely the case. Divorce is litigation. Someone is suing someone. The second you decide to divorce, you are giving up control over your child. You are also giving up control over your finances, and perhaps even where you will live. You may resolve your issues in mediation, but maybe not. Ultimately, a stranger called a judge could be the one to tell you how often you will see your child and how much of your money you will keep. Unfortunately, that stranger doesn't think exactly like you. You may want out of your marriage, but everything points to making a new resolve to find the happiness and love in your marriage that you so desperately desire. Obviously, when there is abuse or outright neglect it's a different situation. This is not the marriage I speak of. My premise is that you have started with someone who is capable of warmth and not an abuser.

How to Use This Book: The Eleven Secrets

There is no remedy for love but to love more.

—Henry David Thoreau

My dear friend and editor, Betsy, told me, "I'm not sure I agree with everything you've written, but you made me think and reconsider. For a book to do that, alone is magical." I realize that I haven't developed the only way to have a great marriage. Yet this blueprint has worked for me and countless others. Give it a chance.

I've divided this book into ten secrets representing ten focus areas of marriage. (There's a bonus secret for "extra credit.") Each focus area builds on the ones before. For example, you can't talk about what you will do for your marriage (Secret #3) before you understand the need to leave the rest of the world behind and offer full focus on your spouse (Secret #1). Here are the Eleven Secrets.

Secret #1. Commitment is the glue of marriage. Insulate and protect your marriage against emotional infidelity by avoiding friendships with members of the opposite sex. This focus area will help you identify the important energy and commitment you will need in your marriage. Often, attempts at making a

Eleven Secrets to a Great Marriage

1. Commitment is the glue of marriage. Insulate and protect your marriage against emotional infidelity by avoiding friendships with members of the opposite sex.
2. Codependence is a necessary ingredient for a great marriage. Spouses must need each other.
3. Spouses need clear, realistic goals and a specific plan of how to achieve those goals.
4. Like any strong working partnership, marriage needs well-defined roles for each spouse.
5. Acceptance is about appreciating, not settling.
6. Your marriage has to come first—before jobs, kids, anything else. Your unconscious assumptions are holding you back from putting in the effort.
7. Your childhood has a great deal to do with your ability to enjoy a great marriage. The more you understand this connection, the better marriage you will have.
8. Great sex comes not from great sexual skill but from sharing your deepest, shyest self while trusting your partner.
9. Your marriage comes before your child. But your child is one of your best tools for creating a great marriage.
10. Time is on your side. A great marriage has many stages and takes years to develop properly.
11. Focus energy on creating a healthy relationship with your spouse's parents.

marriage better fail when much of the marital energy is diluted by outside factors. Commitment to your marriage is the first step you must take to enable all future loving actions to have their full intended impact.

Secret #2. Codependence is a necessary ingredient for a great marriage. Spouses must need each other. It isn't enough to want your spouse. Needing each other is more important than individuality and independence. This focus area will help you learn to see your spouse and your differences in a whole new light. You will see why your mate can offer you so much more in your life than anyone else. Differences will become paths for personal and marital growth instead of points of contention. Codependence is *not* a dirty word.

Secret #3. Marriage must have clear, realistic goals and a specific plan of how to achieve those goals. The difference between a business proposal and a marriage proposal is extraordinary. Couples must understand what it is they are looking for in their marriage. Once they agree on realistic goals, they need to outline what each one of them will do to attain them. This secret will help you create a written marriage document to help each of you focus on what you will contribute to develop a great marriage.

Secret #4. Like any strong working partnership, marriage needs well-defined roles for each spouse. This focus area helps you develop a unique working system to reduce tension while getting the most out of your marital effort. It will also offer you a system to deal with finances and avoid tension in that area.

Secret #5. Acceptance is about appreciating, not settling. Appreciation taps into the very core self-value of your spouse. You will learn to see your spouse in a new positive light and appreciate things about your mate that you never did before.

Secret #6. Your marriage has to come first—before jobs, kids, anything else. Your unconscious assumptions are holding you back from putting in the effort. This focus area offers you a clear plan for carving out consistent time for your marriage while using various methods to connect with your spouse. Using a four-point plan, you will learn to use your marriage as a tool for loving focus throughout your day.

Secret #7. Your childhood has a great deal to do with your ability to enjoy a great marriage. The more you understand this connection, the better marriage you will have. Having a meaningful understanding of your past and how it affects your ability to love will have a great impact on your marriage. This focus area will help you understand this connection and offer you ways to get in touch with this deeper self.

Secret #8. Great sex comes not from great sexual skill but from sharing your deepest, shyest self while trusting your partner. Lovemaking is about the love. You will learn to "make love all day" and make your sexual experiences more pleasurable and meaningful. You will learn about the implicit trust given through the sexual relationship and learn techniques that will greatly enhance your lovemaking.

Secret #9. Your marriage comes before your child. But your child is one of your best tools for creating a great marriage. Don't have a great marriage *in spite of* your children. Take your children on a family journey that will enhance your marital relationship. You will learn to include your children in your marital energy, which will in turn enhance your marital focus.

Secret #10. Time is on your side. A great marriage experiences many stages and takes years to develop properly. Having a long-term vision of your marriage will help you understand what each stage of marriage brings to your relationship and how to use each stage to develop a great marriage.

Secret #11. Focus energy on creating a healthy relationship with your spouse's parents. (This isn't always a fundamental issue in marriages, but I've found it can really cement a relationship.) Don't overlook the importance and potential pitfalls of in-law relationships. Both spouses are responsible for the health of these relationships and can do many things to ensure that they are always successful.

These secrets are the heart of the ten-week program I give couples in my counseling practice: they've proven time and time again to create a dramatic change in marriages. You'll see the results quickly if you do the work and complete the exercises. Each focus area will help you cultivate a loving energy that is the hallmark of successful marriages. I present to you the blueprint for developing a wonderful marriage that suits you and your spouse. *Read each secret and cultivate it for one week before moving on.*

You may feel you're already strong in some of the focus areas. Work on them anyway. Too often, the couples I counsel will try to skip a focus area because they feel they've already accomplished the goals. Yet after greater discussion, they find there was a great deal wrong with their relationship in that area. You, too, may find you've been working under a lot of mistaken assumptions. Take each focus area and make it your job to make it happen.

I don't want you blindly following anything I have to offer. I want you to discuss it with your spouse, mull it over, see what strikes you as remarkable and what strikes you as ordinary. Consider why you feel the way you do and discuss that with your spouse as well. This dialogue itself creates an avenue for marital focus and bonding.

Even if a suggestion strikes you as outrageous, irrelevant, corny, or downright dumb, think about it. Why are you reacting this way? Could your defensiveness be masking other feelings? Consider every focus area from every angle. Discuss what you've done in the past that's worked and why, as well as which failed and why. Allow yourself to become consumed in these secrets and to find the right way to funnel your loving energy into every facet of your marriage. Even if your spouse isn't making this journey with you, you can still work independently and discuss what you've learned with your partner.

After you've completed each focus area, continue to pay attention to it while placing energy toward the next one. You can't forget about any given focus area just because you've already worked on it for a week. You must now integrate it as part of your daily effort to create a great marriage. This is a process of continual building; soon it will feel natural to you. By the time you've completed each focus area, you'll have changed your marriage forever. At the heart of a great marriage is becoming absorbed in the business of marriage. *After ten weeks of regular discussion and focus on your marriage, you'll have taken the most important step: the habit of making your marriage the focal point of your life.*

In addition to these eleven secrets, you'll read comments from "Golden Couples"—couples married a minimum of forty years (our longest married couple, the Lechts, recently celebrated anniversary number 70) who were kind enough to share some of their sage advice. Their stories remind us that even with all the world's innovations, love will always be the same. It's the product of a lot of consistent loving work and patience.

If you're searching for a stronger, more fulfilling marriage, I invite you into my world of reality, one full of love and dreams that do come true.

1

Commitment is the glue of marriage. Insulate and protect your marriage against emotional infidelity by avoiding friendships with members of the opposite sex.

All of us know that adultery—sex outside the marriage—is one of the gravest blows to a marriage as well as a painful rejection for one partner. But you don't have to have *sex* with anyone else to be unfaithful. *Emotional infidelity* is just as—and at times even more—destructive to your marriage. Couples I counsel are absolutely outraged when I tell them that they could well be committing emotional adultery when they flirt with coworkers, send around funny e-mails to colleagues, or hang out with members of the opposite sex at gatherings. But they are, and so probably are you.

You're not going to want to hear this, but stopping this kind of relationship is the single most important thing you can do for your marriage. *It's not about where it may lead. It's about where it has already gone,* far from your focus on your marriage. You may be incensed by what I have to say. You may feel uncomfortable when you hear how I define *relationships* with members of the opposite sex. That's fine. My purpose here is to challenge you to take a close, and almost certainly uncomfortable, look at what you're doing and why, and to help you see how it's hurting your marriage.

When you find yourself getting irritated with what I have to say, consider: Why does it bother you? Why are you resisting the idea? Why not see if I'm right by making some changes? What is it that you're trying to protect by maintaining the kind of relationships you're presently involved in? If these relationships aren't as "damaging" as I say, because you say you don't find them that important and they aren't going to lead anywhere, then prove it to yourself by letting go of them. If they don't mean that much to you, why the irritation when I ask you to cut back on these friendships? Remember what it is you've always wanted from your marriage, and start considering the large, determined commitment that is absolutely necessary to creating a happy marriage.

I love my wife. From the moment I met her, I knew we could develop a wonderful life together. She is my soulmate. We've spent more than fourteen years giving to and receiving from each other. I couldn't recognize my life if she were absent from it. I need little else to calm me than her gentle hugs and wide smile. I fell in love with that smile first—it offered so much hope in a tired world. My wife provides me wisdom for my life, creativity for my work, warmth for my heart, and comfort for my soul. I have kissed her countless times and have held her even more. I've cried with her, for her, and in front of her. I've worried about her dying before me. I've relished her strengths and understood her weaknesses, as she has done for me. We've laughed enough for many lifetimes, and we've been blessed with five children. Together, my wife and I appreciate the life we've been offered and are determined to absorb from it all of the glory we can. She is my best friend and I thank God for her daily.

It is out of this love and the life we have built that I commit myself to my wife and our marriage every single day. I'm dismayed that the world around us seems to have lost the pleasures of commitment, the energy to stick with the responsibility, and the determination to develop the greater goal of marital bliss. When I married my wife, I believed I would never sleep with another woman for the rest of my days. But I also committed myself to offer her a life full of love and attention. This commitment meant much more than never "cheating" on my wife.

Believe me, my wife and I have had our difficult marital moments, times when we let our stress and tensions get in the way of our love. As I describe our positive, loving relationship throughout this book, keep in mind that we've worked hard to know each other and ourselves. I don't want you to start making those finger-down-the-throat motions that say you could vomit from such sweetness. There have been plenty of times that each of us has had to stand back from a fight or disagreement. We've been insensitive, taken each other's actions too personally, found ways to hold back our love in times of stress or pettiness. Like any couple, we're not perfect. However, we have worked diligently to resolve our issues using the techniques and guidelines in this book. We've grown up together and created our own, unique marriage. We feel we've *arrived* in our marriage and achieved a comfort level that works immensely well for us. But at times it's been a complicated road. If our happiness sounds too good to be true, don't tell me your marriage can't be just as good. The difference is commitment. The first commitment we've made is to be faithful to each other— emotionally and physically.

Leon was the first person in my counseling practice to drive home a message often lost in our collective marital minds. Leon had been married for nine years. He and his wife, Maribel, had two handsome sons, ages six and four, a waterfront home, and a golden retriever. Life was going really well until Leon fell in love with another woman. When Leon and Maribel came to see me to see if they could survive this crisis, they both cried in disbelief that this could happen to them. Oddly, Leon had never met the "other woman." In fact, he'd never ever heard this woman's voice. But he knew her e-mail address and had been in private chat rooms with her every night for months.

Leon was distraught and perplexed as he told me his story. He didn't know how or when it happened, but this woman now held the key to his heart. After all, his cyber pal truly understood him. They thought so much alike. She knew the right things to say, or rather write. She had great advice on how to help him reduce his stress at work and seemed so kind and warm. She often inquired about Maribel and the kids and always reminded him that his wife and family came first before her. But Leon's wife gradually took a back seat to his cyber fantasy woman. All of Leon's emotional energy went into his e-mails to this woman.

Leon had never thought it would come to this. Because this other woman lived in a different country, there was no chance of foul play, he rationalized. His marital vows would remain intact as long as he never strayed physically. But recently Leon and the woman had sent each other their photographs. Leon had the envelope at work and had yet to open it, knowing that seeing his cyber love might irreparably damage his marriage.

You Don't Have to Have Sex to Cheat on Your Marriage

When we think "affair," we think sex. Sex outside the marriage can be a knife through a spouse's heart. But an emotional affair can be just as dangerous to a marriage, and often a more complicated situation to remedy. *When a spouse places his or her primary emotional needs in the hands of someone outside the marriage, it breaks the bond of marriage just as adultery does.*

The moment Leon fell in love with this mystery woman, he fell out of love with his wife. Instead of focusing on overcoming the challenges in his marriage, he found excitement in relating to another woman. As he shared his struggles, laughter, fears, and joy with his cyber mate, he drained his marriage of the emotional effervescence and renewal it needed to thrive. He would return home after work and avoid discussing his day with Maribel, knowing he'd have to repeat it all later at the keyboard. With two sons around, it was easy not to find private time with his wife. When Leon and Maribel did talk, it was either about disciplining the boys or money, two unavoidable and unromantic issues. Leon's emotional affair placed his marriage on the brink of destruction. Now that Leon had found fulfillment through his nightly cyber chats, which were devoid of the dull, day-to-day stuff of running a household, he'd stopped making any effort to relate to Maribel. Naturally, she felt rejected.

Leon might sound like an extreme situation. True, most of us won't fall in love in cyber space, yet we find it okay to share a different kind of space with friends of the opposite sex. We discuss our problems, air out our issues, and settle disagreements with our business colleagues. We chat with our friends and neighbors. What's the harm in a man having a casual friendship with a woman when either is married? Surely, every friendship doesn't lead to an affair. Yet we forget the emotional harm of relating to someone outside the marriage when that same energy can be used to relate to our own spouse. Marriage is about relating to a member of the opposite sex with an intimacy felt with no other.

Even if Leon never "fell in love" with his cyber pal, his relationship with this other woman was still whittling away at his marriage. He was closing the door on his ability to relate to his wife in those areas that he chose to share with another.

How Do You Know If You're Being Unfaithful?

Consider your own personal relationships:

+ When you hear a funny joke or good piece of gossip, do you first tell other colleagues? By the time you get home, have you chewed it all over so much at the office that you don't feel like telling that joke again to your spouse?
+ Do you discuss all of your work problems (or issues involving volunteer work or other important things you are involved in) so thoroughly with colleagues that you're all talked out by the time you return home? Do you feel like it would take too long to review and explain the entire issue from scratch to your spouse?
+ Do you go out alone to lunch or after work for drinks with members of the opposite sex?
+ Do you enjoy harmless (by your definition) flirtation with someone of the opposite sex at a cocktail party?
+ Do you believe that getting emotionally excited by flirting with someone of the opposite sex is helpful to your marriage? Do you think it helps educate you as to what you need more of from your spouse? Do you tell yourself that the juice you get from flirting brings more vitality to your marriage?
+ Do you spend as long buying the "right gift" for a colleague of the opposite sex as you do for your own spouse?
+ Do you ride in a car sharing pleasant, personal conversation alone with a member of the opposite sex on the way to meetings or other work-related events?
+ Do you share intimate issues about yourself or marriage with a member of the opposite sex?

If you're doing any of these things, you're being emotionally unfaithful to your spouse. You have only so much energy. If you're spending it with coworkers or outside the home and then getting home and feeling too tired to spend any more on your spouse, that's emotional infidelity. You're effectively relocating vital marital energy into the hands of others. Forget about where it might end up. Even if you never touch this other person, you have still used that person to relate to, and in doing so, you relate away from your spouse.

You may be shaking your head and disagreeing. But I've spent years helping couples pool their energies toward each other, and it has changed their marriage immediately. Stop all of these outside relationships and bring all your emotional and sexual energy home to your spouse, and you, too, will change your marriage immediately.

> *I didn't marry you because you were perfect. I didn't even marry you because I loved you. I married you because you gave me a promise. That promise made up for your faults. And the promise I gave you made up for mine. Two imperfect people got married and it was the promise that made the marriage. And when our children were growing up, it wasn't a house that protected them, it wasn't our love that protected them—it was that promise.*
>
> —Thornton Wilder, *The Skin of Our Teeth*

Unlike many marital experts, I don't believe that divorce occurs more today than ever before in our history because people are more "unskilled" at communication and love. I don't think the main answer lies in your learning the specifics of how to be nice to your spouse, buy those flowers, send that sexy card, or learn to say "I feel" instead of "You imbecile." Although these lessons are helpful, I believe it's more important to help couples first commit to an insular marriage full of concentrated energy that is not allowed to escape into the hands of others. Once you've made this commitment, many of these loving actions become natural to the marriage.

It's not enough to develop "healthy life skills." You must search for the unique marriage that suits your relationship. You'll cement those bonds by discovering the specific ways you'll cope through good times and bad. You two might choose to combat serious stress with humor; another couple might find that very same humor disrespectful and annoying. Each couple needs to find the road to relating that suits them. Such relating can result only when you devote time exclusively to each other. If you turn to someone else to solve your problems, where's the motivation to work it out as a couple? Finding the ability to truly know your spouse starts with a firm commitment to your marriage.

In the remake of the film *The Parent Trap*, two girls who have yet to discover that they are twins have become personal enemies at their summer camp. The camp director places them in an isolation cabin, where they must stay alone with no visitors until they learn to get along. As they are forced to relate to each other, their defenses break down because, after all, they've got no one else. If only we could do this with married couples! Lovers would find the ways to love if they forced themselves to insulate their love by moving into a "marital isolation bunk" of sorts. It might be difficult at times. They might not see eye to eye. They might fight. But if the bunk isn't opened until they're back on the road to loving each other, then 99 percent of couples would find the methods they personally need to create a happy union.

Fidelity Facts

Although 98 percent of Americans believe it's wrong to have an affair,[1] infidelity looms large in our marital world. Statistics vary greatly as to how widespread it is. Research estimates of how many husbands and wives are unfaithful range from 15 to 70 percent.[2] In fact, one poll showed that over half would not consider virtual sex as having an affair.[3] Another study cited infidelity as the number one reason (31 percent) for divorce.[4] When infidelity strikes, there is a 65 percent chance that the marriage will end in divorce.[5] As psychiatrist Frank Pittman believes, "There may be as many acts of infidelity in our society as there are traffic accidents."[6] Dr. Pittman claims that after being involved in seven thousand divorce cases in thirty-nine years, "I've seen only five established first marriages ending in divorce without somebody being unfaithful. Every year I think I've seen the sixth, but I wait, and sure enough the other man or woman surfaces even though they deny and deny and deny."[7] Regardless of any statistic, it is clear that infidelity is a common fear in any marriage. We should never minimize its potential or its danger.

≈≈≈≈≈≈≈≈≈≈≈≈≈≈≈≈≈≈≈≈≈≈≈≈≈≈≈≈≈≈

A Walk on the Moon is a poignant movie that speaks to the issue of the damage caused by allowing outsiders into a marriage, as well as how the mere decision to make a marriage work can determine its outcome. The movie focuses on Pearl, a married woman who has an affair while spending the summer in a bungalow in the Catskills of New York. Pearl is the mother of a fourteen-year-old daughter and younger son, and as she sees her daughter growing up, she is struck by how much of her own youth and aspirations were stolen when she became a mother at age seventeen. The staleness in her marriage causes her to look for excitement in the wrong place—from the man who sells blouses at the bungalows.

The movie is a powerful depiction of how two kind people who love each other can lose sight of the important things in life. Pearl's husband, Marty, is a warm, hard-working man who genuinely tries to listen to his wife's complaints of marital boredom. He makes some attempts to make things a little more exciting, but to no avail. They'd already lost their joy and romance when they stopped placing energy into keeping their marriage wonderful and focused instead on caring for the children and making enough money to raise a family. They forgot about themselves and their personal dreams. Both become sympathetic characters as they get stuck trying to muddle through.

Once Pearl finds emotional joy outside her spousal union, her marriage can no longer compare to the incredible excitement of this new romance. After Marty discovers that his wife is having an affair, they are thrown into confusion. They both desperately want the marriage to work but don't know how to bring back the chemistry. In the end, Pearl realizes that for her kids' sake, she must make the difficult choice of remaining committed to her husband.

By forcing themselves to relate to each other, Pearl and Marty begin to discuss how they've lost their dreams and aged beyond their years. As they begin this journey, the two of them try to learn new tunes, to taste new fruits together. Only then do they discover the unique ways to help each other feel young and full of hope. They could not have done this until both excluded everyone else and attempted to relate fully to each other. No book could have given them the specific answers to their marital distress. As soon as Pearl decides to bring her emotional commitment back to her marriage, she is able to begin to find the solutions to a more fulfilling marital union.

The first step in developing a happy marriage is to close our peripheral vision to others so that we can be fully focused on our mate. We seem to honor this commitment intuitively when tragedy strikes. Recently, there was an unforgettable wedding in my community. After the engagement, the groom was diagnosed with life-threatening malignant melanoma. The wedding was postponed, and the twenty-year-old bride moved in with her future in-laws to help care for her love through his surgeries and subsequent chemotherapy treatments. There were few dry eyes as these two young lovers, wise beyond their years, made a public commitment to each other.

If one spouse becomes physically handicapped, our culture expects the healthy spouse to expend years of energy to stand by the disabled partner, to demonstrate a commitment to love. Why should we wait for that extreme righteous commitment to display itself only after tragedy?

Isolation Makes Sense

I recognize that some may find my idea of marital isolation archaic and unrealistic. Yet we are comfortable applying the same logic to many other areas in life. If we were to start a business, for example, we'd understand the need to focus serious attention on it. If we were to start two businesses simultaneously, others would count the minutes until we filed for bankruptcy. If we started a family, we'd feel obligated to focus our attention on our child. We wouldn't dream of spending large amounts of time alone with another child. We'd know it would be wrong to limit time with our own kid in favor of another kid who seemed "neater" than our own. As a parent, you'd understand your obligation to find the parts of your child you love and to learn to focus more on those wonderful points. You'd want to find activities that brought out the best in your child and yourself.

Marriage needs the same commitment to developing a loving and satisfying relationship. We can't divide ourselves in many directions without losing the intensity in our marriage. Our energy is already split between our jobs, our kids, and our marriage. The only way to keep a marriage strong is to put it first and foremost always. Just because we live in an ever-changing, "enlightened" world doesn't mean we should eliminate healthy marital concepts because they sound archaic.

If you find yourself quick to dismiss my recommendation because it's "ridiculous," "unrealistic," or any other pejorative, ask yourself whether you're being defensive. Challenge yourself to pinpoint the reasons you find my advice so irritating. Could you be avoiding a deeper commitment to your spouse and looking for reasons to excuse it?

I don't touch women other than my wife and mother. I will return a handshake from another woman to avoid being rude, but anyone who knows me well won't offer me her hand. Since marriage, I have never danced with or embraced another woman. I avoid consistent personal conversations with women. I don't "do coffee" alone with other women or have lunch or dinner alone unless it involves a short-term, specific business purpose. Of course, as a psychotherapist, I speak with other women, laugh and talk to them about their problems, but otherwise I do so only in a group or when my wife is a part of the conversation. In today's world, I'm afraid this sounds quite bizarre.

I originally adhered to such a personal commitment to my wife as part of a Jewish observance but found it helped me maintain complete physical and emotional focus on my wife. Now it's a cornerstone of the advice I offer as a marriage counselor. It's a wonderful and needed rule to stand by. I want to grow with my wife. I reap the benefits of my determined focus on our marriage as my wife and I consistently become closer. The more I love my wife, the less desire I have to involve other women in my life. I never want to hurt her or be hurt by her. I can't envision the rejection and deep pain I'd bear if she found regular joy in the conversation or arms of another man. I could never do that to her.

But I realize anything can happen, and it can start with one conversation that is really "refreshing," the word Leon used to describe the first time he met his new cyber love. Whenever life seems to be getting stale or plain overwhelming, my wife and I force ourselves to share that with each other, to find some immediate creative way to carve out the intimate space we need to find our way back to each other, perhaps a dinner or morning alone. It might be easier to laugh with someone else for a while, but I didn't marry my wife to find intimacy outside my home.

∞∞∞∞∞∞∞∞∞∞∞∞∞∞∞∞∞∞∞∞∞∞∞∞∞∞

Affairs Happen in Good Marriages, Too

Many people think that if you have a good marriage, you don't have to worry about having an affair. That's what Leon thought too. Do you believe that affairs happen only to people who've been suffering in a bad marriage for some time? Do you believe that as long as the couple is communicating and working together, they don't need to take these precautions? You're mistaken. Of course, it's more likely for someone to have an affair in the midst of a troubled marriage than in the midst of marital bliss. But I've seen too many divorcing couples for whom an "innocent" emotional affair permanently undermined what both people thought was a good marriage.

Too many people divorce today because they don't understand the concept of commitment. They saw their spouse as kind of a glorified friend. They didn't focus on the responsibility that comes with marrying the person who's supposed to become your soulmate. You don't fight the heavyweight champion of the world on two hours of training a day, and you don't look for a deep, intense love that makes you feel complete in your spousal relationship without a world of commitment.

The "Love Nuptial"

All of us know the cliché: Men seem to be born with a biological fear of commitment. Many men (and women) can barely stand the idea of lifelong sexual commitment, let alone the emotional one I've outlined. The explosive divorce rate has created many marital cynics, even though research shows that relationships between unmarried people are less happy and more prone to dissolution.[8] Skeptical from the start, too many people wonder where their relationship will end up and whether love will last. With prenups and postnups, the message about love is clear: Let's give it a shot. Maybe it'll work, maybe not. Is that all love deserves? How sad that people may never experience marital happiness because of this laissez faire attitude, because their minds have forgotten how to dream and their hearts have forgotten how to love.

Prenuptial agreements are the height of cynicism. Although I clearly understand the legal concept, their purpose is at odds with committing oneself to marriage. The legal document signed by both parties presupposes that this union may get busted. The legal recognition that love may not last has to affect a couple, even if unconsciously. This recognition has to play a role in undermining the commitment made between these two lovers. There has to be some worry, some distance that is created by the notion that we've already signed something that will make it easier and cleaner to get divorced.

In their 1983 study of six thousand American couples (the most recent study on the subject I could find), sociologists Blumstein and Schwartz found that couples who signed prenuptial agreements felt a lack of trust in their union that they believed was harmful to their marriage.[9] Worse yet, the prenuptial suggests an attitude antithetical to marriage—that after marriage we can somehow, if even just financially, revert to the same beings we were before marriage. Marriage is about immediate and effective change through the growth of giving your whole self to another and receiving the same in return. Everything must change: our emotional, physical, and financial selves must service a new kingdom, the one of mari-

The Love Nuptial

We, the undersigned, have jointly decided to make the commitment of a loving, meaningful marriage to each other. We understand this commitment to include the following promises:

1. We promise to maintain daily focus on our marriage. We will place energy into considering how to show love and affection toward each other and help each other do the same. We will diligently and consistently work toward the goals set forth in our "Marriage Proposal" (see Secret #3).
2. We promise to insulate ourselves to allow plenty of private time to continue to know each other and grow together.
3. We promise to find new areas of interest that we can become involved in together. We will become involved in each other's activities. We recognize that our spouse (as well as life itself) will take us to places and to worlds that we have never considered becoming engaged in, but we now will seriously consider involvement in any area of interest just because our spouse finds it appealing and stimulating.
4. We promise to attend lectures, read marital educational books, and consider any other activity that focuses on creating a meaningful and loving marriage.
5. We promise to recognize that each of us may have personal issues that may adversely affect our ability to show or receive love to its fullest. We will consider our spouse's opinion on this matter, and if one requests that the other seek the help of a counselor to better understand these or any other issues adversely affecting the marriage, that one will follow that request immediately, for a minimum of three counseling sessions with the same mental health professional.
6. We promise to jointly attend marriage counseling with a marital therapist or clergy person at any point immediately on the suggestion of our spouse, whether or not we believe it necessary.

These promises bear out our firm commitment to avoiding pitfalls and problems while deepening our love and creating a marriage that brings joy and meaning to our lives. (Sign below.)

tal union. If we could ever go back to the way we were before marriage, then we never knew the genuine meaning of marriage.

I have the engaged couples I counsel sign a new kind of prenup, the "Love Nuptial": a written promise (although not meant to be legally binding) that states a lifelong responsibility to each other, that details an agreement to try new and different things if either person feels love isn't working and to seek objective help from counselors or clergy whenever one spouse requests it. If either party isn't comfortable signing the Love Nuptial, it indicates that he or she needs more time and understanding about love before getting married. I also use this agreement as a postnuptial for those who are already married.

When you make the choice to truly commit to each other, you face a huge obstacle: the world around you doesn't understand commitment. They don't know that you really plan to live the rest of your life with your spouse. No, you don't want to do it in pain and misery. But it can be wonderful only if you learn to be there through thick and thin. When you know that you can be at your very lowest and your spouse will put loving arms around you and pledge undying love, you're married forever. Ironically, marriages have potential to grow the most in times of need and difficulty. When we offer and receive love in times of need, it develops an incredible trust and appreciation for our spouse. If we can just banish the urge to find this kind of love outside our spousal relationship, we'll be forced to put incredible effort into the greatest thing we have going: our marriage. If you feel you are missing that "connection" with your spouse, choose to find the way to create a new bond with your spouse instead of looking to an opposite sex friend to fulfill you.

Countless people have told me that getting involved with members of the opposite sex isn't a problem for them because it would never lead to adultery. They've even believed that a little flirtatiousness now and then is healthy, reminding us that we're still attractive to the world at large. Sex is far from the only problem. You will simply be chipping away at your marriage every time you get that ping of excitement from an emotionally stimulating moment with someone of the opposite sex. It's dangerous to your marriage, and not because it may lead to sex. Rather, it drains your marriage of the immense energy it needs to grow: the energy to flirt with each other, to be emotionally stimulated by a different point of view, to share the excitement with someone who wants to know who you are. When you place your emotional energies elsewhere, without even realizing it, you don't offer your spouse the opportunity to provide you with that same ping of excitement you are looking for elsewhere.

One couple I counseled, Mark and Karen, were both vehemently opposed to this concept. They had attended a seminar of mine and sat there with arms folded, clearly disagreeing with my position. Mark had an assistant who had been his "right-hand woman" for over twelve years, two years longer than he had known his own wife. His wife, Karen, had opened an e-business with a partner the year she and Mark were married. They were so invested in these other relationships from an emotional and business standpoint that they found the idea that these involvements could be draining their marriage of energy quite preposterous. Mark used to say he was thankful for two days: the day he met Karen and the day he met his assistant. Neither spouse had ever had sex outside of the marriage, and they both felt that these other relationships had only positive effects on their life.

Two years after the seminar, Mark made an appointment to see me and related the following story. He'd fallen on hard business times and ended up in bankruptcy, thus ending his business relationship with his assistant, although they remained friends. "I found another business I wanted to start developing, and I wanted to share it with Karen," he told me. "After all, I had no one to really talk to about it, since my assistant was no longer with me. But Karen was never home, and when she was, she was too involved in business with her partner to focus on what I was saying."

Mark explained that especially after his bankruptcy, his wife's focus on her business became even more important to both of them. "It was terrible. I felt so alone, and when I told Karen that we needed to share more, she had the attitude of, like, 'Excuse me? I'm really busy here.' It wasn't long before I began to resent the time she spent talking to her partner when she had such little time to talk to me. And even when I'd ask her to just tell me what was going on with her business, she'd reply that she was tired of it, that she wanted to veg out from it all when she got home. She even once told me if I wanted to hear so much about her day, I should call her partner, because she'd already told him."

Mark had never understood how much time and energy he and Karen were funneling away from each other. Only after life changed and he lost his assistant did he notice that he had lost the most important partner of all. He never thought Karen was having an affair with her partner—far from it. He felt secure that this man wasn't her "physical type." But every night Mark began to notice a certain enthusiasm in Karen whenever she spoke to her partner on the phone, a certain chuckle that seemed to grace every conversation, an excitement about their exchange of ideas, and even stress that Mark quickly began to envy. He didn't have, and realized he had never had, that kind of relationship with Karen, the ease of conversation, the laughter, and the enthusiasm.

When Mark articulated his dismay over Karen's relationship with her partner, she reminded him that he'd done the same since the beginning of their marriage with his own assistant and she'd never complained. She reminded him of his running joke for years of how each of their respective friends kept their marriage together, because these friends offered something that neither of them had for each other in their marriage. He couldn't argue with her points. He knew she was doing nothing wrong according to their marital belief system.

Two years earlier, the idea of limiting those outside relationships had sounded impossible to both Mark and Karen. They even felt that their respective businesses needed the close personal relationships they had each developed with a member of the opposite sex to survive. To have limited those relationships would have taken a supreme commitment and could potentially have destroyed their businesses. But now, even though Mark was plenty busy with the creation of his new business, he had enormous energy and desire to connect with Karen emotionally, but his wife had little interest or energy.

"I had been running from the truth," he told me. "All those years my assistant was as much my confidant as my wife. And our marriage worked. It seemed pretty good. But it doesn't look so good anymore, and I can't help but wonder how much better our marriage could have been if we'd put all that energy into each other. Basically, we found in others what we couldn't find in each other instead of finding a way to have that 'magic' in our own marriage." The relationship deteriorated quickly as Mark resented his wife's outside relationship more and more and she only responded with disinterest whenever he broached the subject. They were on the brink of marital disaster, and it had absolutely nothing to do with sex. Neither of them was remotely sexually attracted to these other friends. Their marriage was being torn apart because of emotional infidelity.

Be cautious not to discount my theory about emotional infidelity. You may find multiple reasons to show how it doesn't apply to you: "I'm not going to have sex." "My spouse and I do talk as much as other couples." "My spouse really isn't interested in that part of my life, so there's no harm in sharing it with someone else." "It's good for my spouse to see that others find me attractive." "I repeat all of my conversations to my spouse." But consider one thing: Why are you searching for a way around this concept? If these other relationships really mean so little to you that they aren't hurting your marriage and would never lead to sex, why resist the idea that you should stop them and avoid them for the future? Perhaps you should realize that you're getting more from these opposite-sex relationships than you're willing to admit and thus have reason to end them.

Refocus on the one you married and how you can get whatever it is you're getting from these other relationships from your own marriage. Find outside relationships with members of the same sex and keep the "chemistry" between you and your spouse.

Emotional Infidelity at the Office

Since men and women work side by side, and with modern technology like the Internet, it has never been easier to meet and bond with others. I'm not asking you to assume a curled-up, catatonic position in the corner of a room every time a member of the opposite sex enters. We are often required not only to spend time with members of the opposite sex but to be sensitive to them and to get to know them. Clearly, we are all unique individuals and have to be honest enough with ourselves to realize when an interaction or conversation makes us feel closer to a person of the opposite sex than we should allow. Be honest: acknowledge the little thrill you feel when you are flirting, being complimented, or being appreciated for sides of yourself that don't come to the forefront at home. Recognize that housework, childcare, and the stress of work have threatened to turn you and your spouse into drudges and that you're feeling less and less excited about returning home and being with your mate. Don't excuse your behavior with the "everyone does it" attitude. If you're not honest, you'll lose the greatest thing you could have going for you even if your office relationships never lead to sex. However, studies show that 73 percent of men and 42 percent[10] to 57 percent[11] of women meet their extramarital affair partners at work. Keep your coworkers at arm's length.

Where Competition Fails

Another reason for restricting relationships with members of the opposite sex is the danger that competition presents to a marriage. For example, if you stare at airbrushed, naked models in pornographic magazines, you may wonder if the person you're getting into bed with tonight is even of the same species. If you develop a relationship with a member of the opposite sex who has a superior sense of humor to your spouse, you may start to realize how "boring" your spouse really is. Your friendship with others can cause you to see your spouse in a more negative light: "He makes me laugh so much more." "She makes me feel like a man." "He takes much better care of his body." "My spouse doesn't have such a strong work ethic." "My spouse isn't that warm." You begin to judge your spouse based on what you see in your relationships with these other people.

It is unwise and unfair to place this form of competition on your spouse. If you dream of trading in your wife for that Playboy model, remember that a model may spend seven hours a day caring for that body. She may be an insensitive person, a boring or dim companion, a rotten parent, a financially irresponsible spendthrift, or someone who would never find you the least bit attractive.

Similarly, the person you're starting to get close to may have a great sense of humor or be much more "spontaneous" than your spouse but then again, he or she may not have so much of what your spouse has. Maybe he or she doesn't have the same concept of responsibility or warmth or willingness to give to you as your spouse does. Everyone has strengths and weaknesses, and it's unfair to judge your spouse on a specific scale without taking the whole person into account. We aren't slices of bread. It's the whole loaf we have to live and grow with.

There will always be people who possess better parts of a personality than our spouses will. Our spouse will never be the best in every aspect of life. That person doesn't exist. We often think that if our spouse were better at something specific, then we'd have a much better marriage. You may even be convinced that it's healthy to hang out with someone else so you can see what needs to be improved in your own relationship. This form of marital growth doesn't work. Nor do more possessions make the marriage happier or more fulfilled. Paul Wachtel, author of *The Poverty of Affluence*, calls into question our reliance on "more is better" as the solution to all our yearnings:

In 1958, when economist John Kenneth Galbraith appropriately described the United States as "The Affluent Society," 9.5 percent of U.S. households had air conditioning, about 4 percent had dishwashers, and fewer that 15 percent had more than one car. By 1980, when Ronald Reagan's successful bid to replace

Jimmy Carter was based on the widespread sense that people were suffering economically, the percentage of homes with air conditioning had quintupled, the percentage with dishwashers had increased more than 700 percent and the percentage with two or more cars had about tripled. Yet, despite the astounding economic growth—despite owning more of the gadgets, machines and appliances thought to constitute "the good life"—Americans felt significantly less well-off than they had twenty-two years before, polls showed.[12]

No matter what we have in life, our happiness is largely going to come from within ourselves. Having a large, elaborately decorated home, expensive cars, multiple vacation homes around the globe, a yacht, and memberships to exclusive clubs and spas offers no added security to your marriage. There is no statistic that declares wealthier couples have better marriages or divorce less. The one statistic we have captured is that divorce rates have soared even with all the extra "happy" items we have in our world. Searching to make our spouses measure up to others doesn't lead to happier marriages. It leads to frustration, anger, and conflict. We often overestimate how much pleasure we would receive if our spouses were better in some way. It's much easier to overlook our spouses' weaknesses if we don't create relationships with others to compare them to.

Remember, too, that measuring your spouse against a friend or colleague will always be an incomplete comparison. What's to say that that scintillating conversationalist you admire at work doesn't morph into the same boring partner obsessed with bills and Johnny's orthodonture the second he or she gets home?

A further problem competition brings to a marriage arises when your spouse is trying to change and become a better partner. Let's say you feel that your mate needs to improve his or her listening skills or better understand your feelings—worthy goals. Such goals take time and energy. Ideally, you should appreciate your spouse's efforts even if the change is incremental. However, once you choose to relate to a member of the opposite sex who is better skilled in these areas, it's likely you'll lose patience with your spouse. After all, even though your spouse may be getting better, he or she may still not measure up to your more accomplished friend. If you had never let yourself get involved with this friend, you might be more understanding of your spouse's efforts. More important than any improvement is the fact that your lifemate is showing such caring for you just by focusing on change. It's not all about the new skill, but about the process and experience of growing together. Involvement with someone outside of the marriage can cause you to lose focus on the important parts of your relationship.

This concept of "no competition" may sound odd or extremely limiting to developing a better marriage. My intent is not to make you stagnate but rather to find healthy avenues to improving your marriage. Working and focusing on your marriage means looking at what will make you feel closer to your spouse. There are better ways than flirting and developing a relationship with others to educate yourself. After all, if you wanted to spice up your sex life, would you sleep around and take notes to see what your marriage is missing and learn some new techniques? Of course, you recognize that even if having outside sexual relationships may teach you a thing or two to help your marital sex life, it's clearly stepping out of bounds. But the same is true for sharing your emotional or spiritual self with others. It is just as intimate and as dangerous. Just as you would do to improve your marital sex life, to improve your marital emotional life you need to educate yourself through reading, talking to a mental health professional, or discussing issues with other happily married couples you feel close to.

I can't underscore the importance to any marriage of befriending happily married couples who are openly warm to each other. From such friends you can see different healthy relationship styles. You can go home and say, "I'd like to have more of that spark that they have. Let's try going out one night a week like they do. Let's touch more like they do." Ask other couples for some of the techniques they use to keep their marriage happy. Most every couple that is genuinely happy with their marriage will have plenty of advice because they will have had to work hard themselves at making their marriage satisfying.

Ten Rules for Avoiding Emotional Infidelity

Keeping members of the opposite sex out of your intimate way is crucial to the success of marriage. In today's world, it takes focus and planning. Consider the following ten rules of avoiding potentially damaging relationships with members of the opposite sex.

Rule 1: Keep It All Business at the Office

What's integral to your job and what's not? You certainly want cordial relationships with all your colleagues. However, being cordial means inquiring of a colleague how her sick mom is doing and how her daughter's birthday party was. It doesn't mean chatting for a half hour and laughing about his recent trip to Egypt. Keep conversations that aren't strictly related to business short and sweet. A person rarely talks to you for any length of time unless you hold up your end of the conversation.

Suppose a colleague of the opposite sex were to say, "My dad is going into the hospital for some tests because he's had some tightening in his chest lately." If you respond, "How terrible, how long has this been going on? What has he been doing to help himself?" you've extended the conversation and allowed a certain bond to begin forming. Of course, you want to be sensitive, but you should be alerted to the fact that you are developing a deeper relationship as you continue to offer emotional support to this person. You can send a card, flowers, and candy and offer support by saying, "I'm praying for your dad," or "Know that you're in my thoughts," or "I hope everything goes well." But avoid becoming the main person from whom your colleague seeks ongoing emotional support. You are not being unkind. This person can receive needed support from his or her own spouse, significant other, or same-sex friends and doesn't need you.

By not being an overly chummy or talkative coworker, you may come across as a not very sensitive person. Some coworkers may even think you're a bit self-involved. But this is a good impression to make. It means

Ten Rules for Avoiding Emotional Infidelity

1. Keep it all business at the office.
2. Avoid meetings with members of the opposite sex outside of the workplace.
3. Meet in groups.
4. Find polite ways of ending personal conversations.
5. Avoid consistency in the relationship.
6. Don't share your personal feelings.
7. Be unflinchingly honest with yourself.
8. Avoid cordial kisses and hugs, or dancing with members of the opposite sex.
9. Don't drink around the opposite sex.
10. Show your commitment to your spouse daily.

your opposite-sex coworkers will feel uncomfortable running to you when they have a problem or question.

One of the nicest "outs" I've found whenever I've worked in an office setting is to appear quite busy. I've left many a conversation around the water cooler after a business meeting or birthday party because "I have an appointment," or "I have a great deal of work to finish up," or "I'm meeting my wife for dinner." I am considerate and appropriate, but I don't stick around for the "fun" after business. Colleagues of the opposite sex don't talk to me about their problems, dreams, or aspirations because I'm not that approachable. I may sound cold, but I think if you knew me, you'd see me as a warm individual who loves people. I'm not aloof toward others. I'm just "very busy." I want my colleagues to think, "Poor Gary—always so busy with his job and wife and kids," not "That Gary, you can always go to him for a shoulder to cry on."

Sometimes we just want to help. A patient once became emotionally involved with a man at work because she "felt so bad for him." His father had Lou Gehrig's disease, and because she was a nurse, she knew more about it than others and offered a great deal of emotional support. She could have kindly shared her concern without becoming so involved, and this man could have chosen to find other friends for support. She could have helped him greatly by referring him to support groups instead of endangering her own spousal relationship. Sometimes we're a little too egotistical and think someone needs *us*, that we can help better than anyone. We love it that everyone sees us as the nurturing den mother or sensitive guy. Although your helpfulness may emanate from a desire to be kind, again, it's not worth the potential danger of losing touch with your spouse by allowing a member of the opposite sex into your life.

In some jobs, idle chatter, wining and dining clients, and "getting to know each other" come with the territory. Such friendship should be reserved for members of the same sex. If you're spending two nights together at dinner followed by basketball and hockey games, you're forming a relationship, and it's hard to imagine you'd feel comfortable if your spouse did the same. You might say, "I trust my spouse." But be honest with yourself: Do you really like that outside relationship? Wouldn't you rather your spouse lavished that attention on you? I wouldn't feel comfortable knowing that my wife was out alone laughing and having a wonderful time with another man, and I think there'd be something wrong with me if I did.

I'd also avoid those trendy "team building" activities that take place outside of work hours. On one of my guest appearances on National Public

Radio's *Talk of the Nation*, a woman called in to criticize such office get-togethers. Her husband's company had taken the employees on a full-day trip by bus to a nearby city to watch a baseball game. It was on the bus that her husband met the woman he went on to have an affair with, the woman he would later divorce his wife for. Perhaps he would have strayed anyway, but this frivolity certainly opened the conversation. The company had invited employees only, no spouses or family. Businesses would better serve their employees by allowing such "team building" events to include family members or by offering intellectual and insightful seminars where people can develop a feeling of teamwork through learning together.

Rule 2: Avoid Meetings with Members of the Opposite Sex Outside of the Workplace

If you have to work together through lunch or dinner, order food into the office rather than go out. Restaurants are far more intimate than your office, and you are much more likely to discuss issues outside of business when you're on the outside. When you do finish a project, avoid the celebratory coffee, drinks, or dinner. Celebrate with your husband or wife at home instead. Share with your partner how much energy this project took. Let your mate into your life more rather than cutting him or her out by bonding a little more with your colleague. You don't owe your colleague dinner or the reward of friendship because you worked together. If someone at the office cracks open the champagne for the group, by all means, join in the toast, but don't linger. Congratulate everyone on a job well done, but make it clear where your attention and allegiance lie by explaining that you have a date with your spouse.

When you do have to meet outside the office, make the meeting in a public place that isn't conducive to intimacy. Avoid long car rides, as the close physical proximity and inability to leave one another begs for idle chatter and potential intimacy.

Rule 3: Meet in Groups

When meeting with members of the opposite sex, try to avoid meeting alone. The addition of even one extra person greatly minimizes any potential for intimacy. Even if it means asking a coworker to tag along for no other reason but to make sure the meeting stays focused on business, it's worthwhile. Group meetings also send the message to others that we're here for a particular goal and then we're through. People hold back from intimacy in a group both because they're naturally more cautious about sharing and because they're not sure if what they have to say will interest the whole group.

Rule 4: Find Polite Ways of Ending Personal Conversations

Learn to bow out gracefully from conversations that you feel are too intimate for comfort. If you feel someone is sharing personal information that is likely to draw you into a more intimate relationship, end the conversation politely. For example, say something like, "This sounds very serious, and I just don't know what to say. I surely don't feel comfortable giving advice on such an important issue. If I were you, I'd talk to someone who really knows me well, or even consider talking to a clergy person or counselor to air out my thoughts." In this way you've referred the person to others who could be more of help and made sure you won't become the shoulder to lean on.

Rule 5: Avoid Consistency in the Relationship

You'd think from these rules that I've never carried on more than a forty-five-second conversation with a female since my marriage. Yet I've had plenty of conversations with personal content. I just don't have them consistently. To tell a colleague about the great time you had on your vacation or to listen to her go on about hers for a while is fine, as long as it ends there and as long as such conversations unrelated to business are inconsistent. What you want to avoid are regular, ongoing personal conversations in which you're developing themes, favorite topics, or a continuing dialogue. Relationships need time and consistency to build. Having an occasional laugh is safe, as long as it stays rare.

Rule 6: Don't Share Your Personal Feelings

When you do find yourself engaged in conversation with a member of the opposite sex, share little of your personal experience or feelings. This curtails the other person's ability to relate to you. This doesn't mean you can't be polite or helpful. If your colleague shares with you that he's learning to scuba dive, you could ask him how it's going and if he's enjoying it without sharing that it's been your personal dream to do the same for years. If you feel the need to share that feeling, tell your spouse that night instead about how you were talking to someone who's begun lessons and that you're frustrated that you haven't found the time to do it.

Sharing our own innermost thoughts and feelings is an easy habit to fall into and a hard one to break. When someone tells you something, it's tempting to say, "Oh, I've felt that way, too." Then you're off to the races. Remember, people love to talk about themselves, so they're not going to feel put out when you keep turning the conversation back to them.

Of course, as a psychotherapist, my job is to engage my patients in conversation to assist them in discussing their struggles and joys. I care deeply for every one of them, but they can never be my friends because friendship is a two-way street. To form a healthy friendship, two people need to relate to each other, to give and take in both directions. With my patients, I only give and they only take. I don't share my personal emotions with them so they won't need to be concerned with my feelings. They can't fully relate to me because they don't know me well enough. Even though I talk "emotions" with them constantly, our relationship is solely for their benefit.

Rule 7: Be Unflinchingly Honest with Yourself

Sometimes people convince themselves that it can even help their marriage to express some sexual energy through "innocent" flirtatious conversations: "Hey, I'm not going to do anything, so where's the harm?" However, ask yourself how uncomfortable you'd be if your spouse found a similar method of "improving" your marriage. Be aware of whether you are ever feeling the slightest twinge of intimacy or attraction, whether sexually or emotionally. Consider honestly why you're looking forward to the next time you meet up again with that person. Be truthful if you have a little bounce in your step as you walk away from a conversation with him or her, or you suddenly have a little more energy after it. You can deny it and no one could argue. It's not about whether you could be "caught." It's about facing that attraction and why it's important to you. It comes down to how much you want your marriage to be wonderful versus how much you enjoy these conversations and experiences with members of the opposite sex. When you face these feelings, call out the reserves and go into red alert. Avoid any more situations in which the two of you would be alone. Consider what it is about this person that's caused this reaction. Perhaps you feel you're missing a certain something this person seems to give you. If you can identify it, try to find it in a safe, appropriate manner. Put your energies into finding it with your mate.

❧❧❧❧❧❧❧❧❧❧❧❧❧❧❧❧❧❧❧❧❧❧❧❧❧❧❧❧❧❧

Greg, who had an affair while his wife, Cheryl, was pregnant, told me that it wasn't the sex that was so wonderful with the other woman. Rather, he felt she appreciated his character in a way his wife didn't. He was turned on by the experience of having a much younger woman find him fascinating and crave his knowledge and common sense. If only Greg had recognized this earlier, he could have talked to Cheryl about his need to feel appreciated, and together they could have found comfortable ways for her to fulfill that need. He might have also had to recognize what Cheryl couldn't do for him—make him feel young again.

After years of marriage, it's hard to be in awe of your spouse or suspect that your mate has some incredible talent that he or she has never shown you. Sometimes we have to realize what relationships can and cannot do for us. Ideally, Greg and Cheryl will work on appreciating each other. But we can also find other ways to satisfy our needs. If Greg needs to feel appreciated and respected, he could teach law part-time, volunteer his legal expertise, and so forth. He needed to discover what he was getting from this affair at the first hint of intimacy to back away and find other methods of receiving it if it meant that much to him.

What Are You Missing?

When you find yourself enjoying conversations with someone of the opposite sex, ask yourself:

1. *What am I receiving from this relationship?* You are feeling good from this relationship. Identify what this person is offering you.

2. *How can I receive the same thing from my marriage?* Be open with your spouse about what you feel you're missing and how he or she could satisfy some of your wishes.

3. *How can I fulfill this need outside my marriage safely?* Perhaps your spouse cannot offer you what you are seeking in this area, or is not capable of doing so at this time. How else might you be able to satisfy this need safely?

Think your flirtation is so innocent? Test yourself: Would you tell your spouse? If you tell yourself that your interaction with a certain person of the opposite sex is fine, ask yourself if your spouse would agree.

Sometimes these interactions are truly innocuous and you can carry on as usual. A friend of mine is an extremely competitive person. Her husband, however, is not. He hated even playing Scrabble with her. She won every time with a huge margin. As much as she tried to coax him into competitive activities, he refused. Finally, she decided to go outside the marriage to satisfy that desire. For the last three years, she's been a part of an all-male softball team (she couldn't find a female league in her area). Every Sunday morning, she's out there sweating and sliding with her baseball buddies. This works fine for the two of them because she is clearly fulfilling a need that her husband recognizes, and in a way he's comfortable with. As long as the two of them maintain a strong, open, communicative relationship, chances are this softball league won't detract from their marriage. It still might be too close for comfort for many other spouses (me included).

However, if she were to tell her husband, "I love going there and laughing with the guys. They get me to laugh in a way I can't laugh with you," or "They build me up with compliments in a way you don't," then her husband would be quite uncomfortable with her method. And if she were to start finding one of her teammates to be less of a buddy and more of a partner, she would need to back away.

Be honest with what you're getting from the relationship and see if you could share it with your spouse openly. If not, end the relationship and find the healthy route to satisfying your needs. Be careful never to rationalize the relationship by thinking you have no choice but to interact closely with this other person. I've yet to counsel a spouse who didn't have a choice.

Rule 8: Avoid Cordial Kisses and Hugs, or Dancing with Members of the Opposite Sex

This may sound extreme, but with even one kiss comes a certain intimacy. Even a cordial hello kiss can be quite a sensual experience. Most often, a simple handshake will do. In the psychoanalytic community, there are clear guidelines that prohibit physical contact, even with same-sex patients. This is not only because of the fear that a sympathetic hug might lead somewhere sexually but because a simple hug immediately changes the relationship and can confuse the perception of both parties. If you ever need a polite excuse for avoiding a kiss or dance, explain that you have a cold and fear it's contagious. You can always clasp the shaker's hand with both hands to indicate extra warmth without introducing intimate touch. I realize that it's become common to hug and kiss even business associates. I join with Miss Manners in disapproving of this unnecessary intimacy.

Rule 9: Don't Drink Around the Opposite Sex

When we drink alcohol, we lose our inhibitions and clarity. I'm not talking just about the kind of dead drunk that'll get you into bed when you don't want to, or aren't thinking straight (although I'm skeptical how much decision making we lose from drinking—after all, I've never heard a heterosexual husband say, "Really, honey, I don't remember anything except waking up the next morning to find *him* in my bed"). Even a single glass of wine or shot of scotch is enough to relax you and lead to a more personal conversation that may be damaging to your marriage at a later time. It's these conversations that leave a door open for later intimacy. If you're at a party and really want to join in the festivities, plant yourself next to your spouse.

Rule 10: Show Your Commitment to Your Spouse Daily

Do something thoughtful for your spouse every single day. This could be a lovely note, a phone call, or a more elaborate effort to plan a getaway. Doing something for your spouse reminds you throughout the day how special this person is to you. Focus on the kind things your spouse has done for you, and remember that relationships take effort and time to grow. Have lots of photos of your spouse, kids, and pets around the office as a visual reminder to you and others of your priorities. Even when I'm staying in a hotel for one night, I place two or three photos of my wife and family around the hotel room. I don't need the photos to avoid an affair. But I do need to be cloaked in love, and photos can help me focus on how much love I have in my life even when my family is far away.

One time while giving an all-day lecture out of town, I called my wife during the two breaks in the day. When the colleague who had arranged my lecture invited me out for dinner, I said I'd be happy to but just wanted to connect with my wife first. Before he could stop himself, he blurted out, "Is everything okay at home?" This is what I get for caring and loving the sound of my wife's voice: a questioning look that assumes I would only talk and think of her that often if there was trouble! I found myself defending my position by explaining that with five kids, I like to call a lot and make sure everything is okay. But I did feel awkward. For a split second, I wondered if I was too dependent, not man enough, or some kind of milquetoast hubby.

If you read this example and think that my wife and I are being sickly sweet, ask yourself why? If you think it's embarrassing to have such a relationship, ask yourself why? If you're worried about "how you'll look," ask yourself why? We need to stay connected to our spouse throughout the day. The world questions those marriages that have a supreme kindness, one that people will find too sugary, too lovey, too much. Admit it, deep down, you want to be that couple, if only you could figure out how to do it.

My brother once confided to me, "You know, I've always felt like you and your wife are a little artificial with your little hugs and kisses and always being so sweet to each other. It always seemed a little much. But now I'm thinking that it's a good thing."

Same-Sex Friendships

You can also undermine your marriage by focusing on same-sex friendships instead of your spouse. Clearly, you can zap energy from the marriage if you tell all of your secrets, problems, and triumphs to your sister, dad, or best friend. You know you've crossed the line if you come home and don't tell your spouse about your day because you're all talked out after sharing everything with your best same-sex friend. On the other hand, marriage doesn't mean we can't share with others at all.

Too many spouses thoroughly check out the opinions of friends and family before discussing ideas or problems with each other. Every marriage is unique, and the concept of growing together means finding your own way as a couple without being under pressure to do things someone else's way. Still, how can we deny the advice of a family member who has known us all of our lives, or the friend with whom we've shared so much history? Often, especially early in our marriage, these people know us better than our mates. We can take their advice, even seek it out, as long as we always remember that, ultimately, we are the ones who have to live with the decisions we make.

Greg's wife, Cheryl, was infuriated at him for his affair, and understandably so. She shared much of her anger with her sister, who was unhappily married herself. They had many men-bashing sessions because they needed to express their anger. But their expression didn't seem to be an attempt to move on. In fact, Cheryl's sister was adamant that Cheryl should divorce Greg. And although I as their marital therapist was quite concerned over Greg's behavior, I strongly disagreed with Cheryl's sister that divorce proceedings should begin in her ninth month of a high-risk pregnancy. Cheryl agreed but refused to let Greg be present at the birth of "her child."

Was Cheryl wrong for discussing the issue at length with her sister? Especially when she felt so betrayed by Greg, it was a natural step for her to confide in someone she trusted, someone who had been there for her a lifetime. Yet her sister couldn't be wholly objective because of her frustration about her own marriage. Unfortunately, our friends and relatives have hidden agendas that they often don't recognize themselves. Cheryl's sister had never had a child (she was only recently married). Convincing Cheryl to restrict Greg's admittance to the birth could have easily been her sister's way of moving herself back into the comfortable sister role that she yearned for and felt she had lost since each of them had married. As it turns out, once Cheryl understood these possibilities, she did allow Greg (and her sister, who served as her "coach") into the delivery room.

The delivery was complicated, the baby was in distress, coming into the world through emergency Cesarean section, and it took three days of tests to find that everything was absolutely normal. But during those days, which felt like years to the parents, Greg and Cheryl worried and cried together. They spoke throughout the nights, and remembered what was so special about one another. They gave each other the support they needed and would ultimately thrive on. They focused on their responsibility to their new family. When the baby left the hospital, Mom and Dad went home together to raise their son and develop their personal commitment to loving each other. Had Cheryl's sister succeeded in getting Greg barred from the birth, the couple would have lost an incredible opportunity to bond.

One husband I knew took his friend's consistent advice to divorce. One year later, I ran into the "friend," who was with his new wife, his best friend's ex. Talk about hidden agendas!

Sharing with our spouse is the lifeblood of marriage. Without it, there are no ingredients to mix. We have to be careful not to share so much with family and same-sex friends that there's nothing left over for our partners. We have to safeguard against the biases of those outside our marriage. Consider the following guidelines before looking to others.

1. *Keep your fights with your spouse out of the headlines.* Of course, it's normal to check out if our friends have experienced the same issues we're struggling with. But be careful that you don't listen so closely to your friend's advice that you develop your own attitude exclusive of the person you are committed to living the rest of your life with. By forcing yourself to air out your issues with your spouse instead of friends, you're actively building your ability to grow together and relate to each other.

   When you air your grievances to a friend, it's natural to seek support and empathy for your side of the issue. The issue is bound to become more polarized ("She did *what* to you? I can't believe it!" Or, "He's such a jerk!"). Then you're less likely to be a good listener when you're alone with your spouse. As Drs. Redford and Virginia Williams say in *LifeSkills,* "You're not really listening unless you're prepared to be changed by what you hear."[13] Your goal is to stay open to your spouse.

   Work on expressing your feelings and thoughts to your spouse and then listening to your mate's point of view. Know how you feel about the issue before you invite another person's opinion. Always remember that your friends don't have to live with the outcome of their advice. You do. And remember that your friends' opinions are colored by their lives and circumstances, which may not be yours. (Cheryl's sister may have given good advice for herself, but not for Cheryl. As much as she meant to protect Cheryl, her own personal issues got in the way and could have caused Cheryl and her son enormous pain.)

   Beware of family and friends who offer lots of advice. When you do share with others, it should be to receive some understanding for your own considered point of view, not to find out what that person would do in your shoes. That's for you and your spouse to consider. You know better about your marriage than anyone outside it.

2. *Keep the personal stuff between you and your spouse personal.* When you and your mate have an unusually serious fight or you feel your spouse has wronged you, discuss it with your spouse or an objective confidential third party, such as a therapist or clergy person. When you take personal issues outside the marriage, you're betraying your spouse's confidence. Also, sharing this personal information creates discomfort in the relationship between your spouse and whomever you've discussed your spouse's shortcomings with. If your husband said something nasty to you and you tell your mother, it will be difficult for your husband and your mother to develop a healthy relationship. After all, your mom will be angry that he talked to you that way. Even if you started it, your mom will feel he was out of line. Typically, you cry your heart out to Mom, and then three hours later you make up with your husband. Great,

except that Mom is still angry. He brought you flowers, apologized profusely, and made love to you, but Mom is left foaming with anger, which may color her opinion in the future, as well as make your husband uncomfortable around her.

It's hard to let others know our weaknesses and mistakes. We share them with our spouses in the hope that the revelation goes no further. Letting our spouses see our whole selves is the most important ingredient of intimacy. Don't breach that intimacy by sharing personal stuff with others. Naturally, there are many small issues you can certainly check out with your friends ("How long does your husband spend with the kids a day?" "Does your wife get mad if you watch the whole Sunday football game?"). If you're not sure what's crossing the line, there's a simple litmus test: Ask yourself whether your spouse would be upset if he or she discovered that you disclosed the issues to family or friends.

3. *Know when it's okay to talk to a relative or friend when you need someone who has known you a long time.* Sometimes our spouses won't do. Let's say you're dealing with an issue between you and your dad. You may want to discuss it at length with your brother since he can understand your frustration and help you identify what's bothering you as well as suggest some possible ways of dealing with it. I'm not necessarily recommending that you discuss it with your brother before your spouse, but it's surely understandable that you would. However, it's important to discuss it with your spouse after you've finished with your brother. Often you leave your spouse out of the loop, figuring you've taken care of it and, frankly, not wanting to revisit the entire issue again. But then you don't give your spouse the opportunity to know you better and help you more in the future. Tell your spouse about your conversation with your brother so that your spouse can learn to be sensitive to you.

4. *Know when the time isn't right to share with your spouse.* As a therapist, I recognize that there are deep emotional issues and scars that psychologists can be sensitive to that you can't always expect your spouse to understand. Sometimes we have to be satisfied knowing that our spouse can't be everything to us, that we need the help of others to deal with tragedies of our past, such as rape, death, or other traumas. In these situations, you should find a qualified, trustworthy therapist to help you work through the issues. When you're ready, your therapist can help you bring your spouse into the picture.

Becoming aware of how much emotional energy may be missing from your marriage, or is being channeled outside of your marriage, will help you focus more of this much-needed energy toward your marriage.

The Sexual Affair

Usually, with sex comes an emotional intimacy that directly abandons the emotional intimacy shared with a spouse. Let's say a husband gets drunk on a business trip, has sex that night, and only knows about it because he wakes up with a woman in his hotel bed. Healing that marriage is generally far easier than in Leon's situation. When people stray sexually, it is the friendship and intimacy shared with an outsider that cause such pain for the excluded spouse. It is not only the fact that your spouse had a physical relationship with another, but the intimacy that sexual contact implies.

Sexual affairs usually develop out of some sort of relationship. Sexual affairs are three times more likely to be the pursuit of a buddy than the pursuit of a better sex life.[14] They aren't about getting "better" sex as much as about getting better companionship and friendship. Many people don't realize the powerful connection between friendship and intimacy. We tend to feel that having a friendship with someone of the opposite sex is harmless because it won't end up in sex. Yet in addition to recognizing the damage an emotional affair wreaks on marriage, we underestimate the attraction between the sexes.

"I feel terrible for what I did, but it really wasn't intentional," was the way Greg introduced himself and his marital problems to me. A successful attorney in his late thirties, Greg was on the brink of divorce because of his affair with a lawyer in his firm. The affair was relatively short: three sexual experiences before Greg found the strength to put an end to it. Greg's wife, Cheryl, couldn't forgive him—understandable, considering that she was in her fourth month of pregnancy with their first child. Greg was greatly remorseful and seemed to be a sensitive and warm individual. He'd never fooled around before and seemed to share a strong relationship with his wife. Most of all, he and Cheryl desperately wanted a family and had experienced extreme financial and emotional pressure in the course of finally being able to conceive a child with the help of fertility drugs. Everything seemed to be going so well.

But because Greg was such a sensitive guy, he was more than happy to offer a listening ear to his colleagues. Nothing "wrong" had ever happened before with these kinds of relationships with women. The woman with whom it went too far was no different than others. Her specific problems involved her parents. She was in her mid-twenties, and he offered her a more mature view of coping with her parental issues. It was all quite innocent. They didn't talk regularly for the first six months they knew each other. In fact, Greg never felt particularly sexually attracted to her. They worked on a case together and would have occasional business lunches, but he just saw himself in an "uncle" kind of role.

However, when Cheryl became pregnant, life changed dramatically. "Suddenly Cheryl could think of nothing else but this baby. It was immediately termed a high-risk pregnancy because she was carrying quadruplets. She was put on bed rest indefinitely. As the days went on, she became depressed, we couldn't go out, have sex, or laugh anymore. I guess that was the first time I went to lunch with this other person and started telling her my problems. I'm the kind of guy who needs a lot of attention, and this other woman simply gave it to me. I never thought anything would come of it. I'm not even attracted to her type of looks usually, but it felt so good to have someone care. The first time we had sex was after she stuck up for my wife when I told her about a fight we just had. I can't believe I did this." Greg's wife lost three of the babies within weeks of learning about her husband's affair and blamed the loss on the stress. She refused to see or talk to him.

Greg underestimated the power of lust and the need to be loved, heard, and cared for. Of course we can control our sexual impulses. We can dance with a member of the opposite sex without it going any further. But sometimes we are extremely vulnerable and confused and apt to look in the wrong places for the love we feel we aren't getting at home. At times, marriage is wrought with trials and tribulations. It's not all about sipping champagne together in the Jacuzzi. In fact, did you ever notice how many romantic movies end after the couple fall in love and get married? Rarely do romantic, feel-good movies drag you through marriage, because it's hard to paint a realistic view of marriage that people will pay to see. What audience wants to hear the stresses of the on-screen couple as they discuss better budgeting plans for the future or whether the Pampers absorb better at night than Huggies? As marriages dip because of life's surprises, spouses are most apt to have emotional and/or physical affairs. And when you already have developed friendships, it can be an even shorter step into bed when things are tough.

When Greg's life "changed," it was easier for him to have an affair because he already had a connection and friendship with another woman.

All Affairs Are Not the Same

In order to begin healing, first identify the type of affair that has occurred. Measures for change will depend on which kind of situation your marriage experienced.

The Emotional Affair. As discussed earlier, an emotional affair is any "close" relationship with a member of the opposite sex. This type of affair may be the most difficult to pin down, since your spouse could deny that the relationship is having any effect on your marriage.

The Cultural Affair. Many live in a culture where having an affair or "fooling around" is not unusual. It is not uncommon for men to disdain the idea of spending fifty years or so with one sexual partner. Such men stray in some part because it is seen as a usual occurrence and they live or work among colleagues who behave in a similar manner. The hope with this type of affair is that the offending spouse can step back and recognize how painful the affair was to his partner, and can promise to do whatever it takes to ensure that such behavior will never continue.

The One-Night Stand. Usually a strictly sexual relationship, the one-night stand is not as much a commentary on the marriage as it is a matter of poor precautionary measures. For example, a spouse who was out of town and drank alcohol, which then impaired his or her judgment, did not properly protect him- or herself from the possibility of straying. This kind of affair is painful because it shows great insensitivity to the other spouse, yet the betrayed spouse usually finds comfort in the fact that there wasn't an emotional relationship involved.

The Multiple Affair. When a spouse has had multiple affairs, despite having promised to stop time and again, it obviously complicates matters. How many times can a spouse trust when there are multiple broken promises? The answer lies in the proper commitment to the marriage and to a plan for change. There are spouses that say it'll never happen again but don't have any real plan to effectuate change. Then there are spouses who are self-saboteurs destined to "cheat" unless they become aware of the deeper emotional issues that drive them to hurt their spouses and destroy relationships.

Had he trained himself to avoid such casual friendships, he would have bought himself much more time before such a friendship could have developed. That time could have allowed him the necessary space to recommit himself to his wife and marital vows. If his marital instinct was to first consider what his marriage needed, he could have been sensitive to his wife and found pleasure in their changing yet potentially more fulfilling marriage.

After the Affair

So how do couples make it after the affair? Can you really have a great marriage after such a blow? Can there ever be genuine trust again? And as many have shared with me, they don't want to return to the way the marriage was. After all, it led to disaster and deep emotional pain. Where do you go from here? Many spouses can't imagine a decent marriage, let alone an outstanding one, once the ultimate rejection has occurred.

The answer is found in your earnest desire to make your marriage work. Your motivation to work with this present relationship is to find yourself along the way. Our greatest asset as human beings is the ability to look deep within ourselves and create a better self, a self that understands its motivations and can learn to grow with change. Naturally, it is hard. It is much easier to say, "He/she went too far and he/she will have to live with the mistake. I'm guiltless." Easier, but not helpful in your desire to grow as a person. Make the commitment to yourself to find love in a healthier way, with the guidelines outlined in the rest of this chapter.

My strongest suggestion is to seek out professional help. The emotional volatility of an affair makes it very hard for spouses to discuss it properly and move on without the assistance of a trained objective third person. Please don't use the following guidelines as an alternative to proper psychotherapy but rather as an aid to recreating your marital relationship.

First, two key ingredients must be present to heal a marriage after an affair:

1. *A remorseful spouse.* When the spouse who has had an affair doesn't fault him- or herself, there's no point in going further. How can the betrayed partner open up emotionally and become vulnerable to a spouse who doesn't feel terrible about the affair? And if the unfaithful spouse finds excuses for the affair, there is greater likelihood that he or she will stray again. To heal the wound, the straying spouse must feel sorry for his or her actions and accept responsibility for them.

2. *The certainty that it's over.* The pain can't begin to heal when a spouse is still involved with someone else. Nor can a healthy return to marriage begin. The first issue is helping the straying spouse find the motivation and understanding to commit to fully returning to the marriage. Otherwise, attempts to heal the affair will be futile and painful. I remember one spouse who continued to do business with the woman he had an affair with. Although he swore it was over, his wife could not accept that this woman was still a part of her husband's life when he had a choice of discontinuing the relationship. The extramarital relationship must end—physically, emotionally, sexually.

The Role of the Spouse Who Had the Affair

The offending spouse must take the following steps.

1. *Apologize.* When another person hurts us, healing that relationship begins with sincere apologies to the person who was hurt. Lower your innate defenses and internal protection mechanism, which may tempt you to minimize your error. Stay away from comments like "If you were more . . . , this never would have happened." I am not saying your point has no validity, but you had an affair and there is no excuse for the betrayal and pain you caused another person to suffer. If your spouse was in fact doing something incorrect or unhealthy, it was part of your marital commitment to do something about it, whether through private discussion or counseling. The moment you decided to add another sexual partner into your marital mix, you were wrong no matter what was going on in your marriage. If there are huge problems in your marriage, deal with them. If you choose not to, or feel there is no option other than divorce, then wait until it is clear to your spouse that the marriage is over before you allow yourself to become intimately involved with another person.

2. *Be willing to listen.* Your spouse deserves and needs the opportunity to share his or her pain. Even if you are extremely remorseful, your spouse still deserves the opportunity to share with you how horrible the situation is for him or her, even though this will hurt your feelings. Listen intently and empathize with what your spouse is feeling. Set your own hurt feelings aside. Let your spouse know that you understand his or her feelings and that you would feel the same if your spouse chose to have an affair.

3. *Discuss the affair.* Your spouse will likely ask a variety of questions about the affair. You may need to share some of the details, but only those that refer to the issue of how the affair came about, and only so you and your spouse can develop a proper precautionary plan for the future. As discussed below, sharing too much can be harmful to the process of healing. However, your spouse

deserves answers that can be used to develop a plan that will protect him or her from such behavior in the future.

4. *Change your lifestyle.* It isn't enough to say, "I'll never do it again." The hurt party needs a lot more to go on than a verbal promise. You both need to put thought and energy into understanding how this affair happened and how you will avoid it happening again. Serious limits should be constructed. You may not like having limits placed on you as if you were a teenager under parental scrutiny, but they are needed to rebuild your spouse's trust.

You will need to go overboard in letting your spouse know where you are and what you are doing, and when and why you'll be late returning home. But would you have it any other way if your spouse cheated on you? For your spouse to make him- or herself vulnerable to you again, your mate will need realistic assurances and checks and balances to make sure he or she is never hurt like this again. Remember the adage, Cheat on me once, shame on you; cheat on me twice, shame on me. It is unreasonable to expect a spouse to return to a former trust anytime soon after an affair.

5. *Discuss the changes you need to make.* You may have many issues with your spouse that didn't "cause" your affair but surely made your marriage ripe for trouble. You need to be able to discuss your needs and what you feel was wrong in your relationship. You should deal with this subject only *after* you've apologized profusely and sincerely heard your partner's pain. Using the techniques in this book, you and your spouse can develop a plan of attack of how you will make this relationship better than it ever was before.

6. *Commit to a long period of healing.* Too many offenders think that after a few weeks their spouse should ease up already and stop worrying. You may know in your heart you'd never stray again, but there is no way for your spouse to know that other than seeing how you act over time. Your spouse has the right to keep a watchful eye out for a long time, commonly a year. It takes many months for a spouse to relax and trust a partner who has had an affair. For some, it takes years before they can await the arrival of a late spouse without first thinking that he or she is straying again. Respect your spouse's need for reassurance.

The Role of the Spouse Who Was Betrayed

The spouse who was cheated on must be willing to take the following steps.

1. *Recognize your role.* Recognizing your role in your spouse's affair is the hardest part. No one is saying you deserved this, but you must be willing to under-

stand that your marriage was suffering. There were things you weren't doing (perhaps not working hard enough on making the marriage better, or not pushing to see a marital counselor) that allowed your spouse to feel unfulfilled or to want to seek intimacy outside of your marriage. I'm not blaming the victim here. But the key to affair-proofing a marriage is consistent focus and effort on your marital relationship—and that includes both of you. It's the only way. If this focus was absent from your marriage and your spouse had an affair, you need to take responsibility for your part in not making this marriage fabulous.

2. *Be ready to change.* Be brutally honest with yourself about your own flaws. Be willing and ready to hear your spouse's feelings and needs. As much as your spouse must be willing to make lifestyle changes to reassure you he or she won't ever stray again, you'll need to do the same. After all, what use is it to return to the way it was, which obviously was unsatisfying for your partner, and was probably so for you as well? Outline your new plan, using the "Marriage Proposal" outlined in Secret #3.

3. *Limit your questions.* This issue is controversial among marital therapists. You're going to want to know details, and it's common for you to be practically hysterical until you receive every answer. Some spouses claim it helps them move through the pain. For the most part, I feel it prolongs the pain and creates deep scars. It's the difference between reading about something horrific and seeing it. The more details you know, the more graphic imagery you will have, and having these images to dwell on will seriously decrease your ability to forget the past and focus on the future.

On the other hand, there are some questions you are entitled to know the answers to, as a means of developing a marital plan for the future and trusting your spouse:

Who is it?

How did you meet?

How long has this relationship been going on?

Do you have any relationship with this person now or do you foresee having one in the future?

Did anyone else know about your affair?

Why did you have this affair? What was happening in our marriage or in your head that would allow you to break our personal commitment?

You may also have specific questions like "Was that why you were late last week?" It makes sense to ask questions that will help you form a new plan that will give you reassurance. If your spouse's good friend "fools around" a lot and introduced your spouse to this other person, you need to know this so your spouse can assure you he or she will no longer have a relationship with this friend.

The questions that are unproductive are the detailed ones:

How often did you have sex? (Even though you won't ask this question, you still need to make sure your spouse gets tested for sexually transmitted diseases.)

What was it like?

Was it better than when we have sex?

Do you think he's handsome/she's beautiful/smart/sexy?

What does he/she have that I don't?

The answers to these questions will torment you, and there are no answers that will make you feel any better. Obviously, the answers are not going to be, "Sex stunk, he/she's ugly," and so forth. The answers will be based on your spouse's wrongdoing and unhealthy behavior. It's unfair to ask your spouse to recount these details because he or she has already admitted it was wrong and decided to return to a life with *you*. No matter how "great" the affair may have been, your spouse has chosen to be with you. The reason behind that decision may not be the one you'd ideally like (for the kids, for example), but it's strong enough to pull your spouse away from whatever he or she saw in this other person. The more details you know, the more difficult it will be for you to love your spouse. You don't want to have an image of him or her having sex with another person every time you two make love. Be kind to yourself and deal with the realistic issues at hand.

4. *Don't bring the affair up again and again.* Your spouse can only apologize so many times without becoming resentful. You want a genuine apology and then the reassurances that it will never recur. It is difficult enough for anyone to admit to his or her error, apologize, and be sensitive to how his or her behavior hurt another. If you constantly bring up the affair, it's simply unfair and manipulative. If you feel a need to remind your spouse of the affair because you feel he or she is behaving in a way that could lead to another affair, then you need to get immediate counseling. But to remind your spouse of the affair in the midst of an argument as a punitive tool, for example, is unfair and will damage your ability to communicate honestly as a couple.

5. *Resolve to move on.* There is no magic to forgiveness. It is the strength of the human mind and heart to forgive and create a new life together with your spouse. If you are satisfied with the new plan to prevent a future affair and create a better marriage, then your job is to let go of the past. It is a decision you must make. No one is asking you to forget it ever happened. Rather, recognize it for what it was: a terrible mistake at a time that your marriage needed a

great deal of help. Look into the future and see you and your spouse happily married years from now. *The past can melt into a rich history that ultimately will help the two of you be stronger, kinder, and more focused on your love.*

There is no easy journey. Your marriage can sustain an affair if you can see it as a devastating mistake that ultimately served as a catalyst to create growth and change in your union. That is the power of love. We find ourselves at incredible lows and crossroads in our marital life, but those who are dedicated to true love will find the hope and put in the steady effort needed to make marriage work for them under any circumstances.

So whatever happened to Leon and his on-line romance? After some therapeutic insight, Leon was able to recommit himself to his marriage. After about five months of counseling, he and his wife happily left my office to enjoy the rest of their lives together. About three years later, I received a letter from Leon. He wrote me how well things were and then added, "Remember that woman? You had me put away her envelope and I never looked at it. I guess I never threw it out, and recently upon clearing out some papers, I found it. I couldn't resist looking at it and then sending it your way. It's enclosed."

I opened the envelope and first read the note.

Dear Leon,

It's been wonderful laughing with you. You are a special man and I wish things were different but this world isn't meant for us to be together. As you can see, it's neither the time nor the place. Who knows, I'll be satisfied if it works out the next time around.

Love,
Cyber Sal

And there it was. The picture of the woman that brought Leon and his wife's marriage to its knees. The picture revealed a beautiful, gentle-looking woman. On the bottom right-hand corner was written, "74 years old and still hot." Her twisted fingers grasped a cane and her white hair flowed over the top of the recliner she sat on.

✳

"Neither the time nor the place." Sage words from one who has lived a long life. Perhaps all of us can learn from Cyber Sal that when we marry, a good motto for getting involved with others of the opposite sex can be summed up with such a simple phrase. It's neither the time nor the place.

Affairs are not about sex. They are about placing vital marital and life energy into the hands of others who don't deserve them and shouldn't have them. They are about rejecting the commitment and abandoning the love we've offered our spouses. If it's marital bliss you seek, start by knowing that bliss awaits those who respect the importance of commitment.

Herman & Celia Lecht

MARRIED: 70 YEARS

How We Met:

It was 1927 and my friends gave a graduation party. We were both there but we didn't speak. The next day I went to Coney Island and there was a banner in the sand so I went to read it. She was standing under the banner and she just came right out and said, "Herman Lecht, how the hell are you?" I liked her right away. We dated and got engaged for two years and then, we married. That was seventy wonderful years ago.

What Makes Our Marriage Work:

I never won an argument. I always told my clients if you win the first argument—either of you, the man or woman—you're on your way out. It's just compromise, compromise, and more compromise. There is no happiness without that.

2 Codependence is a necessary ingredient for a great marriage. Spouses must need each other.

You put me high upon a pedestal
So high that I could almost see eternity
You needed me
You needed me.

—Randy Goodrum

I was on my way to a lecture when I received the call that would change my life. With four-month-old identical twin boys and three other children ranging in age from one to six, home life was complicated enough. But the call would change all of that. It would alter my perception of family, work, and life. It would change my marriage forever. My wife was on the line; she was at the hospital with one of our twins. Minutes after receiving the call, she and I were stroking the arm of our drugged infant as he lay helplessly on a sterile metal hospital bed. Our hopes that his fainting spell an hour ago had been caused by high fever were crushed when we received the results from his spinal tap and bloodwork: bacterial meningitis. We were told to expect the worst. The odds makers pointed us toward death; the optimists pointed us toward unknown brain damage, the least of which would cause deafness as well as other unspeakable complications that the doctors spoke of easily.

My wife turned to me and gave me a look—one I will never forget and never want to. In the midst of tragedy came a most powerful, heartfelt message. The look was one of complete despair and fear as the doctors prattled on. Although the memory of our eyes locking is a sad one, it was at that moment that we showed each other how close we really were. The look said, "I need you," and clearly we knew we hadn't a chance of making it through unless we had each other. I don't mean to be melodramatic. But when you confront the possibility of your child's death, you become quickly aware that life as you know it has ended. You don't think about marriage, making love, dancing in the moonlight. Marriage isn't about you and your spouse anymore. And yet, we discovered it was more about us than we could ever imagine. We learned to lean on each other, cry to each other, be depressed with each other, and know that we were always going to be there for each other. Somewhere in the middle of countless decisions about needles, medications, MRIs, doctors, and caring for four children at home, we found out that we could never live without one another. We held on tight and wouldn't let go. Years later, with our son returned to us miraculously healthy, we still can't let go of the anxiety of that time. Yet it undeniably strengthened our marriage.

Independence has been drilled into our thinking. Bestsellers crowd the shelves, urging you to prize your individuality and let nothing stand in your way as you pursue your goals and dreams. Make time for yourself, pursue your own hobbies, make your own friends, be true to yourself. Financial planning books for women advise a separate account in case your husband leaves you high and dry, an attitude that on some deeper level has to undermine the level of trust in a relationship. You are told to find happiness within yourself: don't look to your spouse to make you happy. All these ideas may have some limited validity, but if your goal is to have a wonderful marriage, you need to surrender this idea of independence for the sake of your marriage. *If you want to be happy, you must need each other and depend on each other.*

Does the idea of needing and being dependent on your spouse make you feel uncomfortable? Why did you marry if you're supposed to find happiness within and be just as happy alone as married? Why did you marry if you want to spend the bulk of your time on pursuits that don't include your spouse? Why did you marry if you want to handle finances on your own? Didn't you marry to get more out of life? Didn't you want a close friend to share life with, who could be there to share in your joys and support you in your times of despair? Didn't you marry someone who would make you feel special? Your spouse isn't supposed to completely define your self-esteem, but don't think for a moment that he or she isn't responsible for making you feel much better about yourself than if you were single. You are supposed to be hearing more praise, having more fun, learning to lean on someone.

You marry to need someone, to become one with someone, to have someone in your life to meld with and create a new life with. That doesn't happen when your focus is on individuality and independence. Put away your fears of being "needy." Neediness doesn't make you weak. It makes you an outstanding marital partner.

Needing your spouse, in part, means that you've developed a relationship in which life's experiences don't mean as much if you're not sharing them in some way with your spouse. Dependence means you look to your spouse to bring something different to your life. It's okay to need your spouse's smile or joke to help you lighten your load, to be waiting desperately for an opportunity to talk to your spouse about something new and exciting in your life, to want to go to a lecture or movie only if your spouse will attend with you, to wait to talk to your boss until you've heard your spouse's opinion. You married so you could do all of these things and more.

Why We Need to Need

Independence is at a premium in today's marriage. We've been scared off by our history. There was a time in the not-so-distant past when spouses needed each other in ways that caused loveless marriages to endure. Women needed husbands for financial stability. Men needed wives to care for offspring. Too many couples were pigeonholed into needy roles that prevented many from finding happiness. As society "grew," couples became convinced that "need" is dangerous. "Never lose your individual identity— your spouse will respect you more if you don't 'need' him/her" has become a kind of motto in the collective unconscious of our culture. However, as couples build these clear lines of individuality and lack of dependence, they also build the foundation for divorce.

In the 1990s, 90 percent of college students would only consider marriage if they were "in love," compared with the 1960s, when 33 percent of college men and 75 percent of college women would have considered marrying someone they didn't love.[1] Today, couples decide to marry because they *want*, rather than need, each other. They are attracted to each other physically as well as emotionally, and the fact that they are choosing to get married when each of their lives could have taken many different directions carries a great deal of weight in our society. This foundation of desire matters. But it cannot be the *only* foundation of your marriage: there will be periods in your life when you will not desire your spouse. Did I "desire" my wife when I learned that my son's statistical chance of survival was a pathetic 19 percent? Did I long and lust for my wife when, after twenty-eight days in the hospital, our infant was allowed to go home, only to relapse a week later, starting the whole process over again?

Will you long for your spouse even though he or she can no longer give you what you're used to? When there is no time for the love and desire you've become accustomed to in your marriage, how will your marriage survive? Moments of high anxiety are a realistic part of life. What will you do when you or your spouse experiences a parent's death, financial hardship, midlife crisis, a child's severe illness? When your spouse is depressed and doesn't want to make love, when you don't have the money to go out to dinner, let alone on a vacation, when you're physically and emotionally exhausted from being up all night with a newborn or an elderly sick parent and can't even think of spending "quality" time with your mate, how will you and your spouse react? And I don't refer only to tragic times. Don't forget about those periods when things aren't necessarily bad, but just stressful. Your business is booming and it requires a great deal of time and energy. You're moving to a better location to be closer to family. Your home renovation has been delayed six months and you still don't have a working kitchen. Even stress that comes from good events can cause some staleness in your marriage while you're adjusting to the change.

If you've chosen to develop a marital relationship based on independence, you risk losing the most important key to the foundation of marriage, *oneness*. If both of you expect to be comfortable and whole within yourselves, you are likely to find your spouse as a burden when he or she can no longer bring you that extra love and happiness and threatens to drain your own supply. During the tough times in life, if your spouse is independent of you and can no longer bring you the satisfaction you've come to expect, then what does your marriage offer you?

It's at these moments when friends may look at you in a confused, sad sort of way and say things like "He's still depressed? But it's been so long since his dad died." Or, "She's still so sad? She had that miscarriage months ago. How long can you be expected to put life on hold?" Then comes the freedom line: "It isn't right. You can't be expected to have this kind of marriage. Anyone would understand if you abandoned ship. You ordered roast beef and you got Spam." Certain friends may never understand how you can maintain a meaningful relationship even when it's gone through drastic changes. They'll tell you that you deserve your freedom. This is pure selfishness. You have a responsibility to work hard and find new ways to create a happy marriage even if all the rules have changed and you don't get exactly what you expected. Some people believe that marriage comes with a clear game plan and when that plan is drastically disrupted, all bets are off. They didn't marry because they ever wanted to become one with another and need that person. Rather, they wanted to "be themselves" with the benefit of having someone else along for the ride who would make life that much more enjoyable. That is the antithesis of commitment.

Codependent Forevermore

You may not realize it, but you may unconsciously be avoiding the intensity of a truly committed marital relationship because you fear being too dependent, too vulnerable. You worry that you'll give away too much power and control, that someone else could break your heart. Yet this fear stifles you from ever having a marriage that will offer the safety and security that you truly desire. The truth is that only when we open our hearts and become interdependent with our spouse do we achieve that security. Dare to love, dare to need, and your marriage just gets stronger. The more you and your spouse fuse together and become one loving unit, the more you will be able to live together through all of life's experiences and learn to change with them. It doesn't work to live scared and hold back in this loving relationship. It doesn't work to hear the word *codependence* as a pejorative, a connotation implicit in books such as *Codependent No More*. A *healthy marriage is a codependent one,* in which spouses feel a sense of completion because of their marriage and don't want to consider life without their spouse in it.

What does work is to listen, learn, and share all you can because you have this one chance to know someone more intimately than you will ever know another human being. It works to fall in love hard and start to see yourself in the other person. Need your spouse and make your spouse need you back. It will keep you together and give you strength beyond your wildest dreams when you least expect it.

❦❦❦❦❦❦❦❦❦❦❦❦❦❦❦❦❦❦❦❦❦❦❦

"I never wanted to be dependent on any man and I never wanted Greg to be one of those guys who needed me to cook him a good dinner and rub his back until he fell asleep," Cheryl told me as she and Greg discussed how to put their marriage back together after his affair. Greg and Cheryl found out that they lacked "need" in their relationship. They had married in their early thirties after both of them had built successful law careers. When Cheryl was suddenly faced with a high-risk pregnancy and confined to bed rest, life changed dramatically. She could no longer work, something she swore mothering would never stop her from doing. She became consumed with the daily issues surrounding the pregnancy. The pleasant lifestyle she and Greg had once shared came to a screeching halt.

During therapy, they discovered that to them, marriage had meant developing a sort of behavioral love for each other. In other words, marriage afforded them pleasures like dinner conversations, friendship, sex, and financial strength. They had lived alone for many years before marriage and were excited about never being lonely again. They spent most of their time together, whether going out with other couples or to professional or philanthropic gatherings. But when all of that suddenly stopped, they felt as if the wind had been knocked out of them. Each of them had come to marriage with an aversion to dependence. They made sure never to become too vulnerable to each other. They shared only the here and now, chatting about the fun they were having while unknowingly avoiding opening themselves up to one another and discussing their innermost feelings and thoughts. They knew very little about each other's childhood, and they never spoke of their past struggles or accomplishments unless it was regarding their law careers.

They knew to stay away from any conversation that wasn't fun. For example, politics brought out an intensity in both of them that made them uncomfortable. In fact, Cheryl had dreams of serving in public office one day but couldn't imagine following through with anything political because she and Greg were so opposite in their views. Although they spent a great deal of time together as husband and wife, they weren't building anything more than a convenient relationship that brought them a relatively superficial kind of pleasure. They were two independent people who happened to share a bed. It was soon after Cheryl was confined to bed with her pregnancy, and the "fun" was over, that Greg had his affair, even though he felt he loved Cheryl and had a "good" marriage.

❦❦❦❦❦❦❦❦❦❦❦❦❦❦❦❦❦❦❦❦❦❦❦❦❦❦❦❦❦❦❦❦

Needing your spouse does not mean you lose your spirit or sense of self. It means, in part, that you give over your whole self to the process of knowing your mate without worrying about where it will take you. By allowing your spouse to know every part of you and focusing on the same in your spouse, you will see life in a completely new light. You will be an inherently changed being and you will recognize yourself largely through the personality you've developed together because of the experiences you've shared with your spouse.

Knowing your spouse is what leads you to needing him or her. The more you open yourself to your spouse and let him or her know who you are, the less vulnerable you feel and the more able you are to depend on your spouse.

Knowing and needing are one and the same. As you deepen your knowledge of your spouse, you learn why you need this person so much, for his or her perspective, for what he or she can offer you.

Be There for Each Other

My husband just can't handle it," a woman in her sixties told me after she'd heard me give a talk about marriage. She told me of her illness. She asked me how she could convince her husband to be more involved in her recuperation. As she further explained, it wasn't that he was uncaring. In fact, she felt he was so caring that the entire situation hurt him too much and he had to distance himself from her. She had to turn instead to a group of friends who acted as her support system, and although she gained great strength from them, it wasn't enough. Sadly, her husband was missing out on a golden opportunity to become closer to his wife than ever before.

Part of why we marry is to have the unconditional love that will show us warmth, kindness, and caring, no matter what. All of us have unfortunate moments in life when we feel a little lost. When we reach out and help our spouse in need, we send the message, "I love you always, unconditionally and absolutely, for who you are and not for what you do for me." When your spouse is ill, whether it's a bout of depression, the flu, or a terminal illness, he or she can't give to you as before, or maybe not very much at all. When you show love during these times, you explicitly state that your relationship and love are not dependent on a what-have-you-done-for-me-lately attitude. They're founded on a feeling of oneness and need.

Imagine how you'd respond if you broke your leg. You would never be angry and emotionally distant toward your leg because it wasn't working properly and was causing other parts of your body greater stress. Your healthy leg wouldn't resent the broken one, because your body is one unit and willing to do whatever it takes to make the unit work even if it means finding new ways to handle life. You want to respond to your spouse in a similar manner. "I'm there for you" have to be four of the most beautiful words in life. They say, "I love you inside and out and am not thinking about me, but only Us."

※※※※※※※※※※※※※※※※※※※※※※※※※※※※※※※

When Peter's wife, Sarah, age thirty-four, was diagnosed with breast cancer, he admittedly didn't have the sympathetic, altruistic reaction he would have liked to have had. The couple had recently moved to a new city for a new job that required Peter to work plenty of overtime. It was the opportunity of a lifetime; he and Sarah had discussed how it would be hard for the next few years but that they would reap the benefits for years to come. "Now what?" was the first thought he had after the initial shock and fear wore off.

Peter had the money to hire full-time nurses, and Sarah's family was willing to travel to be with her while he worked late nights and traveled. He relied on this support system for his wife until the night he was awakened by a faint sound coming from the bathroom. There he found his wife crying, whimpering softly into a towel so she wouldn't awaken him, because he had a very important presentation in the morning. Stunned and saddened, he decided to spend the following morning attending a treatment with his wife instead of giving his presentation.

"I saw her in the waiting room with a scared, lonely look on her face," Peter shared with me much later. "I could only think one thing. What would I want if it were me? I knew I wouldn't want a revolving door of nurses caring for me. I'd want my loved one next to me to share it all." Within two months he was able to find a different job, with a lower salary and less prestige but considerably simpler hours. Through the rest of Sarah's surgery, chemo, and radiation they were together. Over those few months the most wonderful thing happened. They fell in love in a new kind of way. They had thought they had a pretty good marriage to begin with, but neither of them were prepared for what happened. Somewhere in the quiet conversations about life and death, fears and joys, dreams and nightmares mixed with the laughter and tears and in-depth philosophical debates regarding whether Shemp or Curly better served the Three Stooges, they found a oneness.

The following was part of a letter that Sarah wrote to Peter. He found it on his bureau when he returned home after her final surgery.

❋

When I first heard about my illness, I was terrified. I wondered why it was happening to me. I still don't know. But I know that the most special thing has happened to me because of it. Somehow you have given me the most loving, wonderful gift anyone could give. You gave me your whole entire self. I never knew there was so much love in the world. I never knew how far away from alone I could feel. I was always with you, in you, and you in me. I can't figure it all out, but believe it or not, if sickness and even passing was the way we could find each other, then it was all worth it. Because we can never be separated again. I'm sorry to have to leave you now alone. I hope you feel what I have felt so that you understand I'm with you always and waiting for you. Thank you for life.

It was twenty-two days after Peter read that letter that Sarah returned home from the hospital. She had been wrong in her life assessment. She miraculously came through surgery and recovery and has now been in remission for three and half years. Peter and Sarah live every day as one. They used the worst moments in life to be there for each other and to turn tragedy and pain into healing and growth. They now look forward to starting a family and expanding their oneness. They dared to need each other.

Difficult times become lonely when people back away from us because we're not at our best. However, we never forget the kindness offered us during our times of need. It's a kindness that asks for nothing in return. Even when your spouse is mildly ill or down and out, the kindness of taking care of him or her helps to create a strong emotional bond. Even the small acts of caring, like bringing tea or getting a video when your spouse has the flu, making him laugh when he's down and out, canceling your plan to go to the ballgame so you can listen carefully when she's sad all shout the message, "I love you unconditionally and want so much to be a part of who you are." "In sickness or in health, for better or for worse" aren't optional parts of your wedding vows.

Love is like the moon; when it does not increase it decreases.

—Segur

Need Each Other for the Good Times, Too

We don't need support and love only in times of hardship. When wonderful things happen to us, we need friends who can be genuinely happy for us, not jealous of us, or too involved in their own interests to share our joy. That's why it matters so much to have a partner at our side. When we experience a great personal success, we want to share it with someone who loves us for who we are and is genuinely happy just because we are happy. We want a spouse who can hear about how good we feel, again and again, without thinking that we're boring them or making them feel jealous. You and your spouse can make the good times far richer by showing each other how delighted you are for your mate.

Be there in good times by:

- *Talking it up*. Your spouse wants to have the opportunity to share and discuss the details, and you want to be that special person with whom your spouse can share them.
- *Celebrating*. Make a party in your spouse's honor, or have a private special celebration for the two of you when a special occasion arises.
- *Being your spouse's publicist*. It sounds like bragging if your spouse brings up his or her success, so show your mate how proud you are by sharing it with others, thus inviting your spouse to share your pride as well.

Imagine having something wonderful happen to you and not having a single person to share it with. Would that wonderful thing mean as much? We thrive on being able to share our happiness with others, and these good moments can help your marriage flourish just as much as being there for your spouse in times of need. When you are there for your spouse, you actively build a loving history of living life together as one unit.

Sweat the Small Stuff

Love is the irresistible desire to be irresistibly desired.

—Robert Frost

A relationship based on a healthy "need" can develop only through understanding your spouse. If you don't share your inner self with your spouse, he or she can't be there for you. As part of your commitment to building a "oneness" with your spouse, you want to offer him or her your whole self. As you share your thoughts and feelings, you allow your mate to appreciate and understand who you are and how you work. What makes each of you laugh or cry, what gives you feelings of sadness, joy, guilt, boredom, and meaning are unique openings to who you are and have come to be. Your spouse should know this more than anyone else. It is with your spouse that you want to take the time to discuss all of these issues and open up your innermost protected self so that your partner can feel what you feel.

Too often, we focus on the huge events that are supposed to make us close, like having a baby or some career success. But none of that makes any difference if two people are uncomfortable sharing. Closeness is never about the big things. It's all about the constant interaction and messages we can send to our lovers telling them that we want to know them and want them to know everything about us: "I love chocolate," "I was turned off to religion as a kid," "I hate it when people are dishonest," "I'm nervous in elevators," "I really want to spend a little more time alone with my dad," "I want to do something to help out our neighbor." How can you expect heartfelt, meaningful conversations with a person who isn't consistently privy to your heartfelt, meaningful thoughts and feelings?

Ted and Suzy were a simple example of two people who were having fun together yet were often angry and distant toward each other. Suzy was raised by a mother who complained about everything and a father who complained about her mom. Suzy promised herself she would never burden her husband the way she felt her parents overwhelmed her with their negativity. She was determined to be, as she put it, "a low-maintenance gal."

Ted had already suffered two failed marriages. He was so delighted he had found a wife on his third attempt whom he could really have fun with; he wasn't about to spoil it. In fact, his first wife's major complaint to him was that he was a "downer," and this critique had stayed with him through the years.

The result: Ted and Suzy were having fun except, of course, when they wanted to kill each other. One day Ted exploded when Suzy lined up a series of massages for herself and Ted. He was incensed that his business had suffered a 28 percent decrease in income in the last six months and yet Suzy kept spending as though nothing had happened. When I looked at Suzy for her response, she looked stunned. "Your business is suffering like that?" were the first words out of her mouth. The bottom line was that Ted never shared this information because he didn't want to put any constraints on Suzy, didn't want to spoil the "fun," didn't want to be a "downer." Sure, he had said things like, "Things have been tough at work," but when Suzy asked for an elaboration, he resisted. Ted hid the little details and stresses yet became resentful that he wasn't being heard.

Suzy discussed her own feeling that Ted lacked sensitivity. After all, he kept insisting that they scuba dive weekly, even though Suzy had severe back pain every time they finished. Guess what Ted's response was: "What back pain?" Sure, Suzy would say she had a twitch, but she'd quickly cover it up. Ted hadn't a clue that Suzy had to take prescription relaxants to get her over painful moments. They were trying to be the perfect, jolly couple and were losing their relationship quickly. They wanted something deeper than "fun" and had to find it by opening up and allowing each other to learn about the ups and downs of each other's feelings, thoughts, and lives.

We marry to find love within our truest, imperfect, neurotic selves. Perhaps we never realized that our mate could be so flawed, but it should make us feel better about ourselves as we recognize we are not alone in our inadequacies. Couples who share come to understand who they really are: two imperfect souls who love each other for who they are and what they can mean to each other. Remind yourself that both of you have a lot to learn, and thank goodness you each found someone to learn with.

We need to *share* everything, from our needs to our inner thoughts and feelings. This gives our spouse more knowledge about us and more of our personality to relate to. Be willing to repeat your needs, thoughts, and feelings. Don't take it personally if your spouse needs the repetition. It probably doesn't mean that he or she didn't listen the first time. Rather, it takes a long time to learn which part of your message you want your spouse to focus on.

Being Needed

Being needed is as important as needing in marriage. When our spouse seems to have it all together or has others who seem much more helpful than we are, we hurt. Although we can't be everything to our spouse, we should be the first one our spouse turns to to find his or her way. It should be you who can put a smile on his face after a miserable day. It can be your hug that makes her forget getting only three hours of sleep last night. It can be your simple words that remind him that you love him more than words can say, that can turn him into an emotional being again after dealing with a painful experience. Although there will be times when we can't work our magic, we want to know that we can do this for our spouse more than anyone, because we want to feel that close, closer than anyone else. We want to feel that our lover needs us as much as we need him or her.

⸻⸻⸻⸻⸻⸻⸻⸻⸻

Maria came to my office for one reason: to fix her husband, Ken. He was unreliable and did little to help in the home. Although both of them worked full-time, she felt completely alone and responsible for everything from finances to childcare.

"He does nothing, and let me tell you, I don't ask for much. In fact, I ask for nothing for myself, but for our kids, I think he should have to do something when it involves our kids."

But Ken complained that if he tried to do anything, Maria would interfere, take over the job, and do it "her way."

It was telling when Maria said she asked nothing for herself, as though it were a badge of honor. In fact, Maria refused to need Ken in any way, and she didn't even realize it. She had a profoundly "needy" father who was an alcoholic and also suffered from a severe anxiety disorder. Her mom's complete attention had been focused on Dad throughout Maria's childhood. Maria coped by learning to be a loner and never making herself vulnerable to anyone, especially her husband. She wasn't about to offer Ken a chance to "give" to her. She never wanted to become in any way dependent on him for any emotional support. Even when she was mugged and needed help at the police station, she didn't call Ken to accompany her. Instead, she took a friend and only told Ken hours later about the scare. The result of her emotional distance was a husband who had checked out emotionally and learned to avoid trying to "be there" for his wife. After all, whenever he did try to be supportive, Maria found fault with his attempt and would say, "Just forget it. You'll never understand."

Maria's realization that she wasn't allowing Ken to be her partner caused her to start considering ways to let him into her life. She forced herself to share her day's highs and lows and resisted the urge to correct Ken or become frustrated. She even began to tell him exactly what she wanted: "I'd like for you to come with me to talk to the teacher." "Please hold me and tell me you love me." "Come to my parents' home with me and tell me we have to leave when you see them begin to fight." For the first time in her life, she began to rely on someone else. Yes, she had become more vulnerable, but she also became much more lovable. She needed to need, and Ken needed to be needed.

✳

One final example of how need can transform a marriage is when Greg and Cheryl decided to open their innermost thoughts and feelings to each other. It was unnatural at first and took some real practice. In fact, they decided to jump-start this sharing by reserving twenty minutes every night for one week; in this time, they faced each other and talked only of feelings and deep thoughts. It was awkward and contrary to everything they had come to believe about marriage. But they were able to be honest about their frailties and to talk about how each of them could grow. They even dared to share political views, but this time they heard each other and were willing to just listen and understand without caring about their own perspective. They learned to see life together, to teach each other how to be there for one another, to let each other know what each needed.

Life became much more relaxed, and they began to feel like they were meeting for the first time. A therapy session rarely passed without one of them saying, "I never knew that . . .": "I never knew that you liked my humor . . . hated affirmative action . . . read Ayn Rand . . . were bullied by a big girl named Bertha throughout elementary school." Amazingly, all of this loving work was done while they were also raising their first child, which only added to their inability to keep up their perfect façade. They learned to depend on each other.

If you entered their home today, you probably wouldn't even notice the most telling piece of artwork there. Amongst the chatter of children (they went on to have one more child without the help of fertility drugs) and children's artwork framed throughout the home sits a campaign poster with Cheryl's picture. It is the only testimony in the home to Cheryl's unsuccessful bid to a seat in the county commission. But it represents volumes in the changes that she and Greg made in their marriage: in the lower right-hand corner of the poster is Greg's name as campaign manager. They learned to talk politics after all.

Visualize Your Need: Write Your Own Love Story

Buy one inexpensive notebook. You and your spouse are going to share this notebook and write your personal love story. But this story isn't going to be simply about romance. Your goal is to create a story about real love: the moments that you know you are right for each other because of what your spouse means to you, the times when you feel secure and excited that you get to be married the rest of your life.

To help create this "need" and oneness, you and your spouse must begin to visualize what being married might mean to you. Write about the small moments that make married life better than being single. For example: "I came home and looked into your eyes. You smiled and reassured me everything would be okay and suggested we go out to dinner so you could listen to my thoughts and concerns." "I felt your hug and your whispered words 'I love you and will always be here for you,' and I felt all was right with the world." "We lay on the beach in the warm ocean breezes, softly stroking each other as if there were only the two of us in the world." "We laughed and laughed in front of the fireplace." It's all small stuff, and it means the whole world. Record the little things that have happened that are meaningful to you and then record the little things you'd like to hear and feel from your spouse as well as do for your spouse.

Share some personal secrets as you write: "I had never kissed a woman so softly on her cheek, had never felt a woman's touch so gentle, so kind." "I was afraid for much of my life that no one could love me with my frailties, and yet I found a person who cares so deeply for me and lets me know it constantly." "I believed I wasn't very smart because I wasn't well read until you praised me for my creativity and helped me understand my unique 'brightness.'" Write about how life is so much more wonderful because of your spouse. Pour out your love in this story.

Now focus on those moments when you needed your spouse or felt needed: "When my mom passed away, you stayed by me every second." "When my career spiraled downward, you kept letting me know how much you still believed in me." Don't forget the small but meaningful gestures: "You brought me flowers for no specific reason." "You took great pride in my accomplishments of the day." "You made me feel so incredibly special by arranging a wonderful, peaceful evening together with no outside distractions."

Continuing the idea of codependence, look well into your future and spell out your love story. Write about your vision of your children's weddings, the grandchildren, your romantic trips together, and whatever else helps you feel comfortable with the vulnerability that comes with needing each other. Write about how both of you become closer and closer over the years.

Keep the journal in a drawer or out on your nightstand, and be sure that both of you write a few lines in it at least once a week (use some of the time that you will spend together as a result of Secret #6). When it's your turn, pick up in the middle of the story where your spouse left off, trying to keep a fluid story line going.

You Need Your Spouse's Differences

The clearest explanation for the failure of any marriage is that the two people are incompatible; that is, one is male and the other female.

—Anna Quindlen

Men and women are different in myriad ways. Marriage experts often suggest that through understanding and respecting these differences, couples can get along in spite of them. However, these experts fail to explain how these differences are crucial to developing a healthy, loving, and lasting marriage.

Did you ever notice how sometimes when you're indoors, the sun will suddenly peer in, sending a light beam that unexpectedly illuminates countless little dust particles right in front of your eyes? Obviously, the sunlight did not create those dust particles but rather helped you discover what you were blind to only seconds ago. It's hard to imagine that there can be something right in front of your eyes that you don't see without the proper light. Yet there is much we don't see in life, since we are often blinded by our own beliefs and perspective.

How do we let in the sunlight and illuminate our world? When we look at life through the eyes of another, we begin to share a world full of countless lessons, new experiences, and possibilities. Each of us brings a unique perspective to our world, based on our genes, spirit, and history, and we can learn to share this perspective. Sharing is at the heart of living, because it brings new realities into our lives. Without it, we are doomed to learn only from ourselves as individuals and will be blind to what others can see. The more we can see life through the eyes of another, the more we can grow, give, create, love, and understand others.

This is the number one reason you need your spouse. No one else will give you the opportunity to grow as much as your spouse, because no one will be both as different *and* as intimate with you. Consider how much you can learn from your best same-sex friend. Of course you can grow a great deal from such a relationship. But your perspective is likely to be similar to your friend's because men see the world like other men and the same goes for women. But when you marry, you have the opportunity to see a perspective on life that is much different from your own. Even though it is likely you have interests and opinions in common with your spouse, the difference in gender will naturally cause huge differences in perspective.

When I married my wife more than fourteen years ago, I wanted to learn about life with her. I had no intention of learning any one thing, and yet I couldn't wait to learn everything. I learned pieces of things, like what it's like to be a woman, a young girl. I listened to her fears, saw what brought her joy, and heard her dreams. I never knew someone else's sadness so clearly and never experienced another's joy so closely. I learned to solve problems from a woman who never sees "problems," only challenges to which she delights in finding creative solutions. She introduced me to wonderful literature I never would have noticed. I even learned to dress better. The list could go on and on.

And she has heard my innermost thoughts and feelings as well. As a result, she's calmer and more comfortable within her skin. I've helped her feel more confident. We've discovered such a wide variety of things together, including learning our way around the computer world, the stock market, raising children, lovemaking, and even how to make brioche. If my wife and I thought alike and agreed on every matter, we'd have the most boring marriage on the planet. We are different, but we've allowed those differences to fascinate us as we've delved into them so that we could use them as opportunities to grow and know each other and life a little better.

Sergio, like many men who have allowed themselves to grow with their wives, told me he has learned a completely new way to see the world, through feelings. He had always been intensely cognitive, weighing everything in life according to a cost-benefit analysis and common sense. But his wife, Arlene, taught him to listen to the feelings of the people around him. Sergio attributes his great business success to what he learned from Arlene. He feels he can now read people better, ask better questions to find out what kind of people they are. This helps him in every aspect of business, from hiring employees to considering with whom to make deals or partnerships. He never realized how much he hid from his feelings.

On the other hand, Arlene recognizes how much calmer she has become since marrying Sergio. She finds his cognitive, commonsense approach helpful. When she's angry at others for hurting her feelings, Sergio has a way of helping her understand that she shouldn't be taking things so personally. She appreciates his "reality check" and has learned to blend her feelings with a large dose of understanding others around her.

Another wife described her husband's patience and ability to take in a situation calmly. She had been "on the run" her whole life, thinking that being in motion equaled growth. But when she listened more and more to her husband and stopped to smell the roses, she suddenly found inspiration from the simplest of things—a sunset, just watching her child, cooking. Her husband had brought a peace to her life that she never would have known without him. She moved more slowly and, because of him, saw much more. Her husband spoke of the great structure his wife offered him. Yes, he knew how to enjoy life but felt that he wasn't living up to his potential because of his disorganized and lackadaisical nature. His wife showed him how to find excitement along with more activity and an organized day.

One husband told me how he had lost so much money in the stock market before he married. He attributed his incredible success after his marriage to his wife. He explained that he noticed her making important decisions without the amount of thought and research he did before forming an important opinion. He learned from her what it meant to go with your gut instinct, and when he tried this he was met with wonderful success.

A wife declared to me that many people would have died if it wasn't for her relationship with her husband. As an emergency room nurse, she has to make hundreds of life-or-death decisions every day. Sometimes, however, there are disagreements between nurses, or between a doctor and a nurse, about what action to take for a patient. This woman always deferred to others' opinions. But spurred by her husband's genuine respect for her and her knowledge, she began to speak up. He was so fascinated by what she was able to do that she began to believe she was as great as her husband believed. Her change of behavior saved a life in the first week she made the decision to speak up to a doctor she respectfully disagreed with. The doctor wrote her a thank-you for her professional contribution. She promptly gave it to her husband and said, "This thank-you is for you."

These couples learned from the best of each other. Neither was perfect, before or after marriage, but they each began to realize that they were better people because they needed their spouses.

Hearing Your Spouse's Opinion

Jeff and Patrice were planning a vacation, the first in many years. Jeff wanted to take his wife and two boys, ages ten and twelve, to an isolated beach. He just wanted to spend quiet time with his family. Patrice disagreed. She wanted them to visit her relatives in California. Jeff began to resent her opinion and took it personally. He thought, "Why doesn't she just want to be with me?" He then forced himself to focus on the following four steps to understanding his spouse's point:

1. *Think: What is the heart of my spouse's opinion?* Jeff thought Patrice was saying that she wanted to stay in relatives' homes instead of a fun hotel.

2. *Tell your spouse what you think is the heart of his/her message.* Even when you get the heart of the message wrong, it gives your spouse a chance to correct your assumption. When Jeff said, "You'd rather we stay with relatives and spend our vacation visiting with them?" it gave Patrice the opportunity to clarify that she never meant that they should stay with relatives. Rather, she just wanted to spend some of the vacation with relatives they never get to see.

3. *Consider: Why does my spouse have this opinion?* Jeff had to clarify that Patrice wanted to see her relatives, not that she didn't want to spend as much time with Jeff. He had to recognize this was not a personal slight.

4. *Discuss why your spouse has this opinion and ask followup questions.* Through discussion, Jeff learned that relatives were an important part of Patrice's childhood. She wanted her children to have some of that experience and felt this trip could provide that. Patrice never intended to spend all of their vacation time with relatives. She wanted to vacation near them so that they could spend two or three days out of their two-week vacation with relatives. Jeff had made many incorrect assumptions about his wife's opinion that were easily clarified with some calm discussion.

React Differently to Differences

Of course, our differences don't just complete us; sometimes they drive us nuts. As we strive to know and need each other more, there will be inevitable friction. But the next time your spouse states an opinion that is different from yours, resist the urge to fight back and prove your point. Instead, sit back and try to simply understand it from your spouse's point of view. Sounds difficult? Perhaps it will be under stressful circumstances. But when you consider that you ask your children to do the same, it helps keep things in perspective.

When you confront your ten-year-old about something you feel he needs to consider changing, do you expect him to freak out and start hammering you about the flaws in your opinion? If your child reacted that way, you'd explain that you only meant what you said out of love and that he will never grow if he turns a deaf ear to any viewpoint that's different from his own. You'd further explain that if he could explain his own point of view, perhaps you'd see where you could compromise. Sounds like a mature response? Ask nothing less of yourself than you would of your child.

The ability to stretch our perspective is what keeps life powerfully interesting. Understanding your spouse does not mean you will agree. Coming to some agreement is an important task that will be discussed later in Secret #4. But the final decision matters less when both of you realize that you feel a little closer as you've come to understand each other a little better.

This is what I mean by "growing together." Marriage isn't going to change your personality. But it can change your focus and perspective, and for that growth you should be eternally grateful. The moment we stop trying to change, we might as well be dead.

Most people in my office fight this concept of change, especially men. They say things like, "I am who I am. You can't expect me to be a different person." They're trying to rationalize why they should do *practically nothing* to grow as a human being. Likewise, I've counseled people who want to grow so much that they spend enormous time (some traveling to the ends of the world) searching for "spiritual growth" but refuse to read a news magazine to have a more interesting conversation with their spouses. No one likes to have demands placed on them. We aren't very good at seeing our faults and limitations, and one of the reasons we marry is to be with someone who will accept us as we are. But this acceptance isn't the same as the unconditional acceptance a parent should have for a child. Spouses do need to share this role of acceptance, as clearly outlined in Secret #5. But make no mistake about it, your spouse is not your parent or your child. We shouldn't marry so we can be who we want to be and have someone tag along for our ride. Loving someone means being sensitive to his or her desires and needs. And that means we have to accept the idea of change. Often, we have to change to grow.

Change Your Focus and Change Your Life

All of us can change, but change needs to come from a shift in *focus*, not from a *personality* make-over. If I want to be less selfish, I need to focus more on the feelings of others and catch myself when I'm falling into the old trap of being concerned only for my own feelings. *Change your focus and you will change.*

When you realize that you need to make a change in some area, figure out how you want your spouse to support you. For example, if you want to stop criticizing your wife, consider, "How do I want my wife to remind me that I'm criticizing her again and need to stop what I'm doing?" The person who will be making the change should create the signal that the other person will give as a reminder to focus. This way the person is less likely to resist the signal that he or she created. Some people just ask their spouse to make a calm comment about the given situation: "Honey, you're starting to do what we spoke about." One husband asked his wife to give him a big hug when he started to become critical. One woman asked that her husband squeeze her hand lovingly.

The spouse who needs to change in a given area has to create personal reminders as well. One husband who decided he needed to be more loving

Two Steps to Change

List three areas you think your spouse would want you to improve. Under each item list two behavioral changes or actions you can take in the next day to achieve this goal. For example:

1. Show more affection to my spouse.
   - Offer more daily hugs.
   - Listen intently to my spouse without interruption.
2. Be more fiscally responsible.
   - Put away credit cards and use cash only.
   - Pay bills as they come in; don't delay.
3. Spend more time with spouse.
   - Go to lunch once this week (tomorrow) instead of with a colleague.
   - Come home earlier and make some calls from home.

simply made a memo on his Palm Pilot that reminded him daily to call his wife and say, "I love you," as well as to make other loving gestures. One wife carried a bottle of massage oil in her purse to remind herself to touch her husband more when they were together. One man I counseled, who vehemently resisted the concept that he needed to change, finally saw that his marriage couldn't last if he was unwilling to grow in it. He carried around enough coins in his pocket to jingle when he walked. The "change" in his pocket reminded him of his constant need to change. Find your own unique way to stay focused, and change and personal and marital growth will happen.

On your fiftieth wedding anniversary, you should be able to look back at yourself and see a person who had so much to learn. Be appreciative for the personal changes you were able to create within because of a spouse who loved you and needed you enough to share his or her life with you.

Forgiveness: "I'm Sorry" Means "I Need You"

It is hard for so many of us to forgive and be able to get over past pain. In marriage, holding on to past pain and an inability to genuinely forgive is devastating. It keeps us from depending on and trusting each other. Forgiveness is crucial to any life experience, because as human beings we will inevitably make mistakes and hurt others.

Seeing our spouse's effort to change is the key that gives us the strength to forgive and move on. So many spouses express to me, "How will we ever get anywhere if he/she can't forget the past?" What these spouses don't understand is that love makes us vulnerable. Why should you open your loving, tender self to a spouse who has been in your opinion constantly insensitive?

But when your spouse *changes* and shows that he or she is working hard at being a better partner, that allows forgiveness to set in. You can forgive when:

- You feel your spouse understands how he or she hurt you.
- You see your spouse changing so you no longer have to protect yourself from being hurt.

I have a friend whose arm was severely damaged by someone's irresponsibility. He once told me that every time he even hears that person's name he is full of anger. But it was what he told me next that helped me understand this concept of the healing power of change. He told me that there was one point at which the doctors felt his arm was going to make a full recovery. That night, just after this consultation with his doctors, he saw this person in a restaurant and was amazed to feel so calm.

As long as my friend thought his arm would return to "normal," he wasn't as angry at this person. If his arm had been 100 percent better for ten years, he wouldn't have felt a twinge of anger at seeing that person. As much as this person was still just as irresponsible, the problem was corrected. But as long as my friend suffered from the injury, it was a constant reminder to him of this person's carelessness.

If you have hurt your spouse in a specific way in the past and continue to do so, then every time you hurt him or her, your spouse feels some of the pain from every past hurt as well. Your spouse will likely keep bringing it up and feeling it. Your spouse is walking around with a damaged arm like my friend, and every time you inflict a further wound, it hurts the arm all over again. But if you change, if you show that you are focusing greatly on changing as fast as you can, your spouse's pain can heal. Down the road, your spouse will have no need to remember the past because it isn't alive with the pain of today. You cannot expect your spouse to just "get over it" as long as you haven't offered an appropriate, heartfelt apology along with the commitment to change and signs of effort.

However, if you are the spouse who has been hurt, remember that all your spouse can do is to apologize and change. Your spouse cannot erase the past. If you feel your spouse has genuinely apologized for hurting you and is no longer repeating these hurtful actions (or inactions), and yet you still bring these actions up and can't seem to rid yourself of the memory of them, you have the problem. Usually, the offended spouse will tell me, "He never really apologized," "She really hasn't changed," and therefore forgiveness and releasing the focus on past memories are limited. But if your spouse is doing his or her best to change, no matter if it's slower than you'd like, your job is to focus on moving on. Nothing takes the motivation out of a person who is trying to change more than when a spouse takes what is a small mistake and likens it to large mistakes of the past.

For example, let's suppose your spouse used to call you horrible names during fights. He's made a huge effort to change, but he recently slipped and called you one name, whereupon he stopped immediately and apologized. If you treat him as if he acted the same way as in the past and you don't ver-

Forgiveness

Saying "I'm sorry" is one of the most important tools of marriage. But the words alone are not enough. It's the sensitivity behind the words that makes them work.

1. *Before you even say, "I'm sorry," ask your spouse to explain to you exactly what he or she felt.*

2. *Understand your spouse's hurt, not how you would feel under the same circumstances.* Feel what it must be like to be your spouse. For example, you insulted your spouse's family. You may be someone who isn't easily insulted, and so you tend to minimize how your spouse feels. After all, your comment wouldn't have bothered you if your spouse had said it to you. But your spouse is more sensitive in these areas and thus feels hurt, more than you would.

3. *Describe to your spouse what you hear him or her saying.* Repeat to your spouse how you think he or she feels. This gives your spouse the chance to be reassured that you get it and aren't just saying "I'm sorry" to get yourself out of a jam.

4. *Say, "I'm sorry," and then add what you are sorry about,* even if this sounds repetitive after step 3. At this point you may correct any misconception—for example, if you feel your spouse misunderstood your comment or action, or if you want to explain that you behaved badly because of something that happened to you today that caused you to be particularly insensitive.

5. *Discuss how this hurt can be avoided in the future.* Let your spouse know you are committed to changing and working together. What can you do and what can your spouse do to avoid this pain in the future?

6. *Work to make those changes.* Forgiveness and forgetting the past comes from seeing changes in your spouse's behavior.

balize that he's grown (although there's still a great deal of room for improvement), if you suddenly give him the silent treatment for a couple of days, you are trivializing your spouse's accomplishments and his motivation to continue to work at changing. Once your spouse has admitted to faults and is committed to change, your job of releasing the pain of the past begins immediately. If you can't do this after you feel you've received all you should expect from your spouse (an apology, commitment to change, and signs of efforts to change), talk to a mental health professional and discover what deeper issues are stopping you from forgetting the past. The longer the change continues, the stronger the forgiveness and release of the past.

I have an exceptional relationship with my wife, but make no mistake, it isn't that way because my wife or I have the "great marriage gene." My wife and I could easily be divorced today. Each of us has been angry at the other, depressed, tearful, emotionally overwhelmed, and disappointed at various points in our marriage. We have each discovered personal issues and struggles born out of our pasts that we did not even know existed when we first married. *The key that forced us to become a unit was this: We were committed to making our marriage work as a team no matter what we learned about each other.* We never succumbed to the trap of going at it from different corners. If we had a problem, the problem was the focus, not one of us. Whenever we found ourselves in the midst of a difficult marital moment, one of us caught him- or herself and brought the focus back to this commitment.

We learned to apologize, the simple most important tool for a couple in the midst of struggle, and allowed the one who was hurt to fully explain him- or herself so that the other knew what the apology was for. We would discuss what each of us could do to avoid this mistake and hurt from ever happening again. We found that signals or code words were useful for us in knowing that something was important or bothering us early on. And it was never all about just one of us. We each took responsibility for what we both might have done to have brought about a problem. I believe we have argued and hurt each other far less than most. But it was because of our decision to make it that way.

Building Need into Your Marriage

Love does not consist in gazing at each other but in looking together in the same direction.

—Antoine de Saint-Exupéry

Needing your spouse doesn't mean becoming dependent in a way that will trap you, reduce you, or make you into someone you don't want to become. Needing your spouse is a way to experience greater warmth and love in life as your perspective broadens and you learn to share yourself and receive

Six Reasons Why the Marital Foundation Is Built on Need

1. Need will protect our marriage when we do not desire or lust for our spouse.
2. We need to grow. Our greatest growth will come through our marriage, because our spouse is both extremely different from us and will be more intimate with us than anyone else.
3. We need to connect to another through sharing our most personal inner selves.
4. We need to be needed by others.
5. Need will motivate us to put enormous energy toward understanding our spouse. If we only "want" our spouse, we will not find it necessary to truly understand him or her.
6. We need each other to complete our sense of spirit.

the gift of warmth from one who loves you dearly. As spouses become more dependent on each other, more willing to change and grow, more able to forgive and move on, they can share more experiences together and never grow tired or bored of life as a married couple.

Affairs are often occasioned by newness, by meeting someone who offers fresh perspectives and opinions. Keep talking and pointing out your perspective about the important as well as the mundane, and love with your spouse will never grow stale. You will capture that energy and excitement of growth in your own marriage. You will know what it's like to live larger than your individual self.

Step 1: Invite Differences into Your Marriage

One of the reasons we marry should be to find a better self within our collective marriage than if we remained individuals. To continue to focus on our individual point of view would be to sever our ability to develop ourselves.

Greg and Cheryl laughed out loud in my office when I first asked them if they discussed things like politics.

"What am I missing here?" I asked curiously.

"Oh, it's not you. But you've found a real sore spot. We are so vehemently opposed in our political beliefs that we learned even before we got married that we couldn't talk politics," Greg explained as Cheryl added, "Without killing each other, that is. You'll have to come up with a different subject for us."

It would have been easy for me to skip right over politics and find an area that was easy for them to discuss, something they saw eye to eye on. But that would have been reducing the quality and potential "need building" of their marriage. Conversations about politics were the perfect catalyst for each of them to enjoy what the other could offer. They had to appreciate the growth that comes from seeing the world through someone else's eyes.

Avoiding conflict is avoiding need. You can't learn from another perspective without hearing and taking notice of another perspective. The idea of avoiding any meaningful conversation on which Greg and Cheryl would disagree was deadly to their ability to appreciate each other's differences and to find avenues for personal and marital growth. Without learning to appreciate their differences, they never could have collaborated on Cheryl's campaign. They had to begin by learning to listen.

Step 2: Learn to Listen, Not Debate

There are two states of being: talking and waiting to talk. No listening!

—Fran Lebowitz

Whenever Alice and Nick discussed current events, they felt that one was always trying to prove his or her point in an attempt to persuade the other to change opinions. If they didn't agree, Nick took it personally, as if Alice didn't respect his point of view. I asked if there were other volatile issues. "The Yankees." Believe it or not, some of their most bitter arguments began with opinions about the Yankees, because they often avoided any serious topics that they didn't see eye to eye on. Without realizing it, they had found trivial topics safe from strife. The Yankees were an open "fun" topic that they argued about comfortably, figuring it was just baseball. But both finally admitted that they never ended a Yankee conversation feeling good. It reminded them that they were both attorneys who were good at making their points and trying to convince others that they were right. They were dismissive of each other's viewpoints. They didn't know how to listen.

Practice Listening

Each of you takes a turn speaking to the other for ten uninterrupted minutes. Talk about anything you want, from your day's stress to your dreams and aspirations.

The listening spouse must make eye contact and be genuinely interested, putting his or her full attention on what is being said and thinking:

1. What is the heart of my spouse's message?
2. How is my spouse feeling about what is being said (happy, elated, sad, angry, confused, disppointed, frustrated . . .)?
3. How would my spouse want me to respond?

Use these three questions to guide you in your response after your spouse's ten minutes are up. Weave the answer to any one or more of the three questions into your response: "It sounds like you're so happy your boss gave you the extra vacation time you asked for." "How frustrating to have to call the repairman three times for something he supposedly fixed already." "Wow, I'm tired just from listening to how much energy it took to take care of Timmy while he was sick and get everything else done."

Turn off all beepers and cell phones during the conversation. One couple brought new meaning to the term "pillow talk." The person holding the designated pillow would be allowed to speak uninterrupted as the other spouse listened intently until the first spouse gave up the pillow and allowed the other to respond.

My wife and I were engaged on our fourth date. We were married three months from our first date. Because of Jewish law, we neither had sex or even physically touched before our wedding day. Were we crazy? How could we take such a chance after knowing each other for a such short time? How could we know we'd be compatible, emotionally or sexually?

We listened. When we were together, the rest of the world faded away. My wife and I felt a longing to know more about each other. We practically ached because of how much we didn't know and desired to know. When we sent the message to each other that "I want to listen to you, I want to know every detail about you," we knew we could never go wrong. That is what respect is all about.

If you and your spouse listen to each other, it shows how much you value each other's words, thoughts, and feelings. You never have to question your compatibility. The two of you will always find ways to make both of you feel loved and satisfied. Spouses are more affectionate when they feel their lover respects them.

Miriam, a waitress for over ten years at our favorite local restaurant, once told me, "I can always tell who has a good and bad marriage by the way the couple order their meal off the menu. Spouses with a bad marriage are dismissive of each other. He'll be looking at the menu, thinking out loud about what he'd like, and she'll wave her hand, give me her menu and say, 'Just order already.' I often will have a conversation with him to help him decide what he wants. But his spouse should be doing that. The happy couples listen to each other. They try to help each other order, saying things like, 'What are you in the mood for?' or 'What was it you had last time that you really liked?' They don't rush each other."

Be aware of how much you're listening versus dismissing your spouse's thoughts and feelings.

Listening is an often misunderstood art. Think about how often you have your thoughts formulated before the other person in the conversation has finished a statement. You begin to plan your words without realizing it, assuming you have fully understood the other person's point of view and now have something probably more interesting to add or an immediate way to reject it. We often use what we've heard as a springboard for what we want to say. It's easy to understand why this limits personal growth. Listening becomes a means to an end, the end being to state your own point of view.

There is little more important in life than listening and being heard. Why does it feel so good when you share some grief or celebration with another and feel like he or she genuinely understood? Life is about connections. When you find that person who wants to share in every triumph

Steps to Connecting with Your Spouse

1. Listen to your spouse's words: the connection begins.
2. Avoid responding with your point of view.
3. Paraphrase and or express how you think it must feel to be in your spouse's shoes.
4. Allow your spouse to continue and fully explain his or her points or feelings.
5. Ask questions that might clarify your spouse's position or feelings, or say, "Tell me more."
6. Share your point of view.

The main issue that Greg and Cheryl could not discuss without enormous tension and anger was Greg's affair. As hard as it was to hear, Greg was finally able to listen to how betrayed and rejected Cheryl felt because of his affair. He wanted to defend himself by explaining how the high-risk pregnancy was such a drastic change for them. Because he clearly knew in his heart that he was wrong and felt guilty, it was hard for him to listen to Cheryl express her feelings. And the more Cheryl sensed that Greg was not truly hearing her pain, the more she felt a need to focus on it and bring it up.

But Greg did learn to connect. He made the commitment to listening because he began to understand that somehow he was going to grow from listening, and that the marriage would grow from understanding. The moment he did this, their relationship changed dramatically. He allowed himself to hear her pain. For example, he never understood that his affair brought back the intense rejection Cheryl had felt as a child when her father divorced her mom and moved out of state. It hurt Greg to see how much pain his actions caused. But it helped him achieve the proper remorse that the marriage needed. Greg and Cheryl cried together as they connected even from the experience of discussing this painful period in their marriage. But it wasn't about pain anymore. It was about connecting.

After Greg understood his wife, he genuinely apologized for the first time. It wasn't the first time he had said, "I'm sorry" about the affair, but before, his apology had been for what *he felt* he did wrong. Now, he was sorry for the painful feelings he had caused in Cheryl. He could never have felt that remorse until he was sensitive to his wife.

In later discussions, Greg was able to verbalize how alone he had felt when Cheryl was bedridden and understandably consumed with the pregnancy.

Cheryl's earlier instinct had been to attack with, "What did you want from me? And you think that gives you the right to fool around? How about some sympathy for me, the one who had to be chained to a bed?" But this time she didn't take it personally and instead worked to hear her husband's message. He never meant to justify his actions in any way but rather to help her understand his needs and how they would have to learn to cope with life's struggles in the future. He wasn't telling her that she had made a mistake but rather was letting her learn about his coping abilities. Who's right or wrong often isn't as important as understanding the way your mate works.

By the end of the conversation, Cheryl was able to see that Greg needed her and had become somewhat lost when he'd felt she'd abandoned him emotionally. Greg explained that he hadn't shared his needs when she was pregnant for fear of appearing selfish. Cheryl admitted that she would have reacted that way. But they really wanted the same thing in their times of struggle. Had they only been able to discuss their thinking and feelings openly, they would have discovered that they could still recapture some of the romance. The could have eaten dinner in bed together, watched videos, reminded themselves that they'd return to the social lifestyle they both loved once the baby was born. The only reason that Greg and Cheryl were able to correct this wrong and grow from it was because they decided to begin to understand each other instead of trying to convince each other of a position.

Greg and Cheryl also began to hear each other when they discussed other serious issues, like childrearing. They forgot about proving their points and started to delight in hearing such fascinating differences in thought. Instead of remembering how much they knew, they marveled at how much they didn't know. They also learned so much more about each other, since these discussions often brought up personal history about each other's childhood and how they were each parented.

and tribulation, you feel whole. We were made to connect and learn from others, and it is through marriage that we can achieve this completion. Marriage offers us the ultimate connection with a life partner.

Whenever your partner speaks, see it as a form of growth. As soon as a word is spoken, the connection begins. Focus away from the outcome or decision you'd like to see. *It's not about the final decision but about the process of sharing and connecting.* Literally lose yourself in your lover's words as you begin to feel the connection. Look into your spouse's eyes and even reach out and hold his or her hand to increase the connection. Imagine how wonderful it is that he or she is sharing with you.

Avoid responding immediately with your point of view. Instead, focus on your spouse's comment and send the verbal message that you understand. Use the three questions given above, or simply paraphrase the point or make a sympathetic remark involving how your spouse probably feels: "It sounds so frustrating to hear your boss tell you for the fifth time about a mistake you already admitted to a week ago." "It hurts your feelings when I make those little jokes about your driving?" "You're worried the kids will be bored at my mom's house and we've got to figure out some plan to avoid them getting out of hand."

Follow up with questions about your spouse's point: "How did your boss put it this time?" "Is it that the area doesn't offer anything child-friendly or that Mom's place doesn't have many toys and isn't set up for our kids?" Don't remove yourself from this connection until you feel you fully understand it.

Three simple words mean so much: *"Tell me more."* It's a delightful statement that declares your interest in your spouse's comments. We love to be heard.

Unfortunately, many spouses have difficulty listening. For example, men often analyze. When a man's wife talks, his brain chases after why his spouse feels this way, what the real deeper problem is, and what possible solutions are available. The problem is not that the husband offers solutions. Solutions are helpful. The real problem is that to get to the solution, the husband doesn't process how the wife really feels, or search for what the heart of the problem is, by listening carefully and asking for more information. So his wife feels disrespected without having a full chance to express herself. It's disquieting to have someone analyzing you, as if to say, "I know you better than you do and I'll tell you what the deeper problem is." Even if you feel your analysis is correct, your insight is less important than your sensitive listening and understanding.

No matter how mundane or illogical you may think your spouse's feelings or points are, connect and you'll understand something about life you probably never would have seen without sharing life with your spouse. Your spouse doesn't have to share some profound thought or feeling for you to grow dramatically from knowing him or her.

Step 3: Learn How to Fight

What counts in making a happy marriage is not so much how compatible you are but how you deal with incompatibility.

—Leo Tolstoy

Couples fight for many reasons, but the main one is that they don't really listen. We argue when we don't understand each other. We feel hurt, insulted, and unloved. I've witnessed countless fights in my office. Often, they had little to do with the topic that began the disagreement. Most couples can't even remember what started the fight because the actual fight had nothing to do with whatever they originally disagreed about. When couples do discuss the details of the fight, they both usually have valid points. Consider the deeper reason why you're fighting with your spouse. You may feel hurt, disrespected, neglected, or demeaned, so you reacted defensively or aggressively.

Unfortunately, couples have difficulty listening to the genuine messages that their spouses share. So when your spouse says, "I can't believe you made me stand here in the cold for a half hour so you could talk to your friends a little more and pick me up late," you respond with, "It wasn't a half hour, and for heaven's sake, you always keep me waiting, and who knew you'd be waiting outside." Now you're off to the races. Within thirty seconds, you'll be arguing about how your spouse made your parents wait in an airport eight years ago.

How does the conversation degenerate so quickly? Lack of listening. When your spouse shared that you made him wait in the cold, he was expressing his anger over feeling disrespected. The way he sized up the situation, your friends were more important to you than he was. It would have been great if he'd said that clearly, but your spouse isn't going to articulate every feeling perfectly. Instead of focusing on how he was feeling, you heard him attack you and immediately tried to protect yourself with a sound defense and mighty offense, which shows him greater disrespect. In essence you were saying, "You might think you were here waiting in the cold for thirty minutes, but guess what? You're wrong. Oh and by the way"—here comes the offense—"you always make me wait so I have no problem disrespecting you the same way you disrespect me even though I feel hurt when you do it to me." Finally, you hit him with the "not your fault" answer. You didn't know he'd be waiting outside, so you don't have to take any real responsibility.

Change Fighting into Understanding

- *Review the past.* Answer the following questions, then trade responses with your spouse and discuss them together. Give your spouse the chance to correct your answers to numbers 1, 2, 3, 4, and 7.
  1. What was our last fight about?
  2. How many times have we fought about that subject before?
  3. How do I think you felt during this fight?
  4. What do I think was your point of view?
  5. How did I feel during the fight?
  6. What was my point of view?
  7. How would you have preferred me to act during this last fight?
  8. How would I have preferred you to act?
- *Get more insight into your reactions.* Answer the following questions:
  1. Who have I ever seen fight before? (My parents, siblings, children?)
  2. Am I comfortable with their style of fighting?
  3. What don't I like about their style of fighting?
  4. What do I like about their style of fighting?
  5. What do I think they could do that would improve their style of working through conflict? (Be creative and list all possibilities.)
  6. Which suggestions would work for me?
- *Build team spirit.* Imagine yourself and your spouse as a team. When a problem arises, see the problem as the "enemy." Say aloud, "We'll work this out together." Couples in troubled marriages blame each other and feel the other spouse is the problem. Healthy marriages approach the problem with a "we're in this together" attitude. Even if the problem is largely about your spouse—perhaps not properly caring for his or her health or drinking too heavily—think of it as "We have a problem to fix. Let's get to it."

Waiting for each other is not the issue. In the scheme of life, the half hour, even outside in the cold, is not worth such aggravation. Would he have been upset if you were delayed because you had to rush your child to the doctor? Of course not. Obviously a sick child takes precedence. The act of waiting wasn't the problem. Rather, it's the feelings behind these actions that cause the emotional intensity of these fights. Had you listened carefully and connected to your spouse, you would have been able to consider: "What's it like to have been waiting outside in the cold for someone who's late because she's talking to a friend?" If you had taken a moment to consider that, you could have understood his anger and his feeling that he was being disregarded. Had you answered from your heart and simply felt his words, you naturally would have said, "Oh, I am so sorry. You must be freezing and upset. I'm sorry you think I was chatting away knowing you'd be out here freezing."

Before you respond to an angry word, stop and listen and try to feel what it's like to be your spouse. If you were insensitive, say, "I'm sorry," and focus in the future when these situations occur. If you feel your spouse is misunderstanding the situation, explain why he might be taking it the wrong way after you've made it clear that you understand how he feels. "But honestly, I thought for sure that you'd be waiting indoors, and Shelley told me that she just moved her mother into a home as I was about to run out. I felt that I couldn't just leave her right away. After a few minutes, I did tell her I had to go get you and I'd be back to talk to her." This would help your spouse understand why you were late.

If you search for your lover's feelings, you will understand each other and not only avoid bitter arguments but grow from each other. In this case, your spouse might have learned from you how to be there for a friend in a time of need. You might have learned how abandoned a person can feel when he waits for someone who is late because she's found others to converse with. You might have learned how waiting for you really bothers your mate more than the average person. Now you can be aware of being on time in the future or of arranging alternate plans to have him picked up when you are going to be unavoidably detained. You can take control of your arguments with understanding.

Instead of reacting with how you feel, focus on your mate's feelings and message. It will bring both of you closer and make you much smarter and whole.

Step 4: Get Involved in Each Other

Billy saw himself as a simple kind of guy. He would go into an ice cream store and order the same mint chocolate chip cone year after year. He was never looking for much change. So when his wife of three years, Carol, became interested in modern art, Billy didn't share her enthusiasm. Carol, however, became engrossed in the art world and within a year found herself on the board of one of most prestigious art museums in her area. Suddenly, she was off to conventions and nighttime meetings, filled with a greater yearning to express her newfound understanding of art. Billy, however, waved off most of Carol's attempts to talk about it. "I don't know what you see in it. You attach these deep meanings to things that look like they were drawn by a five-year-old," was Billy's common response to Carol's interest in art. They found a way to compromise and felt proud of their ability to do so: Billy agreed not to stand in his wife's way and encouraged her to follow her interests, while Carol felt proud that she didn't pressure her husband into tagging along with her and forcing him to be interested in art just because she was.

However, Billy and Carol's way of handling their differences left them with the following two problems.

1. *They were allowing each other to grow apart.* Carol's new interest was offering her something much more than the simple enjoyment of viewing art. It was helping her feel more confident, become more philosophical, and have more self-respect for being allowed entry into a more sophisticated social group than she was accustomed to. Billy didn't realize that it wasn't just about art.

We take up new interests as a means of self-expression. Carol was verbalizing a great deal about herself through her art interest, and that was why it was crucial for Billy and Carol to be jointly involved in this new interest. That didn't have to mean that Billy learned everything about art with the same enthusiasm. But they did have to find a way to share it. Instead, Billy joked about it and even made self-deprecating remarks about how Carol was smarter and could understand all of that "art stuff." Through therapy, Billy discovered that indeed he felt inferior. He had never understood or felt capable of being a part of the art world. He had found comfort in letting his wife go on her merry way without stifling her. However, it wasn't long before Carol felt there was a huge gap between her and her husband, that there was a part of her that Billy could never understand, and that added a lonely feeling to her marriage.

2. *If Billy wouldn't understand Carol's newfound interest, others would.* Carol found a circle of friends that included men who heralded her efforts and thirst for knowledge. During our second marital session, Carol asked to see me for a few minutes alone and let me know there was a man who was very interested in her and that she returned his interest. She'd brought Billy to marital therapy because everything seemed all wrong. She wanted more out of life, and the art world offered something Billy couldn't.

꧁꧂꧁꧂꧁꧂꧁꧂꧁꧂꧁꧂꧁꧂꧁꧂꧁꧂꧁꧂꧁꧂꧁꧂꧁꧂

Where there's marriage without love, there will be love without marriage.

—Benjamin Franklin

Find Interests to Explore Together

For spouses to build a need for each other, they must continue to learn from each other and to nurture mutual interests. List some things you'd like to learn about. Ask your spouse to do the same. Then pick a few to brainstorm together, and list the steps you could take to get started on a mutual interest together. For example, one spouse's list might read:

Areas I'd like to learn more about

1. Cake decorating
   - Take a class.
   - Download information from the Web.
   - Practice once a week.
2. Colonial history
   - Take a college course.
   - Watch documentaries.
   - Visit historic sights—Colonial Williamsburg, Gettysburg.

Sometimes a new interest can be overwhelming. In therapy, Carol discovered that she'd put her husband on the spot by asking to leave town for so many weekends. Her interest in art had grown so quickly that it wasn't even a year before she was off almost every other weekend. Had Billy recognized the importance to his marriage of joining Carol on her new journey, they could have found a way to step into the art world together. Admittedly, however, Carol made no genuine effort to involve Billy because she felt he would hold her back. She didn't want her husband to tag along and put pressure on her to hurry up or miss out on events because he was too "tired." Leaving Billy behind gave her an opportunity to grow with gusto in a new, uncharted world.

In counseling, Carol learned that she would have to move at a slower pace and enjoy the process of including her husband, while Billy learned how important it was to his marriage to respect and involve himself in his wife's new interest. Carol needed to respect that this area was not one of her husband's interests, and for the sake of the marriage, she needed to help her husband find an interesting path to her new fascination. Perhaps he might find other types of art of some interest. Carol had to be willing to change her exact direction to accommodate Billy and create a path that offered both of them some excitement.

There will always be significant parts of your spouse's thoughts and feelings that your mate will find greater comfort and excitement sharing with others. Looking into new areas of life is healthy, and couples can enhance their marriage and build a "need" relationship through involving each other in their new interests. Spouses have to be willing to allow themselves to become more involved by learning about their spouse's interests. If you're not interested, you create a space in your spouse's life waiting to be filled by someone else.

Whether it's something simple like football or more dramatic like religion, give your marriage an opportunity for incredible growth by becoming involved in your spouse's life. Your spouse's interests and the energy your mate puts toward them represent part of who he or she is. If he plays soccer or she plays volleyball, cheer your spouse on if you can't play. Make yourself a part of the events and the time so you can come to expect to see your other half at every turn of your life.

∞∞∞∞∞∞∞∞∞∞∞∞∞∞∞∞∞∞∞∞∞∞∞∞∞∞∞∞∞∞∞∞∞∞∞

When Hal played basketball, his entire personality changed. This soft, docile man became an aggressive, competitive tiger on the court. His wife, Tiffany, went to every game, and it gave them the opportunity to discuss this aggressive side. When Hal was mad after a game, he vented to Tiffany. It wasn't long before they discussed how Hal was never angry anywhere else except on the court or because of something related to the game.

"Don't you ever get angry any other time?" Tiffany would ask. It was during one of these talks that Hal disclosed that he was afraid to get angry because he didn't really know how. The basketball game gave him a safe way to be mad. As he noticed others expressing their anger on the court, he realized it was an appropriate reaction. But Hal was completely uncomfortable showing his anger anywhere else.

Once this was brought out in the open, Hal and Tiffany were able to talk about making him more comfortable discussing his disappointments without exploding or hurting her feelings. But had Tiffany never been involved in Hal's interest, none of this discussion or understanding would have been likely to happen. As a matter of fact, they probably would have fought about his games because Hal often spent every Saturday morning playing in his league, and Tiffany could have easily requested that he stop. She worked on Sundays, so Saturday was their only weekend time together.

Hal would have been greatly resentful of Tiffany if she had asked him to stop. But because she didn't take it all so personally and was able to see how important Hal's basketball games must be to him, she chose to embrace this side of her spouse instead of trying to squelch it. After one game, she saw a different man out there and knew there was something important about Hal's time on the court.

~~~~~~~~~~~~~~~~~~~~~~~~~~~~~~~~~~~~~

When your spouse has an interest, it is so much more than just "time" that he or she is putting into it. Your spouse is putting his or her personality into it, and the more you are around that focus, the more you can understand and share that part of your spouse's personality.

This doesn't mean that it's wrong for your spouse to have domains that are exclusive to your spouse and his or her friends. Perhaps your spouse loves to watch football or to shop only with friends. At a recent talk I gave on marriage, a couple who had heard me years earlier told me that every year my name is mentioned in their home at least once. They explained that the husband had asked me at the prior talk if it was okay for him to go away for a camping weekend once a year with his male friends, as they had been doing for years. I had told him I saw nothing wrong with it as long as he felt comfortable if his wife did the same with her female friends. Thus, every year when his wife complained about his weekend away, he'd remind her that "Gary said it was okay."

As long as the interests that separate the two of you are few and far between, it's understandable that your spouse might want to use a particular interest to build camaraderie with same-sex friends. But you may miss out on something important to your relationship the same way Hal's wife might never have understood his anger.

If you begin to find any of the following true, it's time to involve your spouse in your activities, or to find other ones that include your spouse.

1. You're unwilling to discuss these separate experiences, or uncomfortable doing so.
2. The time you spend away from your spouse is at the expense of time you could be spending together, especially if you and your spouse feel you don't have enough time together to start with.
3. You find that these experiences are causing you to grow apart.

~~~~~~~~~~~~~~~~~~~~~~~~~~~~~~~~~~~~~

Recently, I was scholar in residence at a weekend for two hundred men aimed at furthering their spiritual growth. I understood the purpose of disallowing wives to partake in the weekend but found their exclusion to be potentially dangerous as well. Some of these men experienced dramatic emotions and insight and then admittedly had no idea how they could relate what happened to their spouses. I suggested that for future weekends there be a separate track for wives and workshops for couples during the weekend as well to help couples integrate these wonderful experiences into their marriage.

Step 5: Taste New Fruits

When we marry, we want to share ourselves and develop new perspectives. Toward that end, learning together in an area that's new to both spouses is a wonderful way to build "need." When you're equal partners in the learning adventure, it offers an exceptional bonding experience. You could do something as simple as joining a book club, or going to baking classes, or learning to dance. Activities lead to discussion and time together. Because growth is an inherent need, we develop an exclusionary bond with those we learn with. We become more reliant on that spouse.

Teaching each other is also a meaningful way of growing. As we lovingly show our partners what we know, we escort them into our world while showing them how much we want them to share in what we know. It also gives each partner the experience of teaching and learning from the other. It helps us respect our spouse for his or her knowledge and ability.

Even if time doesn't permit you to go to a class, find the small things that you can do together. Read a book out loud together, each of you taking turns to read a few pages at a time; learn a new recipe; dance the bunny hop; sing an "oldie" love song together.

One couple had a tutor come to the house weekly to teach them how to use their computer. They were fascinated not only by what they learned but by how much they enjoyed talking about it. Had they not learned together, they would have found someone else to discuss it with. They experienced each other's fascination when they learned how to search the Web and shared disappointing moments, like when they accidentally erased files.

Another couple used the birth of their child as a catalyst to discover more about their spiritual selves. They read and went to various lectures and began discussing their spiritual journey, a topic that was completely new to them. They marveled at how their love for each other grew beyond expectations even though they often disagreed about what they had read. But they learned so much about each other. They shared some stories about their past and how it related to their spiritual selves, points that neither of them had ever considered. It was wonderful for them to think aloud and discover what meaning there was behind some of these past events together. They discovered some large philosophical questions they had never been able to verbalize. They felt a new sense of peace and safety just knowing that they had each other to be close to and continue to search with.

You Need Your Soulmate

Today I begin to understand what love must be, if it exists. . . . When we are parted, we each feel the lack of the other half of ourselves. We are incomplete like a book in two volumes of which the first has been lost. That is what I imagine love to be: incompleteness in absence.

—Goncourt

I cannot point to any one thing in my wife and say, "See, that's my soul or spirit and she's my soulmate." Yet I can't help but point to countless moments in my relationship with my wife when I felt there was something more than our emotional love and adoration, moments when we have held each other, cried, feared, and laughed in a way that was so obviously not of this world. I can't prove it to anyone. I only wish to let myself feel it and become in touch with it. It's another reason I need my spouse. Love is proof that there is far more than meets the eye in life.

I've been married only fourteen years, yet why do I feel like I've known my wife all my life? How odd that we played on the same beach every summer for our entire childhood (I was fifteen hundred miles from home) without ever knowing each other; that my dearest of uncles, a rabbi, had named my wife at the ceremonial service when she was a newborn; that we were closest friends with the same couple without ever knowing of each other's existence (they eventually were the ones who set us up on a blind date).

Arlene & Bernie Silverstein
MARRIED: 42 YEARS

What was your biggest challenge?

Bernie: I'll admit I'm tough, independent, easily angered, and I don't take criticism well. Both Arlene and I had to work at knowing how to build a friendship with each other.

What has worked for you?

Bernie: Arlene tries to understand where my hurt is coming from. She tries to understand me instead of taking my anger personally.

Arlene: I used to just accept him, but I became resentful. I got a job and started to find some personal strength. I began expressing myself to him. At first, he didn't like it but he worked at accepting me and I felt much better. We focus on our friendship and are best friends today. We maintain our romance. We travel and try new and interesting experiences. We create nice memories to keep developing our friendship.

Advice to Young Couples

When you give, you receive. Think less about yourself and more about giving to your spouse, and then you'll have a more rewarding marriage. Remember, it's the trip along the way that counts, not the destination.

Our story of love may not be considered otherworldly, but our feelings for each other are. To believe in a soulmate is to believe in an ultimate sense of connection. If destiny has brought you together, open yourself to the possibility that the spouse you chose was meant for you.

The "need" relationship extends to a spiritual plane of existence. You will need your complete soul to lovingly nurture your vibrant spirit. And guess who carries the other part of your soul? Your spouse.

Judaic literature tells of a heavenly voice that shouts out on high on the fortieth day from conception that "this soul will marry this soul." Interestingly, modern science has proven that an embryo forms its gender around the fortieth day from conception. There is plenty of literature in many religions and cultures on love that points us in the direction of a soulmate intended to form a complete spiritual union. But reading about it or even seeing it is not believing. Feeling is believing. Love breathes within a dimension beyond textbook explanations or chance coincidences. Unfortunately, marriage can be reduced to a business relationship or shallow friendship. If you are willing to open up your whole self to marriage and learn to "need" your spouse, you will easily find something far more inexplicable, the taste of a soulmate. Look for it and you'll find it, just as you'll notice the dust particles in front of your face the next time the sun shines in.

The way you hold your knife,
the way we dance till three,
The way you change my life,
No, no they can't take that away from me.
No, they can't take that away from me.

—George and Ira Gershwin

3

Spouses need clear, realistic goals and a specific plan of how to achieve those goals.

By now, I hope you appreciate why building a "relationship of need" is a must for a successful marriage. Whether you can create that need depends on how well you can work together as a team. *Learning and sharing in the context of marriage don't just happen; you'll have to create a system to work on your unique goals.*

We usually waltz into marriage with high expectations. Unfortunately, so many of those expectations are unrealistic, and worse yet, we often don't even articulate them! I've had so many couples toss out ambiguous terms like "unconditional love," "financial security," and "happiness" as though there were some marital dictionary that clearly defined their universal meaning. I've seen many couples express expectations of marriage that can't be met. In their mind, spouses will never get upset, be insensitive, or get depressed. They want the marriage to be magically responsible for some constant joyful, euphoric mood. Others take it as a given that marriage will provide them with the kind of sex that fantasies are made of. Or that it will provide them with a self-esteem they largely lacked when they were single. They expect to feel cloaked in love immediately on tying the knot, then are surprised when it doesn't happen. It's not wrong to bring expectations into a marriage, but it's a huge mistake not to talk about them with your spouse and make sure you're both on the same planet.

It isn't *marriage* that will make you feel happy. There's nothing magical about the institution of marriage. The magic comes from the commitment. The joy comes from fulfilling expectations together. I see spouses get angry with each other because one member of the couple is waiting for a certain desire to be fulfilled, while the mate was never clearly aware of that desire in the first place. Don't assume your expectations are the "normal" ones and that it's obvious to your spouse what it is you're looking for in this relationship. Our dreams for marriage are drawn from many sources, such as our parents' marriage, the media, and our friends. They're bound to differ for each half of the couple. Our goals for marriage may be unrealistic, thus frustrating us at every turn. Our priorities are almost always different from those of our mates. There's no point in putting great efforts into a marriage before you've clarified all those assumptions, spoken or unspoken.

Marriage Isn't Responsible for Your Happiness

Carla wanted to dream. She believed in her marriage with Sam. But her beliefs sprang from the role model of her father caring for her often depressed mom. Carla had seen great devotion from her father toward a woman who suffered from chronic sadness. As Carla put it, "He always found a way to get her smiling before the night was out." Carla was in for an enormous surprise when her loving husband decided to give Carla her "space" whenever she was in the doldrums.

Carla spent five years being angry with Sam because he wasn't trying hard enough to "help her through the tough times." But "trying hard enough" to Carla meant "doing what her dad did," which was to put everything on hold daily to spend hours caring for and cajoling his wife. Carla misunderstood what marriage was supposed to offer her. She expected marriage—that is, Sam—to make her happy.

Of course, we expect marriage to make us happier as we feel loved, enriched, and a part of a special unit. But marriage isn't responsible for our personal happiness. If you've been generally sad for much of your life, don't expect marriage to wave a magic wand over you and take that sadness away forever. If you feel self-conscious because you suffer from low self-esteem, do you assume it's your spouse's responsibility to praise you often enough to cure your problem? We are justified in having certain expectations. Carla could reasonably expect Sam to cheer her up sometimes when she was sad. You surely expect your spouse to praise you and build your self-esteem. Everyone needs a pat on the back. When it becomes confusing is when we don't stop to determine whether the degree of our expectation is appropriate and if our mate knows what we expect. Ultimately, you and your spouse must decide how much he or she is responsible for your happiness, but you alone are responsible for communicating your expectations.

Developing Realistic Goals: The "Marriage Proposal"

I've always marveled at the difference between a marriage proposal and a business proposal. The business proposal is an exhaustive document that clearly outlines expectations and goals as well as realistic approaches to accomplish the outlined objectives. This proposal is often used to convince others to participate, whether financially or through personal energy, in this new venture. Without the business proposal, the business is doomed, because no one wants to invest in it. Only when we see sound objectives and clear goals are we willing to extend ourselves and get involved.

Compare that with the usual marriage proposal, which consists of a single question: "Will you spend the rest of your life with me?" Here's a plan for an intimate relationship in which partners will combine all assets and act as a unit in every area of life, including the potential to create life itself—all without any clearly articulated objectives or methods to attain them. A ring is all that's needed to seal the deal. If this were offered to you as a business proposal, you'd have to come up for air after heavy laughter. Clearly, the marriage proposal needs work. Of course, I am ever the romantic and don't suggest that we offer fifty-page documents hanging from a ring to our potential spouse. But even if you have already accepted the proposal and have been living for years without any level of detail, it's time to work together to develop a more specific and well-thought-out marriage proposal, in writing.

"It's so unromantic/unspontaneous/clinical/businesslike to put all this in writing," my clients protest. *Writing it down makes it real.* It's time to put that effort into what matters most of all. I realize it may be a departure for you to actually write down the following items. You'd rather just talk about them, or perhaps not clearly focus on them at all. But it's so important for spouses to understand each other and their specific needs. A written document acts as a springboard for discussion.

The written "Marriage Proposal" you will learn to create in this chapter will help you focus on what will make your marriage better by forcing you to offer concrete examples of what is important to both of you. It will also help you discuss what you specifically want from your marriage and how you think you can get it.

Creating a Marriage Proposal

Creating your marriage proposal will take between four to seven days. You can spend moments in your day focusing on a single goal and then take an hour each night to review your lists with your spouse. After your initial week, you'll have a one-month follow-up meeting to further review how it has and can continue to help your marital focus. This marriage proposal will be used to help you focus loving energy toward your spouse on a daily basis. It will serve as an important reminder as to why you are married and how both of you need to continue to make your marriage worthwhile.

Step 1: Write down your goals. Together, discuss all the goals of your marriage: why you married or want to stay married. Then create a single list of no more than seven goals, with a minimum of four goals. Don't worry if your goals sound nebulous. Their meaning will become much clearer to you and your spouse as this exercise continues. If you need to shrink your list, combine goals that easily go together, for example, "Love" and "Friendship." Or combine goals that will likely need the same actions to achieve them—for example, the actions I might take to show love to my partner would likely be similar to the actions I'd take to show friendship to my spouse.

Step 2: Plan your approach. Take two pieces of paper (one for each of you) and write the first goal (usually a variation on "Love") at the top of each piece of paper. Then, draw a line down the middle of the page to make two columns. At the top of the left-hand column write, "Ways I can offer my spouse _____" (fill in the blank with that goal). At the top of the right-hand column write, "Ways I want my spouse to offer me _____."

Next, separately, fill in both columns on your page. For example, under "Love" as a goal for marriage, describe what you think you could do to make your partner feel loved and what you would like your partner to do to show you love. *Be sure to include things that you feel your spouse already does.* Be as detailed as possible. Include not only actions, but frequency: "I want my husband to kiss me at least twice a day—when we wake up and when we go to bed." Or, "I want my wife to support my diet by nicely asking me every day if I've exercised and noticing if I've lost weight."

Step 3: Plan a one-day focus. Each of you should take one day to fill in your page. Look at it several times throughout the day, and make notes. You do not need to repeat certain actions if they've already been included under a different goal.

Also, if you've already listed under "Love" that you want your husband to appreciate your efforts in your career and at home with the children, you don't need to write the same thing under your goal of "Respect." Rather, write a column of items under "Respect" that adds to the column written for "Love."

When you've finished your approach to a certain goal, return to your columns and number each approach in order of priority. The most important aproach is 1, and so forth. This prioritizing tells your partner where you'd like his or her focus to begin.

Step 4: Have a nightly meeting for each goal. Schedule one night per goal for a discussion of each goal. (You'll have a minimum of four nights for four goals, up to seven nights for seven goals.)

First, combine your individual goals and approaches on a new page with four columns. The order of the columns should be as follows:

Column 1: Spouse A's list of "Ways I want my spouse to offer me _____,"
listed in order of priority
Column 2: Spouse B's list of "Ways I can offer my spouse _____"
Column 3: Spouse B's list of "Ways I want my spouse to offer me _____,"
listed in order of priority
Column 4: Spouse A's list of "Ways I can offer my spouse _____"

Compare your list of what you want from your spouse with your spouse's list of what he or she can offer you, and vice versa. Notice the matches: these are the areas in which both of you really know what the other wants and that will motivate both of you to focus on these crucial approaches. Notice also how many

Andrea and Marcus's Marriage Proposal

Here's how Andrea and Marcus created their Marriage Proposal. Their goals were:

Love (combined with friendship)	Respect
Loyalty	Happiness
Family	Sex
Financial strength	

LOVE

Marcus

Ways I Can Offer Andrea Love

1. Listen to her.
2. Look into her eyes when she's talking to me, give her my undivided attention.
3. Tell her I understand instead of giving her advice or solutions.
4. Touch her a lot.
5. Tell her she's beautiful.
6. Bring her flowers.
7. Send her a loving note or greeting card.
8. Let her sleep in on Sunday by taking the kids out early.
9. Be nice to her mom, go to family functions.
10. Give her massages.
11. Make her tea with Sweet 'N Low.
12. Put gas in the car, take over maintenance of the car.
13. Make her feel important by respecting the work she does.
14. Spend time with her.

Andrea

Ways I Can Offer Marcus Love

1. Cook his favorite meals.
2. Find his favorite magazines, like *MAD*.
3. Show interest in his work, ask about it and listen.
4. Show concern about his health.
5. Think of ways to make his life easier: pick up shirts from cleaners.
6. Do more small, thoughtful gestures: bring him coffee in morning, find the drawstring pajamas he likes.
7. Call him during the day to say "I love you."
8. Care for him when he's sick.
9. Find a book I think he'd like to read.
10. Have more sex with him, initiate more.
11. Be light with him: don't bring up intense things when we're having fun.

Marcus

Ways I Want Andrea to Offer Me Love

1. Support me (Andrea found this vague, which forced Marcus to consider more specifically what he meant): listen to my problems, take my side when I'm battling at work.
2. Compliment me about my work.
3. Appreciate how hard I work by telling me so.
4. Tell me how attracted you are to me.
5. Cook meals for me, help me feel taken care of.
6. Be interested in making our sex life better, be willing to try new things.
7. Think of me during the day, phone me just to say "I love you."
8. Give me my space to go to sporting events with friends.
9. Do some things to make my life easier: make a call regarding a bill, tell me to go to the spa while you watch the kids.
10. Take care of the kids. (Andrea helped Marcus see this was an unrealistic expectation, so both discussed how they each saw their roles in sharing childcare).
11. Show me love no matter what. (Andrea considered this an unrealistic expectation. Marcus needed to understand that after a fight in which he said something cruel to Andrea, she could not be expected to forget it all and show him love immediately after.)

Andrea

Ways I Want Marcus to Offer Me Love

1. Listen to me—don't be distracted; make me feel that what I have to say is important to you.
2. Spend time talking and laughing with me.
3. Touch me a lot.
4. Tell me how attractive and sexy I am.
5. Tell me what a good mother I am.
6. Give me massages.
7. Help me problem-solve—don't just tell me what you'd do.
8. Make a date for both of us and plan every detail.
9. Plan little surprises, like getting tickets to a show.
10. Call me during the day.
11. Buy me gifts that reflect my worth to you. (Marcus saw this as an unrealistic expectation, since no matter what he could buy for Andrea, it couldn't equal her "worth"—this was a point of discussion for both of them. Andrea clarified that she wanted thoughtful gifts, not ones that Marcus just purchased because it was easy. The gift's cost wasn't the issue.)
12. Be a full partner in childrearing. (Marcus saw this as vague, and they had a fuller discussion of what would make Andrea feel as though Marcus was a full partner.)
13. Make my birthdays special: remember them, buy cards, cake, gift.

RESPECT

Marcus

Ways I Can Offer Andrea Respect
1. Compliment her.
2. Avoid sarcasm, put-downs, cynicism.
3. When I say I'll do something, do it soon.
4. Tell her how great she is re work and being a mom.
5. Always talk nicely to her, don't scream or call her names.

Andrea

Ways I Can Offer Marcus Respect
1. Talk nicely always.
2. Offer him time to chill out.
3. Limit my criticisms of him.
4. Never mention his poor posture.
5. Compliment him regarding his job and being a dad.
6. Be punctual.
7. Appreciate him by telling him how hard he works for us.

LOYALTY

Marcus

Ways I Can Offer Andrea Loyalty
1. Take her side and try to understand her point of view.

Andrea

Ways I Can Offer Marcus Loyalty
1. Understand his point of view when he's having a conflict with someone else.

Marcus

Ways I Want Andrea to Offer Me Respect
1. When I come home, get off the phone.
2. Don't contradict me in front of the kids.
3. Don't lie about anything.
4. Listen to my problems.
5. When you call me at work, don't take it personally if I don't have the time to talk.

Andrea

Ways I Want Marcus to Offer Me Respect
1. When I say I've had a hard day, show interest. Don't say, "I've had a terrible day, too."
2. Compliment me as a worker and mom.
3. Ask questions about my day to show you're interested.
4. Don't criticize my family.
5. When I call you at work, make me feel like I'm important. (Marcus found this unrealistic and vague, and they discussed further what Marcus could do to let Andrea know he was swamped and under pressure at work without hurting her feelings.)

Marcus

Ways I Want Andrea to Offer Me Loyalty
1. Put me first before your family.
2. Don't divulge my secrets.
3. Take my side in any case. (Andrea thought this unrealistic. After further discussion, it became clear that what Marcus wanted was for Andrea to fully consider and understand his point of view before considering any other perspective and not to play devil's advocate without first fully appreciating how he saw things.

Andrea

Ways I Want Marcus to Offer Me Loyalty
1. Be with me when you say you will.
2. Never look or think of other women. (Marcus declared this unrealistic. After discussion, Andrea explained that she didn't want him looking at other woman when he was out with her or discussing how beautiful other women are to him. She also wanted him to limit his contact with other women (no *Playboy* magazines.)

HAPPINESS
(additions to
"Love" list)

Marcus

Ways I Can Offer Andrea Happiness
1. Spend consistent time with her.
2. Be more positive.
3. Be lighter, more willing to try new experiences and have fun.

Andrea

Ways I Can Offer Marcus Happiness
1. Create experiences that will be fun for both of us.
2. Include him in more of my fun activities.

FAMILY
(this goal is
focused on
the marriage,
not on
the kids)

Marcus

Ways I Can Offer Andrea Family
1. Be home with kids from dinnertime and on weekends.
2. Read to kids.
3. Take children places.
4. Family trips.
5. Teach discipline and offer structure.
6. Have regular meetings with her to discuss how we will parent together.
7. Be physically demonstrative with the kids.

Andrea

Ways I Can Offer Marcus Family
1. Create more festive/relaxed family time.
2. Plan family trips.
3. Nurture kids, do more hugging and kissing.
4. Care for children's nutritional needs.
5. Take charge of discipline.
6. Read to kids.
7. Tell children what a wonderful father they have.

Marcus

Ways I Want Andrea to Offer Me Happiness
1. Develop new interests together.
2. Be included in your interests.

Andrea

Ways I Want Marcus to Offer Me Happiness
1. Be positive: see the glass as half full instead of half empty.
2. Don't walk around making negative comments about people/surroundings.
3. Take me out when I'm low.

Marcus

Ways I Want Andrea to Offer Me Family
1. Present a united front for the kids.
2. Don't contradict me or minimize my opinion in front of the children.
3. Take care of kids' food and schoolwork.
4. Have calm atmosphere: no screaming. (Andrea deemed this unrealistic. They discussed in more detail how they could work together to present a calmer home.)

Andrea

Ways I Want Marcus to Offer Me Family
1. Do research, read books and articles, go to seminars on creating a better family.
2. Get involved in children's schooling. I don't want to feel like I'm in this alone.
3. Teach kids no hitting.
4. Work together to discuss issues.
5. Have regular meetings to talk about the kids.

SEX

(Marcus and Andrea chose to write more generally about their desires while committing to discussing the details openly.)

Marcus

Ways I Can Offer Andrea Sex
1. Have lots of foreplay.
2. Tell her how sexy she is.
3. Touch her more throughout the day and tell her how I've been thinking about her sexually.
4. Buy her sexy lingerie.

Andrea

Ways I Can Offer Marcus Sex
1. Be more focused, think about ways to make it better.
2. Initiate more.
3. Be willing to try new things.
4. Say the things he'd like to hear.
5. Rest so I have the energy to have sex.
6. Dress sexy for him when he comes home at night.
7. Call him during the day with sexy messages.

FINANCIAL STRENGTH

Marcus

Ways I Can Offer Andrea Financial Strength
1. Keep my job.
2. Spend less, think twice about purchasing toys for the children.
3. Record the checks I write.
4. Don't use the credit card unless it's an emergency.
5. Keep to a budget.

Andrea

Ways I Can Offer Marcus Financial Strength
1. Keep my job.
2. Spend less, think twice about purchasing toys for the children.
3. Record the checks I write.
4. Don't use the credit card unless it's an emergency.
5. Keep to a budget.

Marcus

Ways I Want Andrea to Offer Me Sex

1. Initiate more.
2. Be more focused on it.
3. Say certain things we've discussed.
4. Make time for it, rest if necessary so you have the energy.
5. Read more about how to make sex better.

Andrea

Ways I Want Marcus to Offer Me Sex

1. Lots of foreplay/not making it just about intercourse.
2. Tell me how beautiful I am.
3. Nice surroundings, music, lighting, put some thought into it—put on the CD I love.
4. Tell me that you love me during sex.

Marcus

Ways I Want Andrea to Offer Me Financial Strength

1. Be more frugal, spend more carefully.
2. Both discuss nonessential large purchases before making them. (They had to put a dollar amount on what was considered "large.")
3. Create and stick to a budget.
4. Record checks.

Andrea

Ways I Want Marcus to Offer Me Financial Strength

1. Don't offer to pay for everyone else when we're out.
2. Join me/be my partner in spending less.
3. Have weekly financial meetings with me to outline our goals and discuss upcoming expenditures.
4. Agree on a savings plan.

things each of you listed about ways you want the other to offer a certain goal that the other did *not* list in his or her corresponding "Ways I can offer" column. Now you've seen it written as clear as day and know what your spouse wants you to offer. If you don't offer it after this exercise, you need to reevaluate your own commitment and ability to give to others.

Focus also on those requests you don't feel you understand or can gratify. Ask your spouse more questions about areas that seem foreign to you, or areas whose importance to your spouse you don't understand. If you think your spouse is desiring something you don't feel you could or should give (take care of the kids, never look at another woman/man, never work on a weekend), discuss it openly.

Work toward understanding each other and recognizing that there are many points on your list. If there are one or two that you disagree on and can't find some compromise on, pass on them for now and work on everything else. Come back to the thornier issues at the one-month follow up I'll describe after step 5. By that time, you'll have shown each other a great deal of love, you'll feel much closer by following through on these requests, and you'll be better at finding ways to work together on those areas you are having difficulty understanding.

If you don't have many matches on a particular goal, it only means you each want to achieve that goal in different ways. Both of you must focus on what the other needs to receive as an expression of your working toward this mutually desired goal. For example, for the goal of "Love," you may think bringing flowers home is the perfect romantic gesture, but if it means little to your spouse, you're not honoring your commitment to that goal. Your goal is to show love to your spouse in the way that means the most to your partner, not to you. If there is something listed in your column that your spouse tells you will not accomplish that goal for him or her, cross out that action. Remaining on your list should be only the things your spouse would like but didn't think of them for his or her own list about what you could do to achieve a certain goal.

Step 5: Take action. Now that you've learned more about what your spouse is looking for, take time each day to consider how you can provide these loving gestures. For example, the first day after completing your "Marriage Proposal," do the first thing that your spouse wrote under the first goal for "Ways I want my spouse to offer me _____." The next day, do the first thing your spouse wrote for the second goal. When you've finished the list of goals, go to the second item written under the first goal, and continue to rotate through the list.

When you've completed your spouse's list, begin to do one thing each day from your list of "Ways I can offer my spouse _____." This gives you at least one focus every day of something you can offer your spouse toward developing a greater marriage.

One-month follow-up. Review your Marriage Proposal together after a month. Discuss how it has helped. What has your spouse done as a result of the proposal that's worked for you, and vice versa? Be sure to discuss all of the wonderful things that have happened as a result of your both having focused on the proposal. Don't just jump into what hasn't worked and how you have to tweak it.

After thanking each other verbally for specific things each of you has done as a result of the proposal, ask each other how it could work even more. If you feel both of you haven't followed through enough, or if one of you feels you've made a much greater effort than the other, talk about it. But remember the goal, to become closer through feeling more loved. Redirect each other gently and make a new commitment following through on one request daily, as you did when you began the exercise.

Using Your Marriage Proposal as a Springboard

Your Marriage Proposal will help generate discussion about what each of you is looking for and will give you solid ideas on how to begin to respond

Dorothy & Harry Malett
MARRIED: 66 YEARS

How We Met
We met on a blind date. I took one look at her and I was done for.

What Made It Work?
The fifty-fifty way of doing things isn't the answer. Each person must give their 100 percent. You can't split everything down the middle, so to speak.

Learning to have your own fun is very important. Each couple has to know how to laugh. Sixty-six years we've been married, and we still listen to Lawrence Welk and dance in the kitchen.

to your spouse's needs. It will also help you see whether your goals are realistic. Let's say your goal is to be "madly in love." If reality dictates that you stay on the mainland with your two kids, mortgage, and two jobs, and you realize your approach calls for a few years' seclusion on a desert island alone with your spouse, it's time to start erasing. How else can you achieve that love, starting now, from where you stand today?

If you don't really know how your partner could help you achieve a certain goal, consider how the heck he or she is supposed to know what to do to accomplish it. If you "can't explain it" or "it's not as simple as writing it down," force yourself to discuss it further, because you've stumbled on an area of confusion that has great potential to cause hurtful feelings. So many of us think we married mindreaders and prophets: it's so obvious what we need—how can our spouses not "get it"? Unfortunately, true psychics are few, and we often send loaded, mixed messages. For example, you want your partner to be more affectionate, but when he or she moves in to kiss and hug you on returning home, you turn away because you're "busy." You want your spouse to respect you by helping you solve a problem, but you get mad when he or she takes too much control over the solution. The list could go on forever.

We could avoid so much pain if we could describe our needs clearly. And guess what? You may need to repeat your needs many times before your spouse can remember how important they are to you. We need time and repetition to learn anything, including how to love our spouses in a unique way. Men and women often look for different expressions of love. Isn't is wonderful to change through our marriage and become better at love?

Your Marriage Proposal will also help you see how much you are asking of your spouse. Is it reasonable to expect everything? Continue to refine your proposal until you both agree it satisfies your unique needs. Now you have an offer on the table that both of you can commit to. Sign it and keep it handy. At least once a year (I recommend the day before your anniversary), consider if you need to make any changes. Some of my couples frame their Marriage Proposal. At the very least, keep it in a safe place with easy access so that you can review it often. A diamond may last forever, but this Marriage Proposal will make that diamond worth lasting.

4

Like any strong working partnership, marriage needs well-defined roles for each spouse.

Used to know what you were then
Girls were girls and men were men

—Lee Adams and Charles Strause, "Those Were the
Days," as sung by Archie and Edith Bunker

Marital partners have more to argue about today than ever before. From which stocks to invest in to how to decorate the bathroom, spouses have been made to believe that they must share every decision. Because it seems politically incorrect to put anyone into a "role," many spouses feel it isn't right to be in charge of a particular area, even though they may be "better at it" or their time is best served that way. This "management system" based on roles once fell into place naturally. In the past, because men were seen as more capable of managing the financial well-being of the family, they were expected to make unilateral decisions about finances. Since women were seen as better nurturers, they were expected to make unilateral decisions about the children. Each spouse felt a certain amount of power to make decisions in "their" area. Usually, there wasn't a great deal of discussion unless a huge issue was to be decided. Disagreement and fighting were reserved for the "big" items.

Of course, I just glamorized a system that worked so poorly that much of American society has abolished it. The system failed first and foremost because it made assumptions about people based solely on gender. Partners began to resent being placed into a management role that they never requested or that they felt unqualified for. They cheated at the largely unspoken rules for conduct. Father decided to plunge all of the family's savings, which were earmarked for Grandma's operation, into an investment without talking it over with his wife. Mother decided to change little Timmy's school without consulting with her husband. In many cases, Mother didn't have control over even the major decisions that affected the children. Perhaps Father wasn't very involved in the kids' education, but if he had a strong opinion, it trumped Mother's judgment. Women felt that they were far from equal partners in this marital venture.

We now recognize that a woman can be as capable as, or even more capable than, her husband in the area of finance and investment. A man can be as capable as, or even more capable than, his wife in the area of childrearing. The problem is that the presumed antidote to the old stereotypes is a marital relationship in which couples are equal partners in everything. We now live in an enlightened world that recognizes that people have varied talents, regardless of gender. But with this enlightenment comes tremendous confusion. Who should make a financial or childrearing decision if each of us is equally qualified to do so? How can we make these decisions together, and what happens when we don't have the time to make a joint decision? In the last decade alone, the number of full-time working mothers has tripled.[1] The reality is that in any given partnership, one partner really is better than the other in many specific areas. It's absurd and unnecessary to try to make all decisions jointly.

What's critical is that we understand that differences are not necessarily determined by gender, and thus we must challenge and discover where each of our strengths and weaknesses lie. Couples must arrive at a logical division of labor according to ability so they can spend their finite time and energy wisely.

Equal But Not the Same

When Sandy and Sammy first came to me about a three-day-long argument regarding choosing their new china pattern, I thought they meant it as a metaphor for their inability to agree. I said, "So the china is an example about how you argue so much that even the smallest items seem to drag you down."

They looked at me like I was crazy. "No," Sammy said disdainfully, "We just want to know how to resolve this problem. We have very different tastes in china and can't come to some kind of agreement." Thus, the great china debate continued in my office as each outlined how the colors and shapes somehow coincided with the color scheme and meaning of the new dining room. It was Greek to me. I interrupted them with, "How have you managed to get through your day together? If china patterns brought you into my office, how were you able to decide on a house to buy?"

The answer was quite simple. "We've been in therapy for years. We discuss our issues with a therapist, and he or she helps us make a decision." I was the latest therapist in a long lineage of helpers. I was pretty sure that this couple could have purchased a second house with the money they'd spent on therapists, and it was time for them to put an end to their ongoing struggles by understanding partnership.

Partnership doesn't mean equality in skill. It means equality in responsibility and ownership. Show me any business partners who have to meet about every single decision and hash it out until they both agree on a course of action, and I will show you bankruptcy proceedings. How can any business with so many decisions to be made afford to stop everything to discuss and agree on the most minuscule problems? The purpose of any partnership is to bring two people together, each of whom has something the other does not have. This way, the partnership is stronger than the individuals in it. If both partners have the same ability in the same areas, how will being partners benefit the union? Marriage is no different. We marry knowing that we are very different from our spouse but that we share a variety of unique strengths and weaknesses. If we're mirror images in every area, then we haven't made ourselves much better by coming together.

Even if there are areas in which you are unsure if either of you has a better or more skilled approach, you still can't afford the time and energy to discuss every china pattern. Like any successful partnership, you and your spouse will have to create a clear system of management. Although it may seem odd to reduce this system to a written exercise, it is simply good business to develop it on paper for clarification. Unspoken assumptions are the enemy of a great marriage. You'll have to revise your management system regularly. Because we acquire new strengths as we continue in life, we cannot accept roles forever based on the limited self-knowledge of today. We can only try our best and see if we can properly manage our part of the partnership.

Shared Responsibility

Being in charge of your share of the list doesn't mean that you are solely responsible for that area. Remember that, as a partnership, both of you are ultimately responsible. You may well have to help your partner whenever you see the need, or simply when you have the extra energy to do so. But what these roles now offer you is the right to care for the items without

Creating Your Management System

Step 1: Together, create a general list of areas that need care. For example:

Childcare

Work

Food

Clothing (purchasing)

Housecleaning

Home maintenance

Financial management

Social (calendar arrangement, purchasing gifts)

Transportation

Pet care

Next, list responsibilities that take place during certain periods of the year:

Vacations

Holidays

Birthdays

Anniversaries

After you've completed your list, take out a separate piece of paper for each item on the list, then write each item as a heading at the top of its own page. You'll need plenty of room for step 2.

Step 2: List as many duties as you can create under each item. Yes, it's time consuming, but your goal is to be sure you and your spouse understand what is required of each of you. If you only write something general, such as "Food," you may not realize that the category includes making up the shopping list, organizing coupons, going to the store or shopping on-line, putting groceries away, preparing menus, cooking meals, and doing the dishes afterward. The more detailed your list is, the less room you leave for uncertainty and unspoken assumptions. ("I thought *you* were in charge of _____".)

For example, childcare responsibilities might be divided into general care (feeding, clothing, bathing, haircuts); education (supervising homework, reading with your child, hiring tutors, communication with teachers, religious school); healthcare (medical and dental check-ups, visits to eye doctors, etc.); extracurricular activities (play dates, sports, music lessons, class trips); family recreation (outings and other activities); and so on. Financial management might include investing, paying bills, balancing the checkbook, doing the income taxes, reading up on investment strategies, meeting with financial planners, organizing receipts, and so on.

Step 3: Place your initials with the number 1 to the *left* of the specific responsibilities you would most like to be involved in. Place your initials with the number 2 to the *left* of the items you think you are most capable of handling. Even if you already have your initials and number in the same spot, put your initials there for the second time with the number 2 next to it.

Next, place your initials and the number 3 to the *right* of any items you feel you are not capable of being responsible for. Finally, place your initials and the number 4 to the *right* of anything you strongly prefer not having much to do with.

Be honest about your preferences. It's foolish not to choose an area of responsibility you're good at because you don't want to seem "retro," old-fashioned, or stereotypical. Freedom comes from choosing from the heart, not from media messages, the advice of friends and family, or any other barometer.

The two of you are now clear on your preferences and your sense of where each of you could best serve the family union. Begin to discuss which areas you want to temporarily adopt as your own. Start with the areas that you've marked with a 1 or a 2, indicating that you would like to be involved in that area and also feel capable of handling it. You may even want to break down certain responsibilities even more. Perhaps you would like to be in charge of your children's religious schooling while your spouse would be in charge of their secular schooling. Or your spouse will be responsible for math, and you will supervise your child's writing and science.

With these lists, you can also begin to see the items that are of such great importance to the marriage that both of you want to be involved in every decision in these areas. For example, my wife and I discuss all investments before either of us spends our money. That may change in time, but for now, it works, and we enjoy the discussions. Both of you may want to be involved in paying the bills, or doing homework with your children.

Be realistic in your choices. If one of you is home when the kids are doing homework and one is still at work, it would compromise the system for the parent who is home to be unable to make quick decisions about daily homework or to have to wait for the working partner to get home, at which point the kids are too tired to do homework. Make sure you've chosen areas that befit not only your ability but the reality of your time and energy. Just because one of you may be more qualified in a given task doesn't mean that person must take control over it. For example, you may be an actuary, but if you're doing most of the parenting for twin newborns, you're probably better off allocating responsibility for your ten-year-old's math project to your partner. Similarly, if it stresses you out to deal with a particular task, you can opt not to be responsible for it, or at least to create a system in which your spouse helps enough to relieve the stress.

However, if everything else is equal (you both get just as stressed over the bills), you should take responsibility for the areas you feel more confident in. To throw responsibility onto your spouse when you are more gifted at caring for that item is diminishing your marriage's chances for success, just as you'd be hurting your business if you handed off important tasks to someone else who had less capability in that area. For the most undesirable chores (for instance, cleaning the bathrooms), you might allocate according to who finds it less objectionable; decide to take turns (which means you must agree on the length of the tour of duty); or find a third party willing to do the task (e.g., a cleaning person), which means you have to agree on the budget.

There may be some areas neither of you has volunteered to take care of. Perhaps you both love your dog, but not scooping the poop or going to the vet. Start choosing which tasks you will do even though you don't particularly care to, bearing in mind that these types of "sacrifices" are necessary to bring about the benefits we desire from marriage.

Use this document for one week at a time before reconvening and discussing clearly what has worked and what has not. For example, you might not have recognized how much effort it was going to take to plan the vacation and now realize you need to share the task. Adjust as you go at the end of each week. Within three or four weeks you will have developed a streamlined, consistent approach to working well together. However, many responsibilities will not crop up for months (caring for children during summer break, preparing for a vacation trip). Both of you will need to revisit your roles every two months and continue to discuss what works and what needs adjustment.

feeling you have to ask permission or prove your point of view every time you wish to make a decision.

Certain duties are too large not to share: childcare is a simple example. You will probably need to split responsibilities for taking charge of the children's meals; buying, washing, and caring for their clothing; supervising their homework; taking them to activities; and so on. You may find that getting the children ready in the morning is a joint responsibility. Both of you may agree to get up at the same time and work together to cook breakfast, make lunches, get the little ones dressed, and drive them to school.

Childcare is a particularly complicated issue for so many couples because presently women make up more than half the workforce yet are often hog-tied by traditional values that dictate women should do more of the childcare, or make the childcare arrangements. Yet, we know that men are far more capable of caring for children than was believed years ago. We've also learned how important fathers are to children. For example, in my work with divorcing couples, I have seen divorced dads show their gift at caring for their children, and these children have shown wonderful positive responses to their dad's attention. Men, for your child's sake as well as the sake of the marriage, be an involved parent. Challenge traditional roles, and do what works uniquely for you. Don't convince yourself that a wife is simply "better" at parenting. Families benefit hugely from two involved parents. *There will be certain areas of childcare, Sunday family days, for example, that both of you may want to provide jointly.*

The management system put forth in this chapter affords each of you the permission to make daily decisions comfortably without any argument. However, there are two rules:

1. *You must hold weekly meetings.* Just as in any business environment, you must schedule a weekly partners meeting at a definite time when you will have the chance to discuss issues. Too often, we avoid serious issues with our spouses, claiming we're too busy with life, as if there were a more important "life" outside of building our most significant relationship. Couples often argue and resent each other because they don't discuss issues properly, or resolve them. This meeting confirms that your relationship is too important to take a back seat to the mundane details of life. It sets aside real time so you can face each other and discuss the issues that are important to each of you. It is at this meeting that each of you will report on the "state of the union" and raise any decision you've made or are considering that you think your spouse may be interested in.

   The point of clarifying roles is never to reduce discussion but to reduce the tension of differences in everyday life decisions. However, reserving the more emotional issues for a designated time stops you from bringing them up at moments when your partner isn't in a frame of mind to deal with them in a loving, understanding way. A meeting sets the stage for each spouse to listen carefully and focus on the important issues. No one feels blindsided by a bomb dropped when he or she was doing something else important, after a particularly stressful time, or when extremely tired or hungry.

The weekly "state of the union" meeting also allows open discussion on upcoming items that may require you to adjust your roles. Most of all, it confirms the concept of making a set time to work together on your marital union.

2. *You must make major decisions jointly.* As explained earlier, you need to claim appropriate roles to avoid splitting your energy in too many different directions. But this division isn't intended to give either spouse unilateral power in making major decisions. For example, Sammy and Sandy decided that Sammy would be in charge of the kitchen (he was a professional chef and did most of the cooking at home, anyway). This way he could decide on the china pattern, but when it was time to decide on whether to renovate, he needed to talk to Sandy about it. Both of them had to have greater self-knowledge about why they were finding such small things "major" and then set and accept some clear guidelines on who would be in charge of what.

A "major" decision is anything you know your spouse will feel strongly about. Many people may say, "How am I to know what he/she feels strongly about?" or, "He/she feels strongly about everything!" As much as I've heard couples claim to be oblivious of what their spouse desires or what is important to their spouse, I've learned that most couples know exactly what their spouse wants. Generally, you know what decisions your spouse wants to be included in. If you are unsure, talk to your mate before making a decision. As time goes on you will learn what your spouse considers major.

Is It Worth the Argument?

Although I've discussed the importance of inviting differences into life in order to grow through seeing other perspectives, there is a good reason to limit discussion of your differences when it comes to making decisions. There are very few decisions in life worth fighting for. *If it wouldn't show up in your memoirs, it isn't worth the disagreement.* That china pattern or model of TV can't be important enough to upset the one you love or the warm marriage you want. To show each other why you think differently is fascinating and even fun, but when it comes to making a decision, you don't want to feel as though you need to prove your point to your spouse. Respecting differences means listening to and understanding your spouse. When all you care about is winning or proving your point, I guarantee you're not truly listening. So when it comes to a decision, state your opinion, listen to your spouse, and allow the person in charge of that area to make the ultimate decision because your partnership has placed that spouse in that role.

This is how any other successful system works. Partners know that there will be disagreements that will not always be easily resolved. So the

How Important Is It?

Are you the kind of spouse that dominates your partner by finding everything "major"? The following exercise will give you some insight into whether this description is true of you or your spouse.

1. *Make a list of how many things this past month you considered "major"—things you felt strongly about.* Your spouse should do the same for him- or herself. Be honest with yourselves. If you felt it necessary to disagree with your spouse, or if your spouse agreed but you would have made a stink if he or she hadn't, it's "major." How does your list look?

2. *Make a similar list of how many things you feel your spouse considered "major" this week.* Your spouse should do the same in regard to you.

3. *Review your lists together.* Did you find many more things to be "major" than your spouse did? If you and your spouse disagree about whether one of you considered something "major" (for example, you say he found china patterns a major issue and he says he didn't), talk it out. Perhaps your spouse doesn't realize how forceful he is.

    Sometimes people disagree for the sake of disagreeing and not because it means so much to them. They need to realize they are doing this. Create a signal with your spouse that asks if this is a moment when he or she is feeling strongly about something, or if he or she is simply playing devil's advocate. The signal can be something like, "Is this major to you?" On the other hand, look at the possibility that your spouse isn't really making a big stink about things. Perhaps when he asks a simple question like, "Why do you think the boys need to change karate schools?" you take it to mean he's second-guessing you and disagreeing. Maybe it really isn't "major" to him but rather that he just wants to feel part of certain things.

4. *Look deeper within yourselves.* If you realize that you're finding too many things "major," work to understand why. Perhaps you're trying to overpower your spouse so you can feel more "in control." Are you feeling weak in this relationship, or do you feel that others in your past have pushed you around? Are you overcompensating for feeling unheard years before by making sure you're heard too much in your marriage?

Are you following in your parents' footsteps and creating a similar relationship, in which one spouse is the one with the strong opinion? Ask yourself, "Who else in my life had strong opinions?" If you never find anything important enough to have a strong opinion about, consider that as much of a problem. What stops you from having strong feelings about something? Are you afraid to stand up for yourself? Discuss these deeper issues and learn about each other while resolving to help each other change in the future.

person in charge of that department should genuinely listen to his or her partner's opinion, discuss it, and consider all or part of it when making the decision. We can't put all our energy into each decision. So we split the decisions up. We are not avoiding our differences but using them strategically in a way that respects the many demands our busy schedules place on us.

What has always fascinated me about the time and energy we put into decision making is that we seldom truly know whether we've made the right decision. Decisions have a way of finding you years in the future. You can point to something you once thought was a bad decision and then years later realized something great happened because of it. Consider three major decisions you've made in your own life. Were they the "right" decisions? Are you sure that if you had done something differently, it would have been better or worse? Did these decisions cause the exact outcome you anticipated? Few people I've counseled can draw a straight line from point A to point B.

Before making a decision with your spouse, remember that right or wrong doesn't enter into the discussion as much as understanding each other's feelings and thoughts. *Through the ability to make a joint decision, you and your spouse will feel closer. Ultimately, that feeling is more important to your lives than the outcome of any specific decision.* After all, if you and your spouse have a horrible fight over an investment and in the end you make money on the investment, is your quality of life more improved compared with the love you drained out of your marriage? *What is your priority?*

When couples who have children fight about a decision regarding their children, I explain that no matter what the outcome of the decision, it can't possibly outweigh the damage the children will suffer because the marriage had to sustain such fighting. When a couple told me they had fought openly and bitterly for days about what boarding school to send their "difficult" child to, I felt so sad for this "difficult" child. I sympathized with the parents' stress and their wish to do what was best for their child, but they had lost sight of what was really important. Couples like these are not helping their children. Ironically, they forget that what is truly going to help their children more than the "right" decision, is a warm, loving home, which begins with a warm, loving marriage.

You Can Be Right or You Can Be Happy

What good is being right if it comes at the cost of love? So you proved your point, or your spouse admits you're right (which most people are grossly incapable of doing once they've begun to argue, so you usually won't get that satisfaction). Love, respect, kindness, and family are all more important than the specific decisions we make. We often think we're making a decision to benefit our loved ones and consider fighting to be a valiant effort on their behalf. Sadly, fighting sabotages family, love, and togetherness. If it's love you want for the rest of your life, remember that priority when making major decisions with your spouse.

If you need an additional incentive, consider that unhealthy fighting not only detracts from your loving marriage, it affects your health. One study discovered that the more negative or hostile the behaviors exhibited during a thirty-minute discussion about marital problems were, the greater the effects were on the immune system, making the couple more vulnerable to colds, heart disease, and cancer.[2]

The best marriages are the ones in which both spouses reserve strong opinions for very few subjects. These couples are more interested in building love than in wasting life's breath on arguing. *Let go.* Understand that no one knows the future well enough to say, "My opinion is the right opinion."

Following are five ways to resolve a difference of opinion in making a major decision. They all start with listening.

1. *Compromise.* Most decisions can be made creatively to accomplish both partners' goals. That's what listening is about. Just stating your opinion is limiting. *Listening to each other will help each of you understand what the other is really looking for, and usually you can satisfy both of your wishes with an alternative plan.* Compromise doesn't have to mean either of you is giving in somehow; rather it can mean creating a different way to receive what you wanted.

Consider the two parents who were searching for the boarding school best suited for their son. The mother wanted a structured environment that focused on developing critical thinking skills. The father was adamant that the boarding school have an excellent computer education program. But when they found a third school they both seemed to like, it failed in this area. The mother suggested that they arrange a private computer tutorial for their child. It might not have been the best option, but it satisfied this father. His compromise didn't mean his son wouldn't receive proper computer education. Instead, compromise meant he had to find a different solution than his initial expectation.

I counseled a husband who wanted more lovemaking than his wife did. Because of a traumatic past involving sexual abuse, she was reticent to be intimate. Her compromise wasn't to submit to sex she didn't want, but to take control of the lovemaking experience; her husband was more than amenable to having her take the lead.

One couple disagreed about how to spend any income above the amount needed to pay bills. He wanted to invest it all, and she wanted to buy items for the home. They agreed that for every ten thousand dollars saved, they would spend one thousand dollars on home furnishings. They further agreed that if she generated more income, 100 percent of it could also be spent on home décor.

Another couple disagreed about how to spend time together. He wanted to leave the house, as it helped him to clear his head and to enjoy his free time. She was tired of having to go out to "connect" with her husband. They decided to create certain nights when they would go out "no matter what"; they also designated some stay-at-home "nights out." During those evenings, she took over the night routine and put the kids to bed because this helped her husband relax and enjoy their time together at home.

In every one of these examples, no one had to "go without." Yes, each couple had to change their own way of getting what they wanted, but they could largely have their cake and eat it too.

If you are having difficulty finding a creative compromise, consider the following decision-making options.

2. *Allow the spouse who will be most affected by the outcome to make the ultimate decision.* Hand the decision off to the person who will be most affected by it. If your spouse does most of the cooking, purchase the electric stove he or she likes, even though you've read that the greatest chefs use only gas ovens. If your spouse takes care of the family banking, let him or her make the final

decision about moving to a new bank. If one spouse will generally be the one dealing with the nanny, let that spouse make the ultimate decision about choosing the nanny. Whether your points are valid is irrelevant.

3. *Allow the spouse with greater education or skill in the area to make the decision.* If your spouse has a doctorate in childhood education or finance, recognize that his or her opinions in those areas come with a great deal more expertise than your own. It doesn't mean your spouse is right or smarter, or that your spouse's decision will better serve your family. It just means that you should give your spouse the respect that his or her time and energy investment represents.

4. *Accept the opinion of the spouse who feels more strongly about the decision.* If your spouse has strong feelings about this decision and you don't, let it go his or her way. Obviously, it means much more to your spouse than to you, or your spouse feels much more confident about his or her opinion.

This decision-making option assumes a great deal of trust. After all, one spouse can easily take advantage of the other by always being more insistent. This option cannot work if one of you always feels strongly about things or the other never feels strongly about anything. It is the job of each individual to be honest enough with him- or herself to express strong feelings about only a handful of items. If you are feeling strongly about changing jobs *and* china patterns, it's time to reevaluate your thinking.

If every decision is vastly important to you, consider that perhaps you suffer from low self-esteem and may be overcompensating by taking a hard stance and trying to sound confident most of the time. Are you trying to overpower your spouse regularly because deep down you don't feel powerful at all? Did you see your parents fight because of their inability to be more easygoing? Get in touch with your deeper issues (see Secret #7), because spouses need to be able to trust each other. You need to believe that the reason each of you feels strongly about an issue is because of your genuine wish to better a given situation, not because you have a hidden agenda.

If love is your ultimate goal, there should be very few things to feel strongly about other than building a wonderful marriage and family.

5. *Commit to more research and time.* Even a major decision just isn't worth someone feeling hurt or disrespected. You may not realize how much you're hurting your spouse's feelings by your disagreement. When you can't decide together, and love seems to have slipped away as the top priority, step back and agree to give the issue more time. Review your facts and find other possible alternatives. Do more research, talk to people educated in the area you're trying to resolve, or spend some quiet private time to understand the issue more clearly.

If you've truly tried to understand each other and work it out using the preceding steps and can't, *stop*. As wonderful as it may be to talk things over with your spouse, sometimes you must recognize that the discussion isn't helping you make a decision or bringing you closer. *Sometimes you discuss and discuss and discuss until you are disgusted.* Let it go and don't push it anymore.

Stop Pushing/Start Flowing

Place your palm against your spouse's palm and both of you gently push against the other. Your hands are not moving. Then decide that only one of you will push and whenever either starts to push, the other does not resist. You will start to have your hands flow back and forth with each other.

Marriage does not work if both of you are pushing. A flow develops only when you can hear each other, take a step back, and allow your spouse's push to move you. As long as both of you have the ability to push at times, you will develop your unique flow.

Strongly consider your point of view and why it means so much to you that you can't find some middle ground with your spouse. Why is it important enough to cause tension in your home? Try to return to the issue with apologies for being difficult and a new resolve to calmly find the best answer, working from love and warmth.

Uncovering Hidden Agendas

One couple couldn't decide on the right pediatrician for their soon-to-be-born infant. The husband was adamant about a certain pediatric group and even changed the family health insurance to one that had this practice on the plan, without notifying his wife. They locked horns, losing sight of what was really in their child's best interest and instead focusing on controlling each other.

With further discussion, the wife learned that a major reason her husband wanted to send their child to this practice was that he served on the board of a charity with three of the doctors from the group. He felt that it was politically correct to use these doctors and that it would likely lead to business referrals from other members of the charity board.

The problem wasn't that the husband put his business before the well-being of his child. One could argue that ultimately the family as a whole might benefit from the increased business. The problem was that the husband had a hidden agenda, which caused distrust in the relationship.

When you see that your spouse isn't being straight with you, it becomes difficult to trust any of your spouse's opinions. Get it all out on the table. Be clear and honest with your spouse when you are making a decision that affects your marriage and family. Your spouse may not agree with your agenda, but more importantly, you'll be giving him or her the respect needed to trust each other and work out your differences. And don't jump on your spouse if he or she fesses up to an ulterior motive; you have to make it safe for your spouse to disclose the secrets.

When the husband with a hidden agenda about using a certain pediatric group came clean, the couple was able to consider creative solutions. They approached the decision strictly from the perspective of which physician would offer their child the best care, while recognizing that if they felt it was a close call, they could use the husband's "political" connection to help tip the scales. They also learned that the pediatricians his wife preferred offered community classes on childcare. If any charity board members questioned the husband about his family's decision, he could "save face."

What If You Already Have Your Roles?

Many couples have already developed a management system like the one described in this chapter. Perhaps you haven't done so on paper—rather, things have just kind of fallen into place. Do the written exercise on pages

110–111 anyway. Many couples harbor some small or large resentment for the roles that have befallen them. Many feel an uneven system has developed. Creating a management system at this point may be easier because you'll both notice that some of the items are already accounted for and you've been working well together in those areas for years. Even so, you'll find benefits to writing your roles down and having planned time to discuss these roles weekly. One of the greatest benefits is the acknowledgment that you don't have to stay in a role just because you fell into it. Writing it down gives your present role division some light and air, and gives you permission to experiment with fresh roles.

What Are You Really Afraid Of?

I have found that many couples resist the exercise of clearly indicating their roles. It's the same resistance I meet when I ask couples to create a financial budget. We seem to want to shy away from clarity when we are afraid of what clarity might look like.

Couples tell me it's "unromantic" to reduce their "jobs" to paper. What they don't want to do is to take responsibility for their part in the marriage. It's much safer to have an ethereal management system so they can always say, "I thought you were going to do that," or "I always do that. Why can't you do it this time?" Others prefer avoiding any focus on how much their spouse works in the marriage. One such couple was afraid to see how much the other was doing for fear it would make each of them look as if they didn't do enough. It turned out, of course, that listing their roles helped them both appreciate the immense energy each of them was pouring into their marriage. How can you genuinely appreciate each other if you aren't clear about what the other one does? Your energy is finite. Avoiding this exercise will only force you to spend much more of your energy on arguments and disappointments.

When you argue or fight, untold energy is being poured from you as you feel anger, resentment, betrayal, rejection, and sadness. Even if your fight is a calm one and you just don't feel understood, you've spent enormous emotional energy feeling unloved and alone. Have you ever had a rough physical day? You know, one in which you're on your feet all day and then need to carry heavy packages home at night. It really tires you out. But compare it to a day your child was very sick and you were consumed with worry, or any other time when tragedy struck. Remember how tired and drained you were? Expending emotional energy is far more draining than expending physical energy. One unfortunate fight with your spouse could drain you emotionally and physically for days.

Take control now. Create a management system that will offer both of you clarity, and don't be afraid to see what each of you is doing, and need to do, to make your marriage and family the best it can be.

Stop Counting

Counting is when you say, "I got up with the baby last night so you get up with him tonight," or "I cooked dinner last night, so you have to do it now." Lovers shouldn't be looking for ways to give more chores to their partner. Instead you should be considering what you could give and offer to your spouse. With the management system outlined earlier, you've already laid out many of the general responsibilities. But your goal isn't to paint a line down the middle of your relationship and say, "It's settled. That's your stuff to deal with, and this is mine." You should always be looking for ways to assist your spouse in his or her efforts whenever possible. If your spouse is in charge of feeding the baby at night but you happen to have tomorrow morning off, lend a hand and be a kind soul. That extra effort sends the message, "*I love you so much and want to help you take it a little easier.*" That's a message you'd love to hear regularly from your spouse.

You can give without loving but you can never love without giving.

—Robert Louis Stevenson

Are You a Giver?

Do you need to increase your focus on giving? Consider the following true or false questions. Answering "True" indicates you need to grow as a giver. Remember, "giving" is not only about material goods; it includes giving time and energy as well.

1. It's more fun to get a gift from my spouse than to give one.   T   F

2. When I get a gift for my spouse, I don't put in a lot of thought or time.   T   F

3. I feel I should only give to my spouse after he/she
   has given a lot to me.   T   F

4. When I do something for my spouse, I hope to get
   something from my spouse in return.   T   F

5. When I was little, I saw many examples of my
   parents giving to each other.   T   F

6. I have a good idea what my spouse would like me
   to give.   T   F

7. I have a good idea *how* my spouse wants me to
   give to him/her.   T   F

As much as I enjoy drawing business analogies to marriage, your life-time love relationship is clearly much different from a business relation-ship. In business, you do your part and go home. If your partner is still working, that's his or her problem. You have no obligation to be particu-larly sensitive to your partner's struggles or effort as long as you're pulling your own weight. The goal of business is not to be sensitive to your part-ner but to create a successful business. Marriage is about love. The success is in the love, not in how much money, children, pets, or picket fences you accumulate. *When your spouse is struggling, helping out is the immediate goal of your union.* Pick up the slack when you can and give, give, give. If you've got to fight, let it be over who's going to run an errand so that the other can relax. Make the extra effort to help each other in every way possible.

What Is Your General Marital Personality?

In addition to the specific roles we assume in our marriage, we also develop a general personality within our marriage. Usually this happens without too much examination. Do you see yourself more as having to take care of your spouse or as being taken care of by your spouse? Think about when you feel the best with your spouse. Is it a time when you're a caregiver or a time you're being nurtured? Unfortunately, people tend to fall into stereotypical roles. These images can cause damage when we act on them. For example, one husband described his affair as a "situation where I could be myself." He felt his wife depended on him so much that he could never show her his frailties. He found it so relaxing when he could let it all out and tell his mistress everything, unashamed of what she might think of him.

Right or wrong, men often feel they have to be strong and unwavering, and this can lead them to distance themselves from their spouses. There are some women who play into this a corresponding "weak" role and seemingly can't handle being aware of their husband's stresses or lack of strength. In fact, there is nothing wrong with one spouse being "stronger" than the other. But when it turns into a limitation like, "I can't share the way I really feel," then the roles have served to distance the couple. This inability to share can also occur for women as well. In my practice, I've often heard women describing their tiresome days full of work, errands, childcare, and meal preparation while feeling they must maintain a stoic smile and never-complaining attitude.

What messages do you send out about who you are? Consider some of the common personalities we take on in a marriage:

Weak————vs.————Strong

Responsible——vs.——Free and flighty

Serious————vs.——Funny

Organized————vs.——Spontaneous

Deep————vs.— Shallow

Energetic and Fresh——vs.———Deliberate and serious

Deep and philosophical——vs.——Clear and simple

Warm and caring———vs.———Cool and considering

Slow, methodical thinker——vs.——Quick-witted thinker

Family and socially oriented———vs.———Loner

Health-conscious————vs.———Candy lover

Couples don't necessarily fall into either extreme. Rather, each spouse is somewhere along a continuum between the extremes. Try the following exercise to find where you and your spouse fall along the various marital personality continuums.

"Sure, I'll care for the bills because I'm the more responsible one. But don't turn me into Mr. Responsibility who has to always be the serious one because you aren't ever thinking in terms of responsibility," was one husband's frustrated comment. Both spouses were upset. The responsible one felt resentful that he couldn't be more fun. He had to worry about everything because she didn't, so she felt a greater need to be more fun and "lighter" to compensate for her husband's seriousness. He was tired of sweating every detail to get ready for an outing with the kids, and she was equally tired of him obsessing about it all as she entertained the kids while waiting. As they compensated for each other, they became more polarized and more upset with each other's behavior.

Finding Your Marital Personality Roles

You and your spouse should each do the following exercise separately, then compare and discuss your results.

Before you start, together pick one color to represent you in this exercise and a different color to represent your spouse. You'll each use the same color codes to facilitate comparison when you discuss your results. For example, both of you might use red to represent Spouse A on your papers, and black to represent Spouse B.

Using these different-colored pens or pencils, plot yourself and your spouse along each of the above continuums. If necessary, create new continuums that suit your relationship.

When you have finished marking the continuums, consider: Are you much more the strong one or the weak one in your relationship? How big is the gap between you and your spouse? Are you comfortable with that gap, or would you like it to be lessened?

Using "your" color, draw a star on the same continuums indicating where you would *like* to be on each of them. Using your spouse's color, do the same to plot where you'd like your spouse to be.

I'm not suggesting that you and your spouse should meet in the middle for every parameter. The goal here is to challenge whether you're both happy with where you are on the continuums, and to find what works best for your unique partnership. If the extreme works for you in a given marital personality role, so be it.

To have greater insight as to why you fall into certain marital personality roles, use the same continuums to plot your parents' marital personality roles (use "M" for Mom and "D" for Dad). Are you and your spouse falling into the same roles as your parents did? Is there a similarity in the gap your parents had and the gap in your marriage? Perhaps you haven't taken on the same roles as your same-sex parent, but maybe your marriage still borrows from your parents' marriage as far as a lack of partnership goes. Perhaps your mom knew nothing about the family finances and your dad controlled them with an iron fist. Is there a similar gap in your marriage even if you, the wife, are the one who is in complete control of the family finances?

People are naturally different, and it's healthy to bring those different personalities into the mix of marriage. But sometimes your spouse is just so much better at being responsible that you relegate much of the responsibility to him. Or she's just the more outgoing one, so she takes care of the entire social calendar. But too often, the responsible one becomes tired of being totally responsible and would like to have a little fun, if only all of the responsibility didn't rest on him or her. And sometimes the social butterfly wants the spouse to take the initiative and alleviate the constant pressure to plan that memorable night. When we see that our spouse exerts control in an area, we tend to totally drop out of it. It's healthy to allow your spouse control of that area to some degree as you both try to build a management system based on each other's strengths. But it can become tiring and limiting when one spouse is given an entire marital personality role to carry on his or her own.

Consider your role. You and your spouse may have laughed about it in the past: "You're the serious adult one and I'm the fun kid in this relationship." It may not be a laughing matter. It's time to understand your roles and begin to share them in a way that gives both of you a positive feeling about the direction your roles offer your marriage and love.

Take a closer look at how you each plotted yourself and your spouse on the marital personality continuums in the preceding exercise. This exercise will help you begin to discuss how each of you sees the other and yourself in the marriage. Don't be insulted if your spouse places you in a role that you feel is not you. First listen carefully to why your spouse put you there. It's often hard to see ourselves objectively. Maybe your spouse is offering you an insight you should be grateful for. There is no right and wrong here. Perhaps you feel your spouse is wrong. Does it matter what the "truth" might be if that is how your spouse truly feels? Give your spouse the chance to explain why he or she has placed you in each category, and discuss whether change is needed in your respective roles. Every relationship is unique and entitled to develop as it chooses. I only suggest that it be done clearly and out in the open. Sometimes polarized roles work for a couple; more often, the couple finds they need to meet closer to the middle.

Use the role continuums to consider whether your present personality roles are working for you, and how to change them slowly over time if they're not. Discuss realistic behavioral changes that you can each make to help you both become more comfortable in your personality roles: "I'll read up on some of these important issues so I can discuss them." "I'll do the planning for this next outing." "I'll hug you more often." "I'll spend less time upstairs alone." "I'll record every check I write."

Many couples doing the role exercise find that a spouse is uncomfortable with a certain personality role. You may never have realized how tired you are of always being the social one or the responsible one. Now you have a chance to consider how you feel and, by sharing your feelings, to create a more comfortable marriage.

Try switching roles for some time. Doing so can really help each of you appreciate how much effort it takes to be the other one. One husband told his wife, "I'll never complain about work again," after getting their four kids off to school one morning all by himself, a responsibility his wife usually took care of. Likewise, she began to tell him how much she appreciated him after she stayed up until 2 A.M. completing the monthly family financial responsibilities. She was happier getting up early with the kids knowing that her husband was staying up late taking care of other family responsibilities.

Show Me the Money

Defining your marital roles and responsibilities isn't enough to help couples deal with their financial lives. Money takes on a life of its own in marriage, and the more each spouse understands his or her personal relationship to it, the better they can work together to build a strong financial partnership. In one survey, couples admitted that money and children provide the greatest pressures on relationships.[3] No surprises there.

Human beings crave control and power. We want to believe we can secure the life we desire. We expend huge effort and enormous time to exercise, in part because we believe we will live longer and better. We believe staying in shape will help us dodge the bullet of illness, which forces us to feel a lack of control. Consider one of the first things you search for when hearing about the death of someone your age: "How did he or she die?" And what are you looking for? A sign that the person's passing was related to an incident or physical defect that differentiated him or her from you. So if he was thirty-five and passed away of a heart attack, you are somewhat relieved to know he had heart disease in his family, was grossly overweight, and was a smoker. You quietly convince yourself that it couldn't happen to you because there is no heart disease in your family and you are in good shape and a nonsmoker. You hope that you're not going to hear that he was a marathon runner and vegetarian who was never sick a day in his life. Control is so crucial to us that we often think about it, and act on it, without noticing.

Our fervent, almost compulsive desire to control our lives is seen through our relationship with money. Money symbolizes our ability to offer ourselves choices, to maintain control of our destiny. It purchases basic needs like food, clothing, and shelter, but it likely also determines how much free time you have and what you'll be able to do with that time; whether you'll be able to travel or not; the quality of living space, food, and clothing at your disposal; how many others you can hire to assist you with your office work or childcare; whether you'll be dining in or out tonight, going to the movies, or renting a video. Money will determine whether you'll see the national expert in your child's illness or wait for hours in a clinic for someone who will be the first step in many to reach the person you need. Money gives us a sense of independence.

When a husband and wife discuss money, they're really talking about power and control over life. Therefore, any conversation about money can erupt into the worst and most complicated fight, even between two people who deeply love each other and are able to discuss every other aspect of life with warmth. Spouses are caught off guard when a simple purchase turns into World War III. Don't be surprised. It's not about dollars and cents. It's about the biological desire to control every aspect of life.

Sandy and Sammy never made a financial decision without a knock-down-drag-through-the-mud fight. Even though Sammy earned in excess of two hundred thousand dollars a year, they would fight over a ten-dollar purchase that Sammy felt was unnecessary. And it wasn't enough to discuss roles. Money took on a life of its own in their marriage. Even after I helped them determine who would be in charge of spending for what, they both considered most financial items "major" and were determined to discuss them before making final decisions. To get beyond this impasse, they each needed to understand what money meant to them individually.

I therefore asked each of them to complete the following sentence, separately, with the first three things that came to mind, immediately, without any time to consider their answers: "*I would love to win the lottery because it would . . .*"

Sammy wrote: *I would love to win the lottery because it would:*

1. Allow me to work less.
2. Let me worry less.
3. Make me feel like a man.

Sammy and Sandy began to understand that every time Sammy felt Sandy was spending too much, he saw it as an action that caused him to work more and worry more and feel less of a man. Sandy was merely buying a dress or lamp, or even a shirt for Sammy. But to Sammy, Sandy was purchasing stress for him.

When Sammy clarified his third answer, it spoke volumes to the meaning of money for many men. He explained with some hesitance that having money made him feel powerful. His brothers and father were all successful businessmen, and having money helped him feel like he was a part of his family. "Like it or not," he said in a frustrated tone, "having money makes me feel like a man, like I belong somehow." Throughout history, many a man's ego has been tied up in how well he can provide for his family. Like so many men, having money to Sammy translated into belonging with his family of origin as well as walking with his head up high knowing he could care for his own family. It meant that he felt comfortable making a request or getting what he wanted in life because he had money and that bought him prestige.

Sandy never understood these themes and was angered by Sammy's "childish" reaction whenever she spent money. "He can spend a thousand dollars on a suit, but watch out if I buy the kids a name-brand outfit or myself a new hat." But Sammy felt his suit was a business expense and saw Sandy's spending as an extravagance. He worried that his wife's spending literally would cause him to have a heart attack in the coming years when he was older and still forced to work as hard as ever.

Sandy had her own unique relationship with money as well. She answered the lottery question as follows: *I would love to win the lottery because it would:*

1. Offer me financial freedom.
2. Make me feel like a lady.
3. Allow me to do what I want.

Sandy was raised in a home where her father was constantly failing at a variety of start-up businesses. Her mother longed for financial freedom. Sandy recalled dreaming as a young girl of wearing name-brand clothing like her friends wore instead of the hand-me-downs from neighbors that made up most of her wardrobe. She remembered her friends' moms with their beautiful nails and stylish clothing while her own mom's hands were worn and her outfits were tired and often held together with hidden safety pins. Was it any wonder that Sandy felt that money would offer her the ability to "feel like a lady" with weekly manicures and pedicures and stunning, expensive hats? Why wouldn't she want to purchase name-brand clothes for her two children to make sure they never shared her childhood feeling of being "less than"?

Money was a loaded issue for both Sandy and Sammy. It usually is for most couples because of how significant a place it holds in our society, and because of our childhood associations with it.

Your first job is to recognize the significance of money to you personally so that you know the emotional issues you have attached to it. Answering the lottery question will give you an insight. Be brutally honest with yourself and your spouse, and equally sensitive to your spouse's feelings on the matter. Discuss explicitly with your spouse what your parents taught you, by example or observation, about spending, saving, and the meaning of money. Did your family talk about money? Fight about it? Did you grow up amid deprivation or excess? What are your money values?

Planning for Your Financial Future

What do you want your money to do for you? As your individual and joint financial goals become clear, you will need to find creative ways to get as many of these goals realized as possible. Some of your financial goals can be reached immediately, but others will take long-range planning.

The following exercise will help you separate your financial goals into long-range and immediate ones, and will lead you through making a budget that will allow both of you to work together. A budget that both of you have developed will be easier for you to maintain because both of you "own" it. Successfully creating and staying within a budget gives couples a joint sense of direction and control.

Making a Budget

Step 1: Determine your financial goals. Look back at the financial goals you set in your Marriage Proposal (see Secret #3). Use them as a basis for making up a list of your long-range and immediate financial goals. Create this list together.

Long-Range Financial Goals

What do you see money offering you in the future? Your list might include:

Retirement

College education for children

Ability to take long vacations when the kids are much older

Charitable donations

Immediate Financial Goals

What do you want from your money today? Your list might include:

Mortgage

Private school tuition for children

School supplies

Food

Clothing (business and casual)

Household supplies

Summer camp

Vacations

Car payments

Utilities

Dry cleaning

Newspaper delivery, magazine subscriptions

Entertainment (movies, dinners)

Personal grooming (haircuts, manicures, massages)

Step 2: Put a monthly price tag next to each item under the immediate-goals category and a general figure next to each of your long-term goals. Some of these items may be consistent (mortgage, newspaper delivery), whereas others may fluctuate greatly (electricity, dinners). Place a guesstimate figure next to any item that you are unsure about.

Next to your long-term goals, consider a total figure you'd like to get to, and then arrive at a monthly figure that you think will get you there. When it comes to items like retirement, remember that the money you set aside will be earning interest, so your monthly figure multiplied by the years until your retirement does not have to add up to your long-range figure. But do the best you can to come close to that long-range figure.

Add up all the individual figures. This is your monthly budget. Both of you should sign and date the bottom of the budget. Don't duck out of this task because you think it is too time consuming, or figure out some other excuse for not gaining control of your spending and your marital finances. The goal here is to find a healthy way of dealing with money. Resist the urge to just smile and say, "All right, let's just do the best we can to spend a little less." You may as well say, "You know, my emotional issues are a little too intense for me on this money thing so I'd rather pretend it away and risk continuing our dysfunctional way of dealing with it than actually taking responsibility for my actions."

Step 3: Commit in writing to writing down every purchase for the next month. For the next month, each of you must write down in a little notebook every time money leaves your pocket, whether through check, cash, or credit card. When you buy a magazine, shop for food, eat at a restaurant, go to the movies, buy a cup of coffee, or pay bills, have your book ready and simply jot down the date, the item purchased, and the cost. You don't have to itemize the food shopping; just write the date and total cost. If you have a financial record program such as Quicken on your computer, you can just enter these daily totals into your computer records and truly simplify your budgeting.

Step 4: After one month, have a meeting and begin to categorize your expenditures. How much are you spending a month on food, clothing, entertainment, utilities, dry cleaning, and household help? I guarantee you'll have some unpleasant surprises. Fifty bucks just for lattés? Resign yourself to feeling sheepish or embarrassed, or perhaps a little out of control. Forgive yourself and your spouse, and congratulate yourselves on taking a brave step. Now you will have a clearer sense of how much you spend and on what. The two of you can decide on some areas in which you could spend less. If saving money is important to you, decide on an amount that seems reasonable.

Read books like *The Millionaire Next Door* and *Your Money or Your Life* together; discuss the chapters to help you begin to formulate a lifelong plan of how you want to use your money. Begin to be psychologically aware of your personal relationship with money, and commit to creating a responsible financial lifestyle.

Step 5: Revisit the budget you created. From your one-month tracking of expenses, you should be able to create a more reliable budget. Review what your guesstimates were before you started recording every purchase for the month and see how close you were to the real number.

First, add the entire month's expenses and see how this total compares with the amount the marriage earns (after taxes). If you are spending more than you are earning, you must decide where you will spend less each month. Even if you're earning more than you are spending, consider whether you are comfortable with the amount of money you're spending in each category. You may realize that you're spending $250 each month on eating out and that you'd rather spend (or save) that $3,000 a year on something else.

Create a new realistic number for spending on each item that both of you agree to. Commit to your new budget for a month. Agree to use cash as much as possible. For example, if your monthly food budget is $500, take it in cash at the start of the month and place it in an envelope designated solely for food purchases. This helps you regulate your spending. It also avoids impulse purchases of "unnecessary" items.

Step 6: Maintain your weekly meetings, and congratulate each other on taking control of a difficult part of life. Revisit and update your budget every three months. As the two of you start to recognize how well you can approach complicated issues like spending, it will reinforce your confidence in your marriage. It will help you trust your relationship more and motivate both of you to add energy and passion to your relationship.

Whose Money Is It Anyway?

Years ago, odds were that the man made the money and had most of the say over how it was spent. Times have changed. But sociologists Blumstein and Schwartz, who studied six thousand American couples in 1983, found that although 60 percent of wives had jobs, only 30 percent of the husbands thought both spouses should work.[4] Many men still have an attitude of "The money I make is really mine and I'm kind enough to share it with you." Naturally, it's common for their wives to feel offended. Most women who are mothers and do not work outside the home would say there is an unwritten agreement in their marriage that they will not pursue a career so they can care for the children. This trade-off gives the women who have made it a sense of entitlement to their husband's financial success. These women tend to feel grossly underappreciated by their husbands for their daily effort. They often feel they are being treated like children, and their husbands feel as if their spouses are trying to steal "their money," which represents their hard work as well as their manhood.

I have found that this "my money" theory can easily apply to whichever spouse is making more money, with an accompanying sense of greater entitlement. If you are the "my money" type of spouse, recognize it openly. First, identify where it comes from. Most often you can look to your parents' model of money management and see if it speaks to your attitude. Look at your friends and society. I've had extremely wealthy men see it as "obvious" that the money they make belongs to them. They don't ever have to ask if they can spend it, but they insist their spouse must. They've turned money into a way of controlling their environment and spouse. One highly financially successful gentleman told me that he never let his wife work because he didn't want her to become financially independent in any way. Interestingly, it was his wife who worked for the first six years of their marriage to support the two of them while he completed his education.

If there is a part of our lives that we keep secret or manipulate so that our spouse has no say in it, we are effectively dismantling our ability to create a successful marriage. Using money as a means of control distances

Jean & Lou Greenberg
MARRIED: 45 YEARS

What Made It Work?

We weren't limited by staying with only certain roles. He'd cook and I'd paint. We didn't say, "It's your job," but rather we would plan for what had to be done. Both of us were always willing to do anything for the marriage.

People know the right thing to do, and if it's possible, it's always better to do that thing. The Mrs.'s mother lived in our house with us for thirty-one years. It was the right thing to have her there.

What Challenges Face Couples Today?

There doesn't seem to be as much time for talking without interruptions. You have to discuss even simple things, details, current events, a little business maybe, the children. This quiet talking about the small things leads to understanding each other. It's good for the children to see, and it brings you closer as a couple.

Young couples today have to turn off the telephones and the televisions and sit outside a little, talking to each other.

our partner from us. The bad taste of manipulation will taint every part of the marriage, and the lack of giving will become more and more clear as time continues. No matter who brings home the bigger paycheck, your goal must be to plan around "our money for our future."

Your role and relationship with money can be a defining characteristic of your loving marriage. Work hard at making the financial part of your marriage work. Instead of allowing money to disturb the relationship, instead of tolerating your spouse's attitude, instead of avoiding any discussion of money out of fear of what it could do to your relationship, use the area of money to aid and strengthen your marriage. Be honest with yourself and share your insights with your mate. This way, money can be the impetus for greater sharing of feelings and learning, the very lifeblood of a meaningful marriage. Work at developing a better financial management system and your marriage will dominate your finances instead of the other way around.

5

Acceptance is about appreciating, not settling.

Have you ever seen the face of a young child being praised for an accomplishment? There is little as endearing as the beaming smile of a child whose parent has just complimented him for reading a difficult word, opening a jar she struggled with, or making his first scrambled eggs, basketball basket, or Mother's Day gift. It's inspiring to see a small child with a smile and giggle that says, "I can barely stand it. I'm going to burst with delight." Why do all children have the same reaction when a parent takes note of something positive they have done? Appreciation. When we are born, we don't know our value. We are literally built upon appreciation. Every moment our parents approve of us or take joy in our accomplishments or being sends us the message that we are wonderful. We will draw strength from those moments for the rest of our lives. Those moments form our image of ourselves. Even as adults, how much appreciation we receive determines how comfortable we are in our own skin. Appreciation confirms our self-worth.

⁕⁕⁕⁕⁕⁕⁕⁕⁕⁕⁕⁕⁕⁕⁕⁕⁕⁕

Sammy and Sandy, our battling china buyers, found deeper insight into why they fought so bitterly. Each of them felt underappreciated. As a result, they both tried to enhance their strength and sense of control by arguing and trying to make things turn out their own way. When we think our spouse doesn't value us, we feel a need to prove ourselves and practically force our mate to take note of us. We may argue our point not because we believe in it so much but because we want our spouse to stop diminishing our role in the marriage. We may go to great lengths to do things better just to see if our spouse will care. Generally, this results in a vicious circle in which one spouse works ever harder to please the other, continues to feel unappreciated, and feels ever more resentful.

Sammy felt that no matter how much more he worked or earned, Sandy would still focus on what he wasn't doing with the children or how they couldn't take the extravagant vacations their friends enjoyed. Sandy felt that no matter how much money she saved by cutting back on spending or working harder to care for the children, Sammy would never be happy and would always be nervous about money and unwilling to spend it on her and the kids. Feeling that it was a no-win situation drained each of them, and they lost their motivation to try and please each other.

When I ask my marital therapy patients to create a list of everything each one appreciates about the other, I usually get the same type of list, a short one. The couples in front of me are much more concerned with what is *not* happening than with what is. They're in my office to tell me what needs to change, not what needs to stay the same. The mistake every one of these couples makes is that they fail to show love through appreciation. Appreciation helps each of us connect with the little girl and boy inside who yearns to be special and a part of something wonderful.

When you cherish your spouse, it touches your spouse at the core of who he or she is, deep down where appreciation is attached to his or her core self-value. It is that appreciation that motivates us to give more, love more, and trust more. Every one of us desperately desires to be needed and wanted by someone who finds us absolutely spectacular. This is the power of marriage. It can feed our soul and our deepest need to be wanted. There is a serene peacefulness when you feel this loved and cherished. We would do anything for this person who loves us so unconditionally.

We are more comfortable with, and even enjoy, doing things for others when they appreciate our effort. We enjoy seeing another smile and offer us warm hugs. We are greatly motivated to do for those who offer us a sense of importance in return. When we feel appreciated, we feel whole.

Appreciation is much more than being diplomatic. It's not about remembering to "be nice" or about offering a compliment because "he's just a little boy/girl in a big boy/girl's body." It's never about being condescending. It's about understanding one of your mate's truest needs to know that he or she is more special to you than anyone else could ever be.

When I ask couples to create an appreciation list about their spouse, they often leave out things, like the fact that he or she works so hard at a job, cares for the children, makes money, or is kind to the family. In other words, they leave out some of the most important and difficult efforts their spouse makes. When I ask why such monumental feats were ignored, I always hear the same response: "He's supposed to make a living." "She's their mother. It's her job to care for them." Each assumes that whatever the other does as part of being a responsible person need not be appreciated because it is expected. These couples see it as almost childish to appreciate something they expect their spouse to do. In doing so, they take their spouse's energy for granted.

It's unfair to expect things and then be unappreciative of any of the work our spouse puts forth to meet those expectations. It's cold and insensitive. For most, it's a bad habit taught to us by a confused society. It's easily remedied with focus.

~~~~~~

Both my wife and I work hard. There are literally thousands of things each of us does that the other would be unaware of if we didn't take the time to spell them out for each other to appreciate. I'm not suggesting you turn appreciation into a "can-you-top-this?" game. I'm suggesting that you acknowledge what you already know your spouse does, and ask about the things you may not know about so you can appreciate them too. This isn't about a perfunctory "Thanks." It's the time we take to ask with genuine concern what went on in the last day or so, what have been the challenges and struggles as well as the triumphs.

How can I truly appreciate my wife if I'm not even clear on what she does? I want to know that one of my kids made all over the floor while she was cooking dinner after logging hours of billing work on the computer. I want to know how frustrated she was with the workman who only chattered on about fixing our plumbing instead of actually doing the work, and how in the midst of it all she thought enough of me to cook me dinner. I want to know all of this, in part because I want to know how much she loves me and our family. I feel wonderful when I think of how much love and attention she offers us. Deep down, I may expect or hope for no less. But I know that there are many who are not capable of doing what my wife does. And she does it with grace every step of the way. I tell her so. I want her to know how incredible she is. She forgets sometimes. I'm there to remind her.

One of the most wonderful things my wife does for me is appreciate me. Not only does she tell me, she shows me. She tells others. She taught me how to appreciate by listing the wonderful things I do. So it's not, "Thanks for working so hard." It's more like, "I don't know how you do it. I could never do it like you. It must be so difficult to be there for so many people while finding time to be creative and write." *We see each other's strengths so clearly, and we* <u>*magnify*</u> *our focus on them because, after all, this is the best of each of us.* We know we each have plenty of weaknesses, but we feel they are incredibly outweighed by our strengths and the effort we make to capitalize on them. We understand that neither of us has to work as hard as we do in life and in love to be acceptable members of society. But we try to go the extra mile. We feed each other fuel for love with every pat on the back, every "Thank you," every "You're terrific." We make the other feel immensely special, and that just makes us want to give so much more.

So many people, men and women, have told me in my office, "He doesn't appreciate what I do." They practically beg their spouses to recognize their effort. They always say the same thing: "I'm not asking for anything like diamonds for my effort. Just the appreciation." Too many people don't realize how important it is. They misunderstand how far appreciation goes in helping a mate feel special and important.

Make an Appreciation List

Create a list of all the things your spouse does that you appreciate and give it to your spouse. Be as specific as possible. Instead of saying, "Thank you for taking care of the kids," write, "Thank you for getting up at 6:15 A.M. and getting the kids dressed, making breakfast, and taking them to school." Instead of "I appreciate how hard you work," write, "I appreciate that you deal with a boss every day who is rude, that you keep on top of so many people and tasks." Then make it a ritual to tell your spouse one more thing you appreciate about him or her as you say your final goodnight.

The "Manly" Way

Men usually have greater difficulty understanding the importance of appreciation. We've been taught from early on to "be a man," which is often interpreted as "be strong enough to do the really important things in life, like provide for your family." Men are given the message as boys that they must grow up and work hard to accomplish. "You don't have the time or right to cry because you have important work to do. And don't be expecting a lot of appreciation. Only wimps need appreciation. You do what you're supposed to do, and seeing your family well fed is thanks enough."

It's no wonder that men see their jobs as far more important and complicated than their wives may, even if it's the furthest thing from the truth. It's as if these men must believe their work is much more important or else those childhood messages were a lie and they've wasted so much of life negating pleasure and feelings for nothing. So even if one man's wife is getting less sleep at night than he and is working just as hard as he is, he won't see or understand why he has to "build her up" and appreciate her. What's the big deal? Now what *he* is doing, well, that's big news.

If you are this man who finds it ridiculous to have to appreciate his wife regularly, recognize that you withhold the simple kindness of this appreciation. Recognize that finding your wife's work extremely important in no way reduces the importance of what you do. Reconsider your childhood messages as well as the messages society sends you, and allow yourself to find pleasure in the importance of both your and your wife's efforts. Remind yourself how wonderful it is to have a partner who cares to do what she does.

The "Womanly" Way

On the other hand, it seems that many women do not truly appreciate what their husbands do—especially those mothers who are cleaning dirty diapers and wishing they had a nice calm, clean office to escape to. Many women may be correct in assuming their husbands don't work as hard as they do when all is said and done. On the other hand, many women tend to overlook the incredible pressure there is on men to provide for their families. Society places high expectations on men. That pressure causes men to put up with bosses who humiliate, manipulate, and dominate. That pressure causes men to worry and fear about the future.

Many women have told me that it's a joint effort to bring in money. You as a woman might feel there is no reason for your husband to be under more pressure than you to make a living, but let's face it, if your family can't afford food, education, or a nice car, generally no one is looking at the woman in the marriage and thinking, "Boy, she can't provide for her own family." Right or not, many in our society still assign man the role of provider. Appreciate your husband for dealing with that tremendous pressure. It may not add up to extra hours in the day, but when it comes to energy, it adds up to more than you may realize.

Dual Incomes: The New Tradition

Times have changed. Now, so many couples have the high stress of both the corporate world and the family world. I've already talked about developing healthy roles and attitudes in these areas, but many of us are split in so many ways that it's exhausting. That's why appreciation becomes so much more important than ever before. You need to feel that your spouse understands that you're doing what others have rarely done before. Even though it's becoming commonplace for women to be more responsible for family income and men to be more responsible for family chores, it doesn't make the job any easier. It is the ultimate multitasking. Make sure your spouse knows you realize how complicated his or her life can get sometimes, and how much you appreciate your partner's effort.

Give Thanks

Let your spouse know how much you appreciate everything he or she does— and also what he or she *doesn't* do—that's helpful, like, "Thanks for not making a big deal about my little fit." Appreciation will transform your marriage immediately. Start every morning and end every evening with a kind word of appreciation, and you and your spouse will feel like innocent, gleeful children, if even just for a moment. Appreciation is magical. It not only makes your spouse feel wonderful but makes you focus on the goodness of your spouse, which in turn helps you find a deeper love for your partner.

The Triple Crown of Acceptance

Many people when they fall in love look for a little haven of refuge from the world, where they can be sure of being admired when they are not admirable and praised when they are not praiseworthy.

—Bertrand Russell

I refer to acceptance as the crown of marriage because it should be worn as the ultimate testimony of your love and desire to make your spouse feel wonderful and enjoy a meaningful relationship with you. It is the sense that we are seen as special for who we are by the one we love that makes us feel like kings and queens of our castles. Our home becomes a place of refuge where our best selves are focused. Having such a crown gives us the energy to feel special everywhere we go, knowing our marriage is always there to bring out the best in us.

The First Crown of Acceptance: The Mona Lisa Was No Size 2! Change Your Perspective

Our society has become preoccupied with weight, especially women's weight. Most men and women believe that the male brain is wired to be more attracted to thin women than to overweight women. I've had many couples grapple with the issue of the husband desiring a thinner, more attractive wife and the pressures that accompany such requests. When I talk to these couples about the importance of accepting one another for who they are, the husbands believe that their wives have a shortcoming and that they must learn to overlook it or deal with it.

Then I focus them on the most recognized model in history, Mona Lisa, who would never make it today as a supermodel. Not only did Da Vinci choose a large woman to serve as an icon of beauty, voluptuous women have had a long history of serving as romantic images. Picasso's painting *The Lovers* shows a large woman in full view with her lover's arm draped around her tenderly. Rodin's sculpture *Le baiser* ("The Kiss") screams passion as the female model twists her body to meet her lover's lips, her full tummy gathered in a sensuous mound. Let's not leave out the bronze statue of a woman's torso by Aristide Maillol, a remarkably beautiful work that honors the curves of a full figure. Henri Matisse's *Nu allongé* ("Nude Reclining") shows a naked woman lying in bed, her rounded belly and wide hips on provocative display.

Artists with the most wonderful view of life's treasures have consistently chosen large, voluptuous women to portray beauty, intimacy, and passion. These artists and many others prove that society's preoccupation with thin women has been culturally, not genetically, induced. And it is not as though these artists' perspectives are ancient. Picasso passed away in 1973, and Rodin (1840–1917), Matisse (1869–1954), and Maillol (1861–1944) all lived well into the twentieth century.

Acceptance is not about settling. It starts with the recognition that what you see as inferior may not be so. Your wife may be a size 12–14, which would have been seen as much more attractive than a smaller size only a very short while ago. Why don't you find her more attractive? Most probably it is because you have been convinced by countless ads and images of women in the media suggesting that only thin women are sexy. But you don't have to be a product of your environment. Through recognizing that you are forcing yourself to live by society's rules instead of your own intimate ones, you can stop giving society so much control over your thinking and decisions. You can acquire a new taste for your wife's body, just as it is, because her body can be sexy and beautiful *to you*.

I use weight as only one example for a new concept of acceptance. We can change our thinking about a host of characteristics that are labeled "unattractive" by society, such as being bald, unfashionable, or lacking in status. For example, many women are attracted to expensively suited men who seem to have enormous amounts of money and power. Yet you may be married to a man who has dedicated his life to teaching the third grade. He may not be driven to earn massive wealth and power. He may dress rather simply and unfashionably. And if you are told by a therapist that you need to accept this about him, you may take it as having to "settle for less." Yet you can learn to change what you see as your husband's deficits. Should you think less of your husband and lose passion in your marriage because society doesn't choose to see him as a gifted man who is dedicated to forming the minds of our children, and thus the world's future? Don't see it as "settling." See it for what it really is: opening your eyes to appreciate that your husband possesses a certain talent and a willingness to help others instead of conforming to society's stereotypes. That third-grade teacher is an independent, visionary maverick.

My wife and I have largely avoided television for years. We only watch occasionally because we choose not to be brainwashed by the incessant media messages that say you have to be young, tan, prepubescently thin with a large chest (whether man or woman), and sensuously dressed, with a blinding set of teeth, to be considered attractive. Recently a friend told me that she wouldn't purchase *People*'s annual "Most Beautiful People" issue because she didn't want to see how ugly she looked. The media seem to cut men a bit more slack, but the washboard abs and full head of hair still prevail over the bowling-pin physique and bald spot. If you allow these images into your life, you will have no choice but to be less enchanted with your spouse and even yourself. Only about 13 percent of single females and 28 percent of single males consider themselves attractive.[1] But research shows that good looks in one's youth have little to do with happiness or marital satisfaction in middle age.[2]

Protect yourself from being controlled by those images that scream, "You and your spouse aren't good enough." It's not only about thinness. It's about using and appreciating our unique talents and finding those talents in our spouse.

A friend of mine used to love her husband's jokes until she began to notice she was the only one in the crowd who laughed heartily and took such pleasure in his brand of humor. She confessed to me that from then on, it used to practically depress her that her husband's humor was so cerebral. She was an extremely sociable person and started cringing every time her husband was about to open his mouth, for fear that he'd tell one of his jokes that no one would get, or find the least bit funny. Then, a few years into her marriage, her husband became a professor of mathematics at an Ivy League college. As they began to socialize with other professionals at the college, her husband's humor was immediately met with heavy laughter. She realized that his humor hadn't improved, but his audience had. Ever since, she has never apologized nor thought twice about his jokes.

You, too, can acquire a new taste for what you presently see as your spouse's weaknesses. The fact that they don't work for your friends, family, or society doesn't mean they're not just right for you. We acquire tastes regularly. Did you love your first taste of coffee or fine whiskey? Others have learned to love living in a dramatically different location because of work or family. We have an incredible ability to adjust when we feel it's important enough to do so. Unfortunately, society doesn't teach us that marriage is so important that we need to adjust and acquire new tastes to nurture it.

The first crown of acceptance is to change your perception about your spouse and recognize that you can see many of his or her deficits as strengths if you want to. Your spouse's lack of seriousness, for example, is the very thing that has helped you laugh through your hard times and has kept you young at heart. Your spouse's attention to detail is the very thing that has offered you a beautiful home to live in. Your spouse's frugality is the very thing that has helped you rest easier, knowing how much you have saved.

Changing your perspective takes time, energy, and focus. However, there may be parts of your spouse that you don't feel you can change into positives anytime soon. The exercise on page 162 can help.

Change Your Perspective

1. Write down one thing about your spouse that makes you unhappy.
2. Where did you learn that this behavior or situation isn't what you should desire or expect? Consider:
   a. Who in your life told you that this type of situation is unacceptable? (For example, did your mom always give you long speeches about being late and now your husband's disdain for being prompt drives you nuts?)
   b. Who in your life showed you that this type of situation is unacceptable? (For example, did you see your dad poking fun at Mom's weight and now you can't stand the way your wife looks with the "extra" weight?)
   c. What other things have you read or seen that might have given you the impression that your spouse's behavior isn't desirable? (Are you watching a lot of movies that depict love as constant passion and you're finding your spouse rather unromantic?)
3. List the attractive things about your spouse in the same area. (For example, if you are turned off by your spouse's weight, list the things about your spouse you find physically appealing; if your spouse is late, list things like how much fun he is once he arrives; if you find your spouse unromantic, list the behaviors of your spouse that you do find romantic.)
4. List ways you can change your focus to see the great things about your spouse and change your perspective on what you used to find unappealing. For example, you can remind yourself that you're judging your spouse based on the messages you received from your parents or the media, which may be misguided or wrong. You can recall your spouse's good parts when you find yourself beginning to become annoyed with your mate's behavior.

The Second Crown of Acceptance: Redefine Your Spouse

Harry and Lisa sat fuming in my office. They'd had it with each other. Harry made jokes at Lisa's expense whenever they were with company, and it embarrassed her. Lisa also complained that Harry was unsociable, happy to stay home every night. Sure, he'd go out if Lisa arranged everything, but she wanted a man who wanted to have fun as much as she did, who wanted to paint the town red. On the other hand, Harry couldn't accept Lisa's "ditziness": she'd regularly lose her keys to the house or car, her license, or her credit cards. He felt all she wanted to do was to have fun with her friends and take no responsibility at home. They remembered it being different years ago when they were first married, but things changed soon after the honeymoon. Sounds like a pretty serious marital problem? It sure was. But only for one reason. They both had lost focus of what to appreciate and what to accept.

I discovered that Harry was a successful CEO of a publicly traded company and had to do a tremendous amount of socializing for business. When he returned home, he just wanted to rest and not feel the pressure to interact with anyone other than his wife and kids. Lisa cared for their two children practically alone, since Harry worked and traveled a great deal. When he was home, she was eager to have an opportunity to get out of the house.

To me, the "boring" man and "irresponsible" woman seemed like wonderful, well-intentioned people who were both trying very hard to succeed in life in their unique ways. But what did each of them focus their attention on? The other one's deficits, weaknesses, and limitations. Their definitions of their partner were largely the sum of negatives. That was unfair, yet all too common for unhappy couples.

❦❦❦❦❦❦❦❦❦❦❦❦❦❦❦❦❦❦❦❦❦

How we define others and ourselves often depends on whether we are optimists or pessimists. Acceptance is the recognition that every human being has significant weaknesses, carries around so much emotional baggage no airline could lose it all, and often has no clue why he or she acts in ways that sabotages his or her ability to love and be happy. Join the human race. Next time you're looking in a mirror, think of only the worst things you've done in your life. Take away all your effort to do good and restrict your self-image to your mistakes, the lack of sensitivity you've had for others, the things you didn't do that you should have done. It's not a pretty picture. Luckily that picture has nothing to do with your true reflection. But you would never want to see yourself or have your spouse see you only for what you are not. Don't do the same to your spouse. Don't look for Mr. or Mrs. Perfect. Search for Mr. or Mrs. Right, the one choice best for us and only us.

Chances are that your spouse isn't up late at night planning how to annoy you. Like most people, your spouse is trying to give and receive love.

You and your spouse are trying to do the right thing, and deep in your hearts you want to give to each other.

Harry and Lisa weren't trying to get anything but what they each wanted. However, they exacerbated the situation by making countless requests for the other person to change while asserting, "This is who I am and you'll have to learn to deal with it." I asked them, "Did you marry a person or Play-Doh that you expected to shape and mold to your description of perfect?" If you want to see changes, accept and praise the person you married as he or she is right now. Redefine those negatives.

What I'm about to say is so important that I need to draw your attention to it in advance. Every time I've been successful in helping a couple accept each other as they are, the spouses have naturally turned to each other and admitted to their own shortcomings and their desire to change them. I mean *every time*. Any limitation you see in your spouse he or she will also see if you explain it to your mate in a loving, nonjudgmental way (see "It's me, not you," page 169). All human beings have an internal drive to grow and be better. We often can see our own limitations but hide from them to avoid being down on ourselves or becoming depressed. You cannot be very happy today if you focus too much on your shortcomings or what you haven't done. But when the pressure to change is off, you are far more capable of looking deeper within yourself.

When Harry and Lisa heard praise and appreciation from each other, they felt more comfortable considering their own shortcomings. Harry found the strength to say, "I guess you're right. I can be a bit boring, and you shouldn't be punished because I have to socialize so much without you." This prompted Lisa to say, "I understand and I don't need you to be the life of the party. I just want to have fun with you like we used to before life became so complicated with work and kids." Harry apologized for his demeaning remarks and understood that they grew out of his anger over the time he had to spend making up for Lisa's losing things. But now Lisa was able to say that she felt bad for losing things and she didn't want to inconvenience Harry anymore. They both decided to make many car and house key duplicates and discussed other creative ideas to help Lisa get organized. Once they sensed warmth from each other, they could share their inadequacies without worrying they would be met with hostility or greater embarrassment.

Acceptance is a focusing tool. It helps you recognize how wonderful a person you married and how many important things your spouse does. It helps you see your spouse as a human being, a mixture of good and bad.

The Third Crown of Acceptance: You Bought the Whole Loaf

The difficulty with marriage is that we fall in love with a personality, but we must live with a character.

—Peter Devries

Acceptance is also about understanding that your partner's personality is a package deal. If Harry loved Lisa for her vivaciousness and spontaneity, her ability to forget about her stress, have fun, and not be so "serious," it would be unusual to expect Lisa to focus on serious details like financial planning and balancing the checkbook. Harry needed to understand that what he loved about Lisa was her carefree personality, the very personality that did things like lose keys and forget about important details. Likewise, Lisa had to recognize that she loved her husband's ability to be a CEO, make a wonderful living, and be so well respected. But with this ability came a personality that had to be serious and structured. It made sense that Harry wasn't easily given toward spontaneity. The very things Lisa loved in her husband came from a personality that limited his ability to have carefree fun easily.

We don't marry slices of bread. We can't just pick out that deliciously soft slice in the middle and throw away the rest. We eat the ends as well, although we may wait until we've finished every other slice. For those of you who immediately throw away the ends, you may have your work cut out for you in this area of acceptance. For those of you who eat them begrudgingly because you're stuck with them, you're on your way. For those of you who have learned over years that the ends can be rather tasty during those times when you want a little more chew out of your bread, you've got the right attitude. We have to accept what reality dictates: Every personality has its advantages and disadvantages.

The Whole Loaf

This exercise will help you realize that many of your spouse's positive traits are present because your spouse has a certain kind of personality. However, that personality will also carry with it many of your spouse's limitations. When you've finished this exercise, dispose of it so that your spouse doesn't see your list of "improvements." This list is for your benefit, not a "to do" list of changes for your spouse.

Divide a piece of paper into two columns. In the left-hand column, list your spouse's positive traits. In the right-hand column, list the areas you'd like your spouse to improve in. Finally, draw lines to match up the items in the two columns that seem to belong to a similar personality traits. Don't feel forced to match every positive trait to an area that needs improvement. For example, in the following list, "plays sports with kids" was not linked to anything on the right hand side of the column.

The following list, made by a wife who considered her husband too rigid and controlling, can serve as a model for the process.

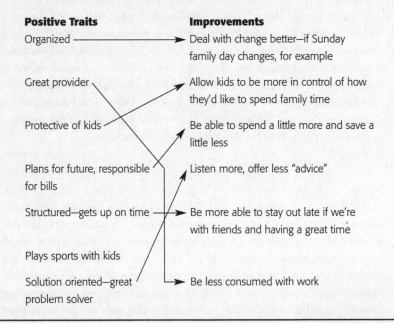

Positive Traits

Organized ⟶ Deal with change better—if Sunday family day changes, for example

Great provider

Protective of kids

Plans for future, responsible for bills

Structured—gets up on time ⟶

Plays sports with kids

Solution oriented—great problem solver

Improvements

Deal with change better—if Sunday family day changes, for example

Allow kids to be more in control of how they'd like to spend family time

Be able to spend a little more and save a little less

Listen more, offer less "advice"

Be more able to stay out late if we're with friends and having a great time

Be less consumed with work

In the above example, the wife realized that the same part of her husband that drove him to be an organized and responsible spouse was the same part that limited his ability to be comfortable with change or with allowing the children to have more control. The same man who's great at planning for the future and concerning himself with the stability of the family is going to be less inclined to spend the family finances on items he sees as "unnecessary." She began to have a much better understanding of her husband's behavior and how the areas he needed to grow in were attached to many of the wonderful things about him.

This exercise will help you appreciate that it's not as easy as your spouse simply "hearing" your request for change and following through. You need to help your spouse find a better *balance* in his or her personality; it's unfair to demand a personality change. You may love that your spouse is great fun to go out with, but you don't feel comfortable leaving the kids with a babysitter every night. You can ask that your spouse tone down the need to be out all the time. Respect the connections you've just made in this exercise and let them stop you from taking it personally when your spouse doesn't change on your request, or changes very slowly.

Encouraging Change

As discussed in the introduction to this book, you can improve many areas in your marriage even if you're the only one working on them. When it comes to appreciation, acceptance, and even identifying and changing your marital personality role, you can hit a solo home run and cause incredible change in your marriage. Work in these areas and there will be a wonderful ripple effect.

Acceptance doesn't mean you can never request that your spouse change. It does mean you have to recognize that none of us likes to feel we have to change because we're doing something "wrong." That's why it becomes your job to encourage change lovingly and sparingly. Be extremely diplomatic and careful with your words so that your spouse leaves the conversation thinking, "He/she loves me so much that I want to try to work on this for him/her, and I'm sure ultimately it'll be good for me as well." In *How to Win Friends and Influence People,* Dale Carnegie offers as his first rule, "Never Criticize." He explains that we automatically defend ourselves when we're criticized, and therefore the criticism doesn't accomplish its purpose of changing our behavior. Following are some positive ways you can encourage change.

1. *Be aware of why you want your spouse to change.* Consider strongly whether society has brainwashed you into believing you need, for example, a thinner, better dressed, or more financially driven spouse. Remember why you married this person, and work to love your spouse for who he or she is. Celebrate your differences, and appreciate everything your spouse offers you. Acquire new tastes. Seek change if the status quo undermines your unique relationship.

2. *Be patient.* Sometimes we haven't given our spouse enough time to show that he or she is working to change.

For example, James was irate when he called his wife, Gloria, to share his excitement about finishing the work project that had consumed him for many months. Gloria's immediate response was, "That's nice, I hope you turn back into your old self now," referring to James's lack of time and tenderness during the previous few months. Gloria's criticism of James was counterproductive in a number of ways. First, he was calling to share his happiness with her, expecting to be met with encouragement and excitement; her response only deflated him. Second, her message was vague. She didn't offer him suggestions on how to "turn back into his old self." Third, her criticism was premature. James had just finished this project; he hadn't been given any time to show his ability, or lack of ability, to "return to his old self."

Of course, anyone can understand Gloria's frustration with having her husband under such pressure for months and how it must have affected her life as well. But her comment was about her feelings and desires, not about her husband's. Criticizing him wasn't going to achieve the goal of her husband changing. She could have waited a day or so to see if he naturally relaxed into his previous ways. If not, then Gloria could have calmly discussed her need for him to change.

3. *Change together.* It is far less threatening when you feel that both you and your spouse need to improve in the same area. Making the change a united effort takes the bite out of criticism. It sends the message that "both of us can be better, so let's try." It offers that most important "teamwork approach" in which we never see our spouse as the "problem." Rather, we see the "problem" as the "enemy" and our spouse and ourself as a team ready to find a method to resolve the issue.

My wife and I have started diets together, not so much to lose weight as to eat more healthfully. But often one of us changes eating habits to support the one who wants to try something new. As a result, my wife and I cook together much more, because we both are on the same diet plan. If we weren't, we'd spend far less time together cooking and be fending for ourselves a great deal more. We discuss our food selections and how we've each done that day. It becomes a partnership builder when you work together on projects instead of living separate lives.

As another example, if one of us feels the other is being too critical of our children, we will both commit to being more easygoing. It may be more my problem than my wife's at the time, but she will still approach it as a unified problem. This makes me feel much more motivated than if my wife were to send the message that I alone am hurting the children in some way. This unified approach to change helps keep each of us from becoming defensive, because we don't feel criticized, and it causes us to work together. If I tell my spouse, "Please change," it becomes her problem to deal with. But when I say, "Let's change," we both take responsibility. Together we discuss ways of changing, and we regularly check in with each other on how we're doing.

Not only will changing together benefit you because of the actual changes you make but once again you will have formed a stronger, loving bond with your spouse through working together to grow. I can't underscore enough how important this form of growth is to a marriage. It builds a shared history of learning and becoming better people. It teaches a couple to come together to find new ways of living instead of finding private ways that can cause them to grow apart. When change is needed, make it happen together.

4. **"It's me, not you."** When you need something to change, blame yourself whenever you can so your spouse doesn't feel as though he or she doesn't measure up. This isn't just about diplomacy. You have to realize that if you are the one requesting the change, you are the one who wants change. *Another person in your shoes might not need the change even if your request is reasonable.*

Convey to your spouse that what you are asking is largely about meeting your personal needs, and not solely about your spouse's behavior. One woman discovered that her husband's jokes about her were so devastating because of how she felt her father mistreated her mother. Even though it was clearly unhealthy for her husband to make little jokes at her expense, she realized her reaction to it was much more intense than she would expect. She was able to translate that discovery into a nonblaming approach with her husband that helped him recognize how important and hurtful this was for her. Instead of "How disgusting of you," she turned it into, "It really hurts me because of how it reminds me of bad stuff."

If you think this is too soft an approach, keep in mind that you have an agenda: to help your spouse change. If you take an all-out-attack approach, you may be right, but if it doesn't cause change and you both end up fighting, you haven't accomplished your goal. Let's suppose you feel your spouse isn't spending enough time with the kids. Perhaps some of your friends would agree, perhaps not. You might or might not be able to prove that you're right in a court of law. *But that's not the point.* Explain to your spouse that his or her behavior may not be unreasonable, but you're requesting a change because it's important to *you.* Change isn't about your spouse's problem as much as it's about respecting each other's point of view and trying to develop a better team. Take responsibility for your inability to accept your spouse's behavior and make sure your spouse knows that.

Psychologist Thomas Gordon, pioneered the concept of using "I" language. Frame your requests in terms of how your spouse's behavior makes you feel: "I'd like you to call if you're going to be late, because I get worried," rather than, "It's so rude of you to be late."

5. *Plan and know your goal.* Plan carefully how you want to explain your request. Never bring it up spontaneously, as you're likely to hurt your spouse's feelings through careless words. When you don't plan, you are apt to be harsh and blaming. You must also be sure of your goal. What exactly do you want to change? Will you know the result when you see it? It can land a devastating blow when you criticize your spouse and can't articulate what you want. It's like saying, "You're really messed up and unattractive to me and I have no idea what you could do about it."

It's just not good enough to say, "I want you to be nicer," "more fun," "more loving," "sexier," "happier," "more responsible," "more easygoing." Imagine if your spouse sent this message to you. It's a terribly limiting approach because if you aren't specific, your spouse must define what he or she feels is "nicer," and that may be quite different from your definition. So your spouse could work hard at changing and do nothing to help you feel better. Ambiguous references only underscore how we're failed. I have to be sexier, nicer? This means I'm not so sexy or nice.

The only way you can understand each other's meaning is for you and your spouse to describe what you want in detail: "I'd like you to help me out more with bathing the kids when you're home." "I'd like you to get me tea when I'm sick," "I'd like you to bring me a cup of water when you bring one for yourself." Or, "Please give me more hugs throughout the day and tell me loving messages. That's sexy to me." These requests don't say, "You're not sexy or nice," but rather "Here are some areas where you could be even sexier or nicer." If you don't know exactly what your spouse could do to improve, discuss some things that could be tried to see if it makes you feel any better. As outlined on page 166, dedicate yourself to the same task and become an active participant in loving change. By understanding your goal and describing it, you have a greater chance of effecting change. That's your goal, not just to let off steam at your spouse's expense.

A cautionary note: Discussing change in the midst of a situation that you realize is unlikely to allow for much change at that time only serves to cause friction and conflict. For example, if your wife just had a baby and you want to talk to her about being more sexy or taking over the family finances, you're setting yourself, her, and your marriage up for failure. If your husband just claimed bankruptcy and you need him to be more fun, your goal may be unrealistic. Reserve requests for change for when your spouse is most likely to receive the message and have the energy to make the change.

6. *"This is what you are doing right."* One of the most loving ways of requesting change is to state what you love about your spouse. Instead of saying, "I'd like you to help me out more with the children's bath whenever you're home," say, "I really appreciate it whenever you help me out with the kids' bath time when you're home." Instead of, "Please give me more hugs throughout the day and tell me loving messages. That's sexy to me," say, "I find it really sexy when you give me hugs and tell me loving things throughout the day when we talk." This is a great motivator as it says, "You do this great, keep it up" instead of "You don't do this very well and here is what you could do to be better."

Make a list of *"Three things I've enjoyed that you've done for me and have made me feel loved."* Then add three more things under the heading *"Three things I've enjoyed doing for you recently."* Leave the list on your spouse's nightstand, mirror, or somewhere else where your spouse will happen upon it.

7. *Listen carefully to your spouse's response.* If your spouse disagrees with your request or is having difficulty accepting your point, don't respond with an argument. Rather, discuss with your spouse what he or she is thinking and feeling. Does your spouse feel your request is unreasonable? Why? Does your spouse have a valid point?

For example, you asked your wife to stop spending so much time with her sister three days before her sister was set to return to her out-of-state home. Perhaps you're right that Sis has consumed too much of your family time, but asking your wife to tell her to leave two days early might not be the best way of dealing with it.

Be open to other creative solutions. One wife was upset when her husband resisted her request that he spend more time with the children. But when she just listened and tried a teamwork approach, she discovered her husband felt self-conscious being at home with the kids while the nanny was around. He also felt his wife scrutinized everything he did, and it made him nervous as a relatively new dad. They came up with a creative solution—he would take the kids out alone, or send the nanny out on errands when he returned from work so he could be alone with the kids.

The situation had developed from an honest misunderstanding. Mom had increased the nanny's hours because Dad wouldn't spend time helping out with the kids, and Dad spent less time with the kids because of the nanny's presence. But he couldn't articulate what really was making him feel uncomfortable until his wife lovingly raised the issue and was willing to discuss it as a team.

8. *Avoid the ouch points.* Be aware of those areas in which you know your spouse is hypersensitive.

One husband told me how much he hated it when his wife told him to tuck in his shirt because it reminded him of his critical father, who constantly told him the same thing. His wife never said it in a critical tone, but it was just too overwhelming for him to hear it from her, as he'd told her many times. She needed to understand that even though he may have needed to improve his manner of dress, she couldn't be the one to help him with it. Her goal was not going to be realized through her request, so she needed to find alternative ways of dealing with this issue: buying him more casual clothing that didn't need a "tucked in" look, asking his brother to talk to him about it if they were emotionally close, even giving up on her husband's dressing perfectly.

As I've mentioned, a lot of couples quarrel about the wife's weight. Any man who answers anything other than, "What, are you crazy? You look like a twig," when his wife asks him, "Do I look fat?" deserves what's coming to him. *Honesty is not the best policy when it comes to ouch points. Diplomacy is.* Respect your spouse's ouch points, regardless of whether you think your criticisms are warranted. Pressuring your spouse in these areas will rarely result in the positive change requested. Criticism of an ouch point almost always results only in your spouse experiencing painful feelings of rejection.

Honesty is the foundation of a marriage. If you can fake that, you've got it made.

Comedian Richard Jeni

9. *Get a friend to help.* When you're worried that your spouse will take your request for change much too personally and be hurt, call upon someone else to help. Obviously, your request must be crucial to your relationship with your spouse for you to enlist the help of a friend or family member. Start with your spouse's closest family member or friend—someone you feel will have your spouse's best interests at heart.

One wife told me she could never tell her husband that she worried he was drinking too much. She felt he'd be angry and defend himself, especially since his father was an alcoholic and it would be devastating for him to accept that he, too, had a drinking problem. She finally spoke to his brother, who had dealt with alcoholism in the past. He was willing to approach her husband since he had significant experience with this problem and understood his brother's situation. It would be harder for the husband to resist his own brother's intervention than his wife's. Additionally, if her husband became irate with his brother and reacted by not speaking to him for a period of time, it was better than the same happening between the wife and her husband, who had to continue to live together and love each other.

10. *Don't overdo it.* If your spouse says he or she feels that you are consistently overly critical, heed the message.

One friend used to love to criticize, and he loved to be criticized as well. He saw criticism as a kind of constructive report card from someone who cared enough to try to help him grow. But the criticism he threw around was overwhelming, even though he criticized with altruistic intentions. He was flabbergasted that his criticism could hurt others so much. He defended himself emotionally from recognizing his hurtful ways by rationalizing his hurtful comments. He later discovered that it was a part of his controlling nature and had less to do with helping others.

When your spouse is feeling overwhelmed by your criticism, step back and try not to make one single critical remark for a full seven days. Can you do it? If you can't, you're the problem, not your spouse. If you can, continue to temper your tongue and only criticize with the sensitivity just outlined.

Change Can Take You Many Places

When your spouse does change in part because of your request, do everything you can to encourage him or her, even if the change doesn't reflect your personal vision. Often, change requires a personal journey to overcome certain struggles.

Hannah and Peter walked into my office to discuss their marriage. Peter confessed that he'd put a great deal of effort and time into working on himself for the sake of his marriage. But Hannah simply didn't see enough change. Every time Peter had a setback, Hannah saw it as though nothing had changed and all of Peter's personal efforts were for naught. Even if it was understandable that Hannah was at the end of her rope and desperate for immediate, drastic change, she needed to appreciate that genuine change takes time. Making the commitment to change takes less than a second. Once Peter made that commitment, Hannah needed to see that his efforts reflected his love for her, even if they didn't result in the drastic change she sought.

You may not understand why it's so difficult for your spouse to change. Because you don't share that issue in question, change may seem like such a simple thing. But we are complicated beings, and change doesn't come easy. Change is the hardest thing we do. You need to look at the desire and energy your spouse is directing toward change. Love your spouse for not taking the easy road and deflecting responsibility. Be patient in the same way you'd want to be treated.

Believe it or not, some spouses sabotage healthy change, as in the following example.

One husband wanted his wife to be more sensitive and loving during lovemaking. Through therapy, she was able to properly discuss with her husband her sexually abusive childhood and how it contributed to her inability to make love the way he desired her to. But instead of becoming more sensitive to her struggle, her husband became more demanding and abrasive, making it even harder for her to take the softer approach he was requesting. As it turned out, he couldn't handle his wife's abusive past. It made him feel like he didn't have a partner, but rather "damaged goods." He set out on a course to ignore his wife's past.

When we ask for change, we have to be ready to deal with the complicated issues that may arise from it. We have to use love as our guide to understand the deeper parts of our spouse and ourselves.

When you see your spouse attempting to make changes, be extremely supportive and encouraging. Sometimes, a client tells me he or she has come to see me because of a spouse's request. As I work with this person, I notice that some spouses are wonderfully encouraging and patient while others are upset and "can't understand it" if there aren't quick, dramatic behavioral changes. *The most your spouse can do is try to change.* You may feel your spouse isn't trying hard enough, but it really isn't for you to say, because you can't identify how much energy your spouse is really putting into this change. If you have difficulty with your wife's family's involvement in your life, for example, you may feel the solution is as easy as her telling her family to butt out. After all, you'd have no problem telling that to your family. On the other hand, you haven't spoken to your brother in ten years and moved six thousand miles away from your parents. Just because it may seem easy to you doesn't mean it's easy to your spouse. You will motivate your spouse the most by acknowledging his or her efforts, even if they seem far from where you'd like them to be.

Appreciating your spouse is one of the simplest things to do, and yet it's so powerful. Appreciating and accepting your spouse sends a clear message of how much you love and adore your partner. It means never taking your spouse for granted. It means giving your spouse what all of us want, to be accepted for who we are. Our marriage is the one place we want to be able to show our whole selves without hiding. We want someone to love our gorgeously flawed selves. As much as we always want to better ourselves, at the same time we want to believe we are still "great" as we are. No one else can give us the amount of approval our spouse can, because no one else will know us that intimately.

Make an immediate change in your marriage. Find the goodness in each other and remind yourself of it all the time.

Al & Freddy Scheinfeld

MARRIED: 52 YEARS

How We Met

It was in the summertime. I went to a dance because that was what young people did in the evenings. I was dancing with a girl when I saw her on the dance floor with somebody else. She saw me and gave me the wink. So I winked back and it was love at first sight, really. I got rid of the girl I was with and cut in. We danced and that was it. I was working as a waiter and saving money to start a business but we got married three months after we met. That was fifty-two years ago and we're still happy together.

What Makes it Work for Us?

I'm the boss and she's always right. Seriously, trust and respect aren't just nice ideas, they make it all right to argue. We argue a lot but I respect her point of view. We can listen to each other and appreciate the other person's mind.

What's Different for People Getting Married Today?

Today married couples work every bit as hard as my generation. I built a business, worked twenty hours overtime a week. But money is a problem for people today because they feel they have to spend so much. Everywhere they look there is pressure to buy, have, and get. The value of saving has been exchanged for one of spending. And of course you have the credit cards, which we never had years ago. So she sees something on the television or she wants it and she can charge and he gets mad and everyone feels deprived or in debt. It puts a lot of pressure on people and makes them unhappy. Couples should put away the charge cards and be proud to save together.

6

Your marriage has to come first—before jobs, kids, anything else. Your unconscious assumptions are holding you back from putting in the effort.

Love is about peaceful, quiet times together when you hold each other in the silence of the night and feel each other's warmth. Love is about dancing to new music while laughing at how pathetically the two of you dance. Love is about paling around while holding hands and going to the movies. It's about finding new adventures, reading to each other while sitting in the warm sun at the beach. It's about laughter, smiles, gentle hugs, and warm "I love you's." Love is about building friendship and enjoying each other's company but understand that it only happens with a great deal of attention. But you're not putting in that effort. Why not? Because you've made some unconscious assumptions that are holding you back.

Unconscious Assumption #1. Our Marriage Will Run by Itself While We Deal with Everything Else

Frank and Helen were communicative. They had been in love. They were insightful, educated, and outstanding parents. Yet, they were in my office to discuss how to divorce without traumatizing their two young children. They spoke so highly of each other. They could point to nothing dramatic that caused them to be so miserable together. They'd started fighting a few years before. They hadn't had sex in over a year. They'd been to marital therapy and hadn't learned anything new. They were tired of each other and felt like heavy anchors were tied around their necks.

The anchor metaphor caught my attention. Where had this burden come from? Neither of them seemed to make any requests of the other. There didn't seem to be any kind of pressure that either of them placed on the other. I explored with them what gave them the feeling of this weight bringing them down. They took turns telling me in detail about how complicated their lives were. Frank had begun a new, thriving business three years ago, and Helen was working as his assistant, in addition to taking care of their two preschool children. They were in the process of building a dream house. It was in its third year of development. I was getting tired just listening to the amount of activity. And it never stopped. Weekends were filled with errands that couldn't be completed during the "work week."

I asked, "Think back to when you fell in love. Remember what you talked about? Remember the loving conversations you had about whether you had enough money to pay the full balance on your credit cards or should carry the debt further, or how you needed to spend less money so you could pay the bills this month? And, oh, can you recall the sensual, fun conversation that really turned both of you on? You know, the one about the dirty diaper that your kid pulled off and smeared on the floor. Those romantic moments at dinner when you each interrupted your conversation at least six times to answer your cell phones and discuss important business?" They smirked. They understood that they'd never had those conversations back then because if they had, they wouldn't have fallen in love. In fact, they would have run away from each other as fast as possible. Yet this was their life today. It consumed them and their marriage, and yet they expected to be happy and in love.

It's the number one myth of marriage: "After you fall in love, you don't have to work at it anymore." Countless couples have told me, "If it takes so much energy, we must not be made for each other." Somewhere we have been improperly taught that true love is supposed to come easy. Once we've committed to each other through marriage, our love will take care of itself while we get on with life. We can now focus on jobs, kids, and acquiring things: house, cars, appropriate furniture. We see our spouse less as an individual and more as an extension of ourselves: a team dedicated to keeping the physical plant of our lives hale and hearty. We begin to figure that whatever we're doing is understood as serving the greater good of both of us. This should be enough to keep us madly in love, sexually attracted to each other, and wanting to be together forever.

There isn't one obvious theory that keeps this unfortunate pattern believable, but I think many desperately want to hold on to it to resist having to work so hard at love. It takes enormous energy to create and maintain a wonderful marriage. Great marriages are about a type of absorption, a kind of fully engaged connection that requires constant attention, a deep, soul-searching understanding of yourself and how it affects your ability to love. Giving it everything you've got sounds exhausting and disquieting.

We may say we want that wonderful marriage, but deep down we recognize that being sensitive to another human being is harder than most things we do. If all you're giving your spouse is the energy left over from balancing work and family, you're cheating your marriage.

Putting your marriage first is about a state of mind. It's believing that everything else that you feel is important is dramatically impacted by your marriage. Whether you feel in love or lonely will affect every decision and action you take today. Marriage is a foundation for your world. With love in your heart and a sense of someone who cares deeply for you as your partner, you have greater energy and greater abilities to handle all of life's tasks. Aren't you a better parent on the day you feel close to your spouse than when you've just had a fight? Aren't you more focused and energized at work the day after a romantic, loving evening with your spouse? Don't you want to live more passionately when you feel loved and able to give love? You should and you can. For every ounce of effort you put into your marriage, you will benefit tenfold, not only from the direct love you feel but from the energy and focus you'll have for everything else in your life.

The idea that you need to focus more on kids, work, or friends than your marriage is an excuse for running away from having an exceptional marriage. You didn't marry to be absorbed by everything else but your marriage. You'll never lose from any other part of your life when you make marriage your priority. Obviously you may have less time for your kids today if you go out to dinner alone with your spouse. But you will be offering them a supremely better parent on your return. Start at the top—the love in your marriage—and allow that intense love to flow into the rest of your life.

Unconscious Assumption #2: Marriage Is First About Knowing the Other Person, Not Yourself

Sensitivity to your spouse starts with understanding yourself. How are you going to appreciate what your wife does as a mother to nurture your children if you have unresolved anger at your own mother for leaving you and your dad to go live with another man? How will you see your husband as sexually exciting when your mother told you when you were only ten years old that your dad slept around on her and was completely untrustworthy? The ability to truly give and understand your lover is tied up in your ability to understand yourself. Being forced to confront your own emotional issues is the greatest gift of love. (I'll explain more about how to overcome these issues in Secret #7.)

Sid had been in therapy for years and was progressing rather slowly. But his emotional life took a dramatic change after he asked me to help him have a better relationship with his wife and children. Six months later, he was a different being. I did nothing special. But he did. He allowed himself to focus on painful issues that he only tapped into because he was desperate to connect with his family. He learned to feel what he had never felt before. He cried when he saw his wife and children's pain. He had never seen the pain before because he had protected himself from seeing it.

On his journey, he confronted his own pain as well, the struggles of his own childhood that he hid from. Suddenly it all made sense to him at once, and his struggle to feel alive with a host of joyful and painful emotions took him by surprise. If Sid didn't have a wife or kids, it would have been many years before he understood himself the way he did after six months of focusing on his marriage. He was responsible enough to force himself to feel for his family even though it meant a crash course of knowing himself for better or for worse. He used his family as the motivation he needed to confront himself.

We are able to make much faster progress when we feel that there are others depending on us and that we are responsible to our loved ones to become healthier. In marriage, our foremost task is to know ourselves so that we can heal the emotional issues that stand in the way of our union.

Unconscious Assumption #3: If I Don't Invest in My Marriage, I Can't Be Blamed If It Fails

Another reason why so many people avoid the work that marriages need is that being in love demands that we be true to our spouse and give. We unconsciously hold ourselves back because if we make this ultimate commitment and fail at it, it might truly break our hearts and push us into a deeper understanding of ourselves and our shortcomings. It's easier to simply "give love a shot" without the intensity of deep love. That way, if things go wrong you can blame it on things like, "I was young," "I married the wrong spouse," "We didn't know what we were doing," and avoid looking deeper within.

There is little else as hard as confronting who you are and why you act the way you do. Once you open up to yourself and see some of your deeper issues and frailties, you can never pretend them away. For example, if you realize that your mother and father didn't have the marriage you pretended them to have, you have to live with that perspective. Too many of us deny our innermost feelings and don't give to our spouse the way we could precisely to protect ourselves from that deeper understanding of ourselves, which can be painful. However, you can't possibly know or truly love another human being without learning a great deal about yourself along the way. It's a spectacular, albeit difficult, journey that takes bountiful energy and concentration.

And it isn't even easy once you do understand yourself. Ask couples who have been genuinely happy in their marriages for twenty-five years or more and you won't find one who says, "It was easy." Sound depressing? We would prefer not having to work at it. We'd like it to just flow easily. But is there anything else worthwhile in your life that came easily? We don't expect parenting or creating a thriving business to be easy. We don't even treat important friendships with ease. We know that we will have to be there physically and emotionally for our dearest friends, our children, and our family if we want to reap the benefits of a loving relationship. But when it comes to our spouse, too many of us don't believe we need to put forth the same energy. We think our relationship should be able to thrive on what's left of us after we've given to everyone else.

Unconscious Assumption #4: Being Vulnerable Is Dangerous

Yet another reason you may shy away from putting in the daily effort to develop a wonderful marriage is that it makes you extremely vulnerable to your spouse. Your spouse knows you better than anyone else. You can hide somewhat from your children or from your parents. But your spouse will know every detail of your weaknesses and strengths. Your spouse will know what you really think about your parents, boss, friends. He or she will know the truth about who you are deep down, even when you've been able to fool the rest of the world.

Being close to your spouse means being an open book. Perhaps you're not as comfortable with yourself as you think. Perhaps you're hiding from yourself emotionally and are therefore avoiding the closeness of a loving bond, as it will force you to deal with your issues. Perhaps you're afraid to become so close to your mate. Closeness will make both of you depend on each other. Maybe you can't handle that, or you're afraid you'll disappoint your spouse. Maybe you feel deep down that you're just not good enough to deserve a wonderful marriage. When we love deeply, we lose control, and we're apt to get hurt and suffer deep emotional pain.

I'm not suggesting any of us consciously uses these fears to sabotage our marriage. I don't believe you get up in the morning and say, "I'll put time and effort into every other relationship except my marriage because that closeness makes me uncomfortable." I am merely pointing out the potential push-pull struggle of being close to your spouse. In front of your spouse you are naked, plain and simple.

People are surprised to learn that they may be shying away from the very thing they say they desire. But we are complicated beings. We say we want to eat more healthfully and then sneak a candy bar. We say we want to work harder but find ourselves leaving the office early. We say we want a fabulous marriage but don't do a whole lot to make that happen. You can only challenge this contradiction when you see it clearly. When I explain to couples how much work marriage takes, they respond with comments like, "Who has the time?" You *do* have the time to dedicate if you want to. We always find time for the things we see as a priority. If your child had an accident that required hours of physical therapy, you'd find the time to do whatever you needed to do to care for your child. Make marriage the priority it deserves. You're not as busy as you think.

Your Marriage Must Come First

I don't mean to suggest that every couple that doesn't make time for marriage has some deep, dark problem. It's just that as a society, while we see work as a given and positive ethic for every other area of life, we denigrate the work of spousal love. I ask you to consider any possible roadblocks to making the decision to dedicate time and energy to your marriage. It's understandable how we get caught up in so many details in life at our spouse's expense. It's understandable that life gets so busy that we simply lose our sense of priority. Understandable but not excusable. You and your spouse deserve better. You deserve true love.

Frank and Helen were busy. Besides their obligations to business and family, they were on many boards and important committees. And they were very needed. What would happen to their causes if they stopped spending nights at meetings and volunteering on weekends? Perhaps those causes would suffer the same way their marriage suffered because of how busy they were. Frank and Helen had to let go of so many things they were doing. They began to leave work on time and stopped discussing business every second of their day. They even started leaving their children with a babysitter after the kids fell asleep so they could go out alone together and recapture what they once had. Yes, it meant that their reputation as selfless pillars of the community took a little beating, but they realized that they'd discovered a higher priority—their marriage.

Make up your mind today that you want, that you *must have*, a great marriage, and understand the energy commitment that comes with such a decision.

Daily Love Makes Every Other Part of Life Richer

Not only did Helen and Frank take control of their marriage and begin to return to the loving relationship they once had but they found every part of life was better. They didn't realize how much creativity they had lost, whether in work, dealing with the kids, or any other aspect of life. They forgot how much more energy they could have when each of them had love and warmth in their hearts. They never knew how drained they were from the stress of an unhappy union. For every hour they left work early to focus on their marriage, their business sense and competence improved. For every night they went out and left the kids with a babysitter, they enjoyed many more nights with their children because the kids became less whiny and more fun to be with. They hadn't understood that their lack of marital effort had been having a negative impact on their kids, and their new commitment to love was changing their children back to the fun-loving kids they once were.

Love doesn't just sit there like a stone. It has to be made like bread; re-made all the time, made new.

—Ursula K. LeGuin

The Four-Point Connection Plan

Every marriage needs a plan, a focusing tool to make sure the marriage is getting the attention it needs and deserves in the midst of the most hectic lifestyles. Following is a four-point program to ensure that you and your spouse are consistently placing daily loving energy into your marriage. This "connection plan" will help you and your spouse feel closer, warmer, and more connected.

Connection Plan #1: Have Five Touch Points a Day

Touch your spouse lovingly at least five times a day. Kissing, hugging, and hand holding are all healthy touch points. (If your spouse kisses you and you kiss back, or calls you to say "I love you" and you say "I love you too," that is not considered one of your touch points. Your touch point must be a gesture you originated.) Try to make each touch point meaningful. Instead of a peck on the cheek, give a gentle kiss on the lips. Give a real bear hug—hug and count in your head for six seconds—that says, "I love every inch of you." Let yourself feel as though you are melting into each other. Touch points also include any caring activity: bringing your spouse a drink, writing a loving note, making a phone call just to say "I love you," cooking a favorite meal, getting a favorite magazine, taking a phone call on your spouse's behalf that your spouse wishes to avoid, or sending a greeting card or note of thanks, a flower, or a balloon. Don't let a day go by without thinking, "What simple thing could I do for my spouse that would put a smile on his or her face?" Then do it. Let your lover know that he or she is in your thoughts and heart every day.

Leave a Love Note

To help yourself focus on loving and connecting consistently, create a loving note like the following example (or use your own ideas) and place it on the fridge, in your spouse's briefcase or drawer, or anyplace where your spouse will happen upon it.

Just Because . . .
- ❑ I love you.
- ❑ Thank you for_____.
- ❑ I am looking forward to_____.

I can't wait to . . .
- ❑ Hold you.
- ❑ Kiss you.
- ❑ Talk to you.
- ❑ Take a private walk with you.
- ❑ Run a bath for you.
- ❑ Give you a ten-minute massage.
- ❑ Make a romantic dinner for you.

Last night I dreamt we were on a deserted island and we _____
_____.

Connection Plan #2: Have Four Talk Points a Week

The average couple talks only four minutes per day.[1] It's no wonder spouses don't feel close and loved.

Four days a week (at any point in the day or night), plan at least forty-five minutes when you can be alone together and do something you both enjoy. And no, sleeping does not count. This could be a walk or other form of exercise, watching a video, reading to each other, dancing in your home, making love, playing a board game or cards, cooking, having a cocktail, massaging each other, shopping (only if it's fun for both of you), or anything else that will take you away from the stresses of life and into each other's arms. These activities add spice to life and lead to great relationship-building conversations about politics, gossip, interesting thoughts you've had after reading a book or seeing a movie, some deeper thoughts about your past or dreams, spiritual thoughts, how to help your kids grow.

These aren't the times to talk about problems with the kids, financial woes, work headaches, and so on. The purpose of the talk points is to increase your easygoing time together. Talking about the lighter things reminds you that the person you are married to can be the person with whom you enjoy life.

Connection Plan #3: Have a Weekly Date Night

One night a week, come hell or high water, you and your spouse should go out alone to enjoy each other's company. You can do anything, go anywhere, and talk about anything except three things: money, children, and work (unless it's exciting stuff—I got a promotion, our child has been selected as valedictorian, let's plan our trip to Europe). Many couples laugh and tell me there's nothing else to talk about. I reassure them that they'll find something—they didn't fall in love because of scintillating conversations about kids and money. You fell in love discussing what was interesting to you. On your date nights, it's time to return to that place in yourself where you are interested and interesting. It is this night, the same each week, that no one plans anything else without first clearing it with the other.

If you have young kids, make a standing arrangement with a babysitter or family member for that night of the week, or swap babysitting with a friend, if necessary. And if you must miss date night because you have to attend an event on the assigned evening, you must make it up on another evening that week. The date must last a minimum of two hours. If a date day works better for you, go for it. If you have a newborn and are uncomfortable using a babysitter, take the infant with you if you must, but get out of the house. Avoid meeting any other couple for at least the first two hours of your date.

The date night is about one thing: enjoying each other's company. It's about kindness and tenderness. Talk to your spouse about the things he or she loves to talk about. Be quiet and listen. Enjoy your lover's voice, perspective, and life energy. Tell a joke. Laugh at yourself. Hold your mate's face in your hands and smile. With every giggle comes a deeper love and bond. Take turns planning the date night or create a a "grab bag" of ideas for dating fun: Each of you writes three dates you would like to have on

Ideas for Dating Fun

Following are some ideas for dating fun—doing or learning—that you can find in even the most boring towns (look for classes in some of these areas at your local school or college).

Cooking/baking (really fun and sensual)

Cake decorating

Dancing

Massaging

Art/painting

Photography

Swinging on swings at the park

Drinking cocktails at a club—learn how to make them together (with or without alcohol) at home

Writing a short story together

Reading

Going to a comedy club

Visiting a bookstore

Playing board games

Rollerblading

Bicycling

Boating

Fishing

Playing instruments

Listening to music—going to a music store and listening to CD's together—find "our song"

Creating with clay

Swimming

Walking

Playing a sport (where both of you are equally talented)

Planting a garden

Flying a kite

Eating ice cream or snow cones

Buying a camera, and enlisting strangers to take an entire roll of pictures of the two of you on your date night slips of paper to put in a bag. Pick one slip of paper out of the bag three or four days before the date and start planning it together. One couple's grab bag ideas included painting, reading *MAD* magazines, and bicycling—three things they had never done since getting married seventeen years earlier. This way you avoid that stale moment in the car when both of you look at each other dumbfounded and say, "Whaddya wanna do?" "I dunno. Whadda *you* wanna do?" which is another way of saying, "I'm not taking this date thing too seriously."

Get yourself a little charged up about spending alone time with your lover and soulmate. Make some nights a surprise, in which you don't tell your spouse what you've planned until you're already on your way out together. Every time out doesn't have to be dazzling, just thoughtful enough to say, "I put some effort into this and wanted to find something different to do. Let's find some new fun together."

Your date night doesn't have to be an extravaganza. Sometimes my clients tell me, "I live in a town that closes at 10 P.M." But walking is a wonderful way to connect—it lessens the intensity of a dinner, where couples have to face each other, and it gives you the outdoors to focus on. If it's cold, walk in a mall and have fun people watching and window shopping. Cooking is a creative and sensual experience: research recipes and purchase the ingredients together. Many megabookstores are perfect places for exploring. Have a coffee, play some Scrabble, and scan books together. Even a small bookstore offers a wide variety of reading. Sit on the floor between the aisles and share interesting points on many topics. Read each other some jokes as well as some lovemaking tips.

Spirit comes from inside: focus on fun and you'll find the perfect play activities to enjoy together with laughter.

Getting to Know You

On your date night, use the following two lists to take a "crash course" in your spouse. Each person can ask two questions from each list.

Getting to Know Where You've Been

Who was your closest childhood friend?
What was your favorite adventure or act of mischief?
Who was your favorite teacher and why?
Who was your worst teacher and why?

What is one of your saddest memories?

What is one of your happiest memories?

What was your favorite holiday? Explain.

Who was your most loved pet and what did you love about that pet?

Where were the most exciting places you've been and what was so wonderful about them?

Getting to Know Where You Are Today

What was your high and low of the day?

What are your dream and wishes?

Name three qualities you like the most about you.

What is sexy?

What is passionate?

Name one thing you'd change about yourself.

You could feel closer to me if I _____.

Describe your perfect day.

Where's the place you want to visit the most and why?

If you were an animal, you'd be a _____. Explain.

Connection Plan #4: The Honeymoon Night

At least once a month (you may make this coincide with date night), plan a fabulous night of romance and lovemaking. Plan the details: a wonderful meal; a fun time out on a date; lots of sensual touching, hugs and kisses while out on your date; the music both of you love; a bowl of fruit, flowers, candles in the bedroom; a shower/bath or swim together; a romantic movie—anything that screams "romance" to each of you. This is the recharging night that will advance your relationship beyond words. But it works best (often, it will *only* work) in conjunction with the rest of the daily connection plan.

The four-point connection plan is meant to encourage the two of you to gaze into each other's eyes and speak of your undying love for each other. If that seems like an impossible goal, remember that it doesn't happen just by speaking the words on cue. It comes with the ease of relating to each other. That ease begins and ends with time spent together.

For those of you who think this plan is extravagant, keep in mind that the entire plan takes only about six hours for the entire week (considering each touch point is thirty seconds on average, and counting a half hour a week for the two-hour honeymoon night once a month). With 168 hours in the week, that's less than 5 percent of your week. I wonder what you'd say if I told you that you have only six hours to spend focusing on your business or parenting for the week.

The time isn't the only issue. The main growth comes from using these times consistently to connect with your mate in a way you haven't before. For many couples, it's like riding a bicycle, learning to return the relationship to where it once was before life became so overwhelming and complicated. For others, it's like learning to ride for the first time. Some couples never enjoyed much daily love and sensitivity.

The following two guidelines will help make this plan or any focus on your marriage work.

1. *Insist on uninterrupted time.* When my wife and I slip away for a two-night vacation alone, we realize that much of our ability to relax comes from knowing our time will not be interrupted. Granted, you can't get the same exact feeling in one date night or in a forty-five-minute talk point, but you can get much closer. Turn off and put away the cell phones, the beeper, the computer, and the Palm Pilot. Know that for this next block of time, you have only *one* focus: the love in your marriage. Too many people can't remember when they took an hour and focused on only one thing. We've all become inveterate multitaskers. When you're in an audience to hear a speaker, what does the announcer request? "Turn off all cell phones and pagers." Interruption is not only a killer of your train of thought, it reduces your ability to relax because you know at any moment your entire focus might change. On your date night, make it clear to your kids that they shouldn't call to ask a question about homework. Unless they smell smoke or see blood, it can wait. Teach them to respect private marital time.

2. *Remove the television from your bedroom.* A client once explained to me that my plan "sounded" great, but she and her husband really didn't have the time for it. "After coming home from work, dinner, kids' homework, and cleaning, I barely have enough strength to watch the news for a half hour before I go to sleep." Her half hour of news viewing every night was "an absolute must." But there it was: a full half hour that she and her husband could spend together any way they wanted. She didn't even realize until we discussed it how much of her life she gave to TV. She also explained that her husband had to "unwind" by watching sports every night.

Television has become an incredible interruption in our marital lives. Everyone seems to focus on how detrimental it is for kids, but we should focus on the detriment for marriages. Over a lifetime, the average person will spend thirteen years watching television.[2] Naturally, getting cozy together in bed to watch a favorite video might be your thing now and then. But we often turn on the television just to fill air and space, and once the set goes on, it stays on, and suddenly the evening's gone. In addition to stealing precious marriage time, the television offers us models that are often counterproductive to a strong marriage. For example, only 15 percent of sexual acts on prime-time television are between married partners.[3] Plus, it's usually hard to find any show that both spouses really enjoy. Marriages need private interaction; television is a distracting third eye. Consider reviewing your TV guide at the start of the week to see if there is any program you don't want to miss; then limit yourself to that program, or tape the show so you can watch it when you have some spare private time. If you create a "TV budget" at the beginning of the week, you'll discover that there's a lot of programming you can let go.

Return to Woo

When we marry, we often become stale at loving. When we were wooing our prospective mate, we were much sharper. We read up on interesting things to discuss on dates, dressed nicely to be attractive, listened carefully to what was interesting to our date, and created lively conversation around those topics. Then we married and figured our spouse would live happily for the next fifty years on the memory of how scintillating we once were. We became two-dimensional, predictable people. We began talking about the same things, people, and problems, over and over.

Obviously, we cannot be expected to look our best every second of our day nor live with daily pressure to have scintillating conversation. Yet there should be some balance. If you're a man and haven't shaved or showered today yet expect your wife to fall all over you after dinner, guess what? You're not going to be very appealing. The same goes for women. Both men and women like to feel their spouse is making an effort to be attractive. And I don't mean only in a physical way. We're flattered when our spouse wants to share something he or she read that day or heard on the news. You may be pleasantly surprised to note how endearing it is when your spouse makes a mental note to share something with you. It's always exciting to know that you're in your spouse's thoughts. You don't have to go to sleep wearing makeup or have toothpaste-fresh breath in the morning, but you do have to make attempts to woo your partner. Don't dress up only for functions where you'll see others. Put on your finest, most exciting demeanor for the special one you love.

I once met a couple in a restaurant who were dressed in formal clothing. They were a handsome pair, he in his classic black tuxedo and she in a floor-length sequined gown. It was a rather odd sight. Formal wear is usually reserved for formal, black-tie occasions, not restaurants. They told me that every wedding anniversary they dress formally for their evening out. It sends a thoughtful message when you choose to present your best self to your spouse instead of waiting for the right public occasion.

Being your best for your spouse is also a personal journey. It is the need to live with and please your partner that will drive you to change for the better. It's time to woo your lover again.

Too many of us have worn ourselves into a groove of expressing our worst side to our spouse. After all, this is the person we don't have to put it on for, right? Negative just attracts negative. Focus on the positive energy. This doesn't mean you should fake it. Rather, learn to see more and more of the goodness in life and people. Say more positive things: "What a beautiful day," "It's great to feel healthy," "I had such fun last night," "I'm lucky to have a job to pay the bills." "The kids are so cute."

Bring out the poet in yourself. Write a list of things to be happy about, or write a poem or letter as if you were a teenager delirious with love. Connect to that kid inside.

Search for happiness. Find a fragrance you love and bring it into your home, whether with perfumes, candles, scented soaps, or flowers. Find those places that give your spirit a little lift, such as a nearby creek, an old shack surrounded by wildflowers, or a handsome building, and visit them with your lover.

"But We're So Busy with the Kids"

Many couples don't realize that they put their children's interests ahead of their marriage. Today's parents believe that unless their child studies piano, soccer, baseball, ballet, and karate simultaneously, they have failed. Satisfying our children's bare-minimum needs can be a full-time job. Adding extracurricular activities can overwhelm the most well-intentioned parent. You can expect your marriage to change drastically because of the time, energy, and pressures that come with children. But be aware that couples tend to put much more frenetic energy into childrearing than is necessary. It's wonderful and healthy to have your child learn piano or ballet. It's not wonderful or healthy for your child to have parents who fight, limit their loving relationship, or divorce. No one gets divorced because their kid takes piano. Obviously, it's not one lesson or activity that causes marriages to fall apart. But the misunderstanding that our children come before our marriage is deadly. Part of healthy child development is being surrounded by caring parents who are in love with each other. Your children draw great strength from your marital love, and you should take great care to preserve it.

As a father of five, believe me when I tell you that a considerable amount of my life's energy and time is devoted to my children. But when it comes to extracurricular activities, my wife and I find limits. The one extra skating lesson or basketball practice combined with two birthday parties can wipe out a weekend. These events can tire me and my wife out so much that we've got nothing left to be loving toward each other and our children. My kids were in a baseball league for one season. After it was done, my wife and I and two other couples went out to dinner to celebrate. We toasted our newfound energy and ability to reconnect as lovers. Our kids don't go to baseball league anymore. It's not as if they never enjoy extracurricular activities. We carefully select what we can and cannot be involved in and as they've gotten older, they've been able to ride their bikes to the skating and piano lessons. And sometimes I worry I'm not giving my children everything I can. But then I remind myself that my children have grown up in a household of loving parents in a loving marriage. I remind myself that such an atmosphere is far more important to who they will be in life than any other activity.

I can't do it all. No one can, and that includes you. Granted, we have five children. But you can occupy enormous amounts of extracurricular time even with one child. So, find the time for your marriage even if it means cutting back on taxiing your kids around or limiting your community activity obligations. Do it for yourself, your spouse, and your kids.

It is not lack of love but a lack of friendship that makes unhappy marriages.

—Friedrich Nietzsche

Find the Fun

∽∽∽∽∽∽∽∽∽∽∽∽∽∽∽∽∽∽∽∽∽∽∽∽∽∽∽∽∽∽

A husband hired a private investigator to spy on his wife because he sus-
pected she was having an affair. Two weeks after the P.I. was on the job, he sat
down with the husband to show him his findings.

"I'm sorry to have to do this," the P.I. opened the conversation as he pulled
8 × 10 photographs from his briefcase. "Here is a picture of your wife and
this man at the ballgame. This next one of the two of them flying a kite in the
park was on the following day, and these others are of them dancing at this
nightclub they frequent."

"I can't believe it," the husband said as he held the pictures in his hand and
examined them. The P.I. tried to console him, "Even when you suspect, it's
still a surprise to find out your wife is cheating."

"That's not what I can't believe," the husband broke in. "I can't believe she
can have so much fun."

∽∽∽∽∽∽∽∽∽∽∽∽∽∽∽∽∽∽∽∽∽∽∽∽∽∽∽∽∽∽

Never underestimate the power of fun. Sometimes we think of it as friv-
olous, but it's crucial to life and love. Couples resist my mandatory date
night and say, "Yeah, but life is about bills and pressure. So we go out one
night and have a fun, light time. That's not reality." What these couples have
forgotten is what fun and laughter do for us. They change us. The same
stress can look totally different after a fun time or a good night's sleep.
*When we are happy and in love, we are more creative and able to cope with life's
complications. Every second you and your spouse have fun, you are building your
relationship, which will directly affect your ability to deal with the serious issues later
today and tomorrow.* Find the ways to let go and enjoy each other completely.

Becoming a Kid Again

List three things you loved to do as a kid. When you were a kid, you knew how to
have fun. You need to reconnect with those times and include your spouse in them.

Reality Check

The fact is, we're not always at our best. You or you spouse may have a bad mood, a headache, or other ailment. You may be overtired, hungry, premenstrual, nervous about the in-laws coming to visit, or anxious over a sick child or a host of other issues that could cause either of you to be off your "love game." It may sound like a downer to think that after all your hard work, you still will have many times when you and your spouse are not excited, joyful, or happy. It may have nothing to do with you personally. When you live with another human being, you'll see many moods, and the most you can do is work to change for the better. Be relaxed about your expectations of what your spouse is going to bring you. You married a human being with all the splendor and frailty that comes along with one. Forgive each other for the little lapses.

Learning from Others

As part of your dedication to daily focus on marriage, search for others who can teach you more about a strong marriage.

1. *Happily married/monogamous friends.* At some point in our teenage years, our parents told us, "You become like the friends you hang out with." If you spend consistent time with another couple who bicker, make jokes at each other's expense, and are disrespectful toward each other, watch out. You will develop part of your marital attitude from them. The marriages our friends model for us are powerful images. Find friends with good marriages. Focus on creating close friendships with couples whose marriage you admire. Limit consistent time with same-sex friends who are cheating or think little of cheating. Hang with people who see cheating as terribly wrong. Get close to those who have intense respect for their marriage and yours.

2. *Mentors.* As you can tell from the "Golden Couple" interviews I've included throughout this book, I have great respect for life experience. Too many people think they know so much more than the older generation or that things are so different today that they can't learn from older people. Love is timeless. Those older couples have seen the highs and lows from life and learned a great deal from them. If you know or meet an older, happily married couple, invite them to be your friends. Have them for dinner. Double date. Create a close enough relationship that you can ask them questions about marriage. It is such a relief to hear from someone older and wiser how normal it is when you and your spouse feel overwhelmed at certain life stages. It's equally important to hear that you may be making some mistakes that need

attention. Older couples can serve as a valuable objective resource to help you in your own marriage.

The Cool Guy Menu

As the final course in my plan for daily focus, I offer you a proven menu from my own marriage.

In my experience, women find a man who cooks for them sexy. Whatever the reason, they feel cared for, and they enjoy seeing a man take over in the kitchen. Men, take heed. I offer you here my splendid dinner for two that only takes twenty-five minutes to prepare. One rule to really make it meaningful: no sexual advances before or after. In other words, make it clear from the start that this dinner is for her, with no strings attached. Avoid the idea of, "I made you a great dinner—you owe me one." Surely, if your wife wants to make love, then feel free.

Baby Greens Salad with Cherry Tomatoes and Hearts of Palm

1 bag washed organic baby green
   salad mix
1 can hearts of palm

10–12 cherry tomatoes
Salad dressing (a jar of her favorite)

Mix together greens, hearts of palm, and tomatos. Pour dressing into a dish and serve on the side.

Fish en Croûte

1 pound tilapia (grouper or snapper
   can also be used, although the
   cooking times vary depending on
   the thickness of the fish)
¾ cup crushed nuts

1 egg
½ teaspoon salt
¼ cup extra virgin olive oil
2 tablespoons flour

Stir together crushed nuts, flour and salt. Spread mixture on a large plate. Beat the egg by hand and place in shallow pie pan.

Wash and dry fish thoroughly. Dip the fish into the egg (this helps the breading stick to it) and then coat both sides of the fish with the nut mixture. Heat the olive oil in a frying pan on medium heat until it begins to sizzle. Place the coated fish in the frying pan and cook for approximately 6 minutes. Turn the fish and cook another 6 minutes. The fish is done when it is white and flakes easily with a fork. Remove from pan and serve.

Optional: Smother fish in Creamy Mushroom Shallot Sauce.

Creamy Mushroom/Shallot Sauce

If you're willing to spend a little more time, gather the following ingredients:

3 shallots

¼ Vidalia onion (if Vidalia onions are not in season, just use the shallots and skip the onion)

6 tablespoons extra virgin olive oil

2 tablespoons heavy cream

2 portobello mushrooms, stems removed (or ½ cup shitake or any other mushroom)

Finely chop shallots and onions and set aside. Finely chop mushrooms and keep in separate bowl. Heat olive oil in small pan. When the oil begins to bubble, add shallots and onion pieces and sauté for 5 minutes, stirring occasionally. (If you like your shallots more well done, just let them sauté longer.)

Quick and Easy Asparagus

1 can asparagus

For extra points, heat and serve next to the cooked fish.

Mix-and-Match Ice Cream Sundaes

Offer a selection of different ice creams and toppings. Make your own sundaes and feed them to each other.

Sydney & Betty Feinberg
MARRIED: 54 YEARS

How We Met

It was 1938 and a friend suggested we go to a lecture. I saw Sydney there and he asked to walk me home. I said okay. My friend said it wasn't so nice, I hardly knew Sydney. But I didn't care. He asked if I would mind going on a date with him. He told me he was sorry, but could we go to the inexpensive movie house. I knew money was tight everywhere and that he lived in a poorer section of Williamsburg, so I said I wouldn't mind at all. He surprised me instead by taking me to Radio City Music Hall.

We dated and I saw his character; every penny he made he gave to his mother. Before he went to help fight WWII, he gave me a watch to show we were engaged. I waited, of course, and when he came back from the army we got married. We lived with my sister at first and I helped by working as a secretary. Soon we had a son and a daughter. I just made him a party for his eightieth birthday and we had our great granddaughter there to celebrate with us.

What Makes It Work For Us?

We've never slept on an argument. We fix it early, before it becomes a mountain. When we get upset, we start to talk and talk and pretty soon it becomes clear that I didn't mean what I said and he didn't mean it the way I thought he did. We always live for each other.

Advice for Couples Today

Take time to be alone together. We always traveled together if he had to go on business. We found a way to have quiet time to be with each other. That's very, very important.

All of us come to marriage with certain assumptions about how it should work. We don't realize that most of those assumptions are not the result of long, hard thinking but are rather messages we've easily accepted from our parents, the media, and our culture. Challenge yourself to think it through and understand the unconscious assumptions that may be getting in the way of your giving your marriage the best chance it can have. Start considering how much real time and energy are going toward your marriage in contrast to the rest of your life. Review your personal goals for your marriage and make a commitment to attain them with consistent focus and time. Prepare your mind and soul for love and make it happen.

Your childhood has a great deal to do with your ability to enjoy a great marriage. The more you understand this connection, the better marriage you will have.

The role that our childhood plays in our adult lives is a delicate subject, one that is often misunderstood. Recently, I attended a lecture given by a friend/mentor of mine. The topic was taking responsibility for yourself, one of the most common themes of pop culture. I was understandably dismayed when my friend described psychology as a convenient system for placing blame on parents. His description matched so many others I have heard that belittle psychology as an unscientific field that says, "It's your parents' fault you are the way you are, so there's nothing you can effectively do about it." On leaving that evening, my friend offered me his apologies if he had offended me with his comments. I told him I wasn't offended because his description had absolutely nothing to do with my work or beliefs in the psychological field.

I believe in the power of childhood. We come into this world with nothing but a genetic code that science is just beginning to comprehend. We enter as infants, completely dependent on our surroundings. What we believe about ourselves and life will largely, if not completely, depend on our surroundings. How does a six-month-old know she is special? It depends on the amount of hugs and kisses, loving words, and good nutrition she receives, as well as a dry bottom. How will she know when she is three whether she is wonderful and smart, or lazy and a troublemaker? It depends on the same hugs and kisses and reactions from her environment. When she is six, are her parents showing her how smart and beautiful she is, or are they reminding her how much she does wrong? Are they loving or cold and distant?

I respect children. I respect the power parents have over their children's lives. If parents are generally loving and warm and satisfy a child's needs, that child believes she is special. By the time she starts first grade, she is already expecting good things from herself and her environment. She is more likely to do well scholastically and find a healthy peer group because she believes she deserves it. She is more likely to marry someone who loves her dearly and brings her joy and meaning. She is more likely to find the job that suits her aspirations, to find motherhood meaningful, and to enjoy loving and giving to others. She expects good things out of life because her parents showed her by giving her love that she was worth loving. She took their message extremely personally. Her mind developed while being surrounded by love. Although it wasn't necessarily a conscious thought, deep down she figured, "If I'm getting all of this positive attention and love, it must mean I am a worthy being whom people want to give to and love." The little girl can't separate the actions of her parents from the feeling she has of herself. Maybe her parents are acting this way only because they had indulging parents who modeled good parenting skills. Their positive regard may not reflect this little girl's qualities at all. It doesn't matter. The little girl feels wonderful and deserving and will always draw strength from that feeling because of her parents' actions.

As wonderful as this scenario is, it is unlikely for many. Unfortunately, many parents don't offer their children the love and sensitivity that helps them believe they're special. When parents limit their love and warmth, don't meet a child's needs, are withdrawn from their child, or don't connect or understand their child, the little girl again believes that it reflects on her personally. She develops a sense that she isn't deserving of joy and wonderful things. This inner voice can cause her difficulty in coping, scholastically and socially. It can make her overly serious and tense. Her unconscious voice may cause her to marry a person with whom she fights. It may allow her to pass up good employment opportunities while settling into a job that brings her a personal sense of disrespect. She may have difficulty being warm to her children and criticize them bitterly as was done to her from birth. She may never be able to separate the problems that caused her parents' emotional disengagement from the personal values she came to embrace as a result of that distance. For the first six years of her life, she couldn't understand any reason for her parents' behavior other than that it spoke to who she was and what she deserved. And it wasn't a conscious thought. She didn't think, "I could be getting better treatment from Sally's mom but instead I'm stuck here." It's simply a natural mental development for a kid to believe that she is as valuable and special as her surroundings have made her feel.

The little girl doesn't know that her dad hits her because he had an abusive childhood or that her mom had a postpartum depression that lasted the first three years of her life. The little girl never criticizes her parents or depersonalizes their actions. She isn't capable of thinking, "I'm great and my parents don't know it because they're pathetic, irresponsible individuals who must have suffered themselves at the hands of their parents." Instead, the girl takes their messages personally and swallows it hook, line, and sinker. She deserves what she has been made to believe she deserves as a result of her parents' actions toward her.

Of course, there are no perfect parents, so we are always a mix of the best and worst of our parents. We can never compare tragedies. Our personal belief system, this internal voice, is dependent on so many factors besides our parents' actions. A parent's single action could affect two children in completely different ways. How we as children translate and interpret those actions depends on many factors, including our birth order as well as other support we may have received from siblings, relatives, friends, or others. For example, one child who is abused goes on to abuse herself and others, while her sister goes on to dedicate her life to protecting children. Childhood is never black and white. Myriad factors cause us to create this internal self-perspective from which we will draw personal definition every day. The one thing I am sure of from all my years of counseling clients is that it's a mistake to downplay your childhood and its effect on who you are. I've heard people defend their childhood and minimize the impact of major blows a thousand times before: "So my mother died when I was eight." "So my father criticized me every day." "So I never knew my dad." Then comes the protective defense: "It wasn't like I was molested or something." Allow yourself to be more aware of what your childhood could mean to you. You can understand its powerful effect only if you allow yourself to.

Countless people have told me, "When things are going well in my life, I start to get nervous. I wonder, 'When will the other shoe drop?'" It's often difficult for even the healthiest of us to feel completely comfortable with joy, success, and love. We may have received or created messages about ourselves we're unaware of. Yet we continue to act on these preconceived notions about ourselves: "I can never get it right." "I can't handle this." "I'm afraid to love or allow myself to be loved." "It's got to blow up in my face eventually." We usually don't recognize that this inner voice is directing us as we make millions of decisions a day. When we awaken, do we smile and kiss our spouse, or grunt and go into the bathroom without saying hello? Do we pick our kids up and hug them in the hall as they pass us in the morning, or not? Do we share anything about the fight we had with our spouse when we talk with our sibling that day, or not? Do we prepare a healthy lunch or leave in a hurry and figure we'll grab something at work? Are we well scheduled or are we doing one more thing that will cause us to show up to our next appointment late and harried? These endless decisions, made in a split second, seem meaningless yet are often powerful displays of who we are deep down.

If you refuse to recognize that many of these unconscious decisions arise from self-impressions you received in your childhood, you will be limiting your ability to change your behavior. Or you may change for a short while until you bounce back into your old ways because your unconscious self-identity is often more powerful than your conscious will to change. If you have a stomach ailment, the first thing you consider is what you've been eating lately. If you continually have flat tires, you want to determine what's causing the problem. Of course, you can just keep taking medicine for your stomach or buying new tires. It's often easier to do that instead of the long and costly investigative process to determine what's really causing the problem. To ignore your past and expect to change is like trying to drive your car with only three good tires because you're afraid to get out and see what's really going on. You'll have to keep dealing with the problem until you find the cause and resolve the issue at its root.

The Real Meaning of Taking Control

If you want to take responsibility for your actions and change the ones you dislike, first understand why you act the way you do. Look back to the time when you defined who you were and would always be. "Blaming" your parents doesn't mean that you aren't responsible for your actions. Searching your childhood for answers means that you recognize you are acting today as an adult to uncover those messages your parents sent you about yourself. You merely want to respect the power the past had on you as an individual and reconsider whether those messages truly speak to who you are or are mistaken messages you received or created about yourself. You want to take control of your actions by deciding that as a conscious adult, you can determine who you are and who you can be rather than relying on those messages received as a child. Uncovering the messages you accepted about yourself from your parents isn't about telling your folks how rotten they were. It's about recognizing that they had their own personal struggles as well. It's about appreciating that you might have done no better job if you were put in the same circumstances they were.

Understanding the power of your childhood is about making new choices based on who you are and want to be and not solely on your parents' messages to you as a child. That is taking ultimate responsibility for your actions.

Connecting to Your Past

Answer the following questions regarding each parent:

1. How did you learn to love as a child?
2. How did you learn to care for and give to others as a child?
3. How did your mom love you?
4. How did your dad love you?
5. I didn't like it / hated it (circle one) when my mom/dad _____.
6. I liked it / hated it (circle one) when my mom/dad _____.
7. What is your fondest memory of yourself with your mom/dad?
8. What is your saddest memory of yourself with mom/dad?
9. What is your angriest memory of yourself with your mom/dad?
10. How would you hope to be exactly like your mom/dad?
11. How would you hope to be different from your mom/dad?

Write a memory from age ten and under for each of the following feelings:

1. Sad
2. Mad
3. Happy
4. Scared
5. Lonely
6. Disappointed
7. Guilty
8. Joyful

9. Loved
10. Calm/peaceful

Review each feeling and remember with whom you shared it. What did that person do? Did you feel he or she understood you?

Silent Messages

1. Write down how you feel about yourself: your own personal messages about yourself. List your strengths and weaknesses.
2. Consider all the messages that you were sent as a child. Don't judge yet which messages you accepted or not. Simply list the messages. Remember that messages are sent by inaction as well as by action.
   For example:
   I feel my mom sent me the following messages about myself: _____.
   I feel my dad sent me the following messages about myself: _____.
3. See what similarities you find between #1, your personal feelings and messages about yourself, and #2, the messages you received from your parent(s). Those similarities show that, for better or for worse, the way you feel about yourself in those areas is largely built on the messages you received about yourself as a child.
4. What areas and beliefs about yourself are you uncomfortable with?
5. What will you do to change the areas of your personal belief system that are not working for you? How will you remind yourself not to act, think, or feel based on that definition of yourself? How will you remind yourself "in the moment" that you no longer wish to operate on the basis of mistaken messages from your past?

Feelings: The Ultimate Time Travelers

If you doubt that your childhood could have had such a lasting effect on you, consider how feelings travel through time. By conjuring up a single memory, you can feel the same way you felt when you were four years old. The situation and causes may be dramatically different, but the feelings are similar. If you grew up with an overwhelming sense of sadness, then it makes sense that when you feel sadness as an adult, it will be familiar to you and you won't fight it. You may even feel comfortable inviting it into your life (without consciously intending to do so). Not only are you used to it, you may even find comfort in it. After all, you know how to be sad. You've lived it all your life. Your mental self is safe with sadness. This may sound outrageous, but we are creatures of habit. We gravitate toward what we know, even when it hurts, and avoid change because change brings with it a host of anxieties about the unknown. If you grew up feeling happy and peaceful, you will likely seek out life situations that feed those feelings, and you will find comfort with the happiness generated by your actions. Child-hood feelings tell us it's normal to feel a certain way. When you were seven and generally felt lonely, you thought that feeling lonely was normal and spent many years without realizing that you put yourself into situations that would lead you to loneliness.

Yvonne grew up with parents who were largely available to her financially but were quite absent from her life otherwise. As her servants tended her every need, taught her to ride a bike, and explained to her what sex was while her parents traveled the world, Yvonne felt lonely. But she always protected her image of her parents by focusing on all the neat stuff they gave her and the indulgent experiences of her youth.

Yvonne came to a seminar on relationships because she had little luck with men. Or rather, she had great luck with men who had an almost protean abil-ity to suddenly turn cold and distant to her and break her heart. Through her stories of how she consistently failed at love, she finally noticed a pattern. She fell for a certain kind of man, one who didn't come after her but rather forced her to rope him in. She fell in love hard and quickly well before the man gave any indication that he was that interested in her or even looking for a long term relationship. She was making herself much too vulnerable too early in the relationship.

When she told me, "What the heck, I've always been lonely," even she began to understand the deep connection she had to this feeling. She found it hard to believe that her internal connection to loneliness could cause her to uncon-sciously seek out certain types of men and fall in love with them quickly. But the proof was in her life. There were other men, ones who thought she was wonderful and who fell in love with her. But she found them wimpy, needy, boring, simply unattractive. Yet this, too, was her unconscious way of staying lonely. Again, this didn't mean that the men who were unkind or manipula-tive were excusable in their behavior. Rather, Yvonne's struggle with loneliness left her unprotected from their inappropriateness.

Understanding our childhood can be an intense personal journey. It can be unpleasant and uncomfortable as it may reveal insights into our behavior that we'd rather focus away from. Consider that the next time you disrespect the impression childhood makes on all of us.

Your childhood has profoundly affected who you are, and appreciating its role will make a considerable contribution to your ability to create and maintain a great marriage. There are countless unique examples of how looking into our past can help us effect change in our marriage. I offer a few to help you understand this power; then it's your turn to write your own example of how childhood made you who you are today. Don't discount what your childhood means to you by drawing differences between your experiences and the following examples. Everyone is unique, but we can still learn from others how connected we are to our past.

⁂

Douglas admitted that he needed to loosen up, but he felt his wife was overly critical. They had fought bitterly for over twenty years, seen countless therapists, yet were directionless in their marriage. Doug was a huge man with a soft heart who had married an encouraging yet anxious woman, Matty. She told me privately that he would get so incensed that she was literally afraid he would strike her, even though he had never done so. She explained that no matter what she said or how nicely she said it, if she said anything that was the least bit critical, Doug couldn't handle it and would have a violent reaction. The only way she knew to deal with it was to disengage from her husband and never discuss anything of importance with him. Their marriage was reduced to talk of the weather and other subjects that had nothing to do with money, kids, or work issues. When they were forced to deal with one of their children because of misbehavior, for example, they fought. Doug had been on antianxiety medication for years. They were both at their wits' end and couldn't see any other way out but divorce.

Doug decided to go to therapy alone to try to resolve his own issues. He described his childhood as "miserable" because of a tyrannical, critical father and a weak mother who did nothing to protect him from his father. But Doug didn't want to believe that his father could be "causing" his marital problems. He wanted to believe that his childhood trauma happened a long time ago and he couldn't keep going back to Mommy and Daddy for blame. It took him weeks to understand that he had a burning anger at his parents that he had never resolved. He was displacing his anger toward them onto his wife and kids whenever they dared to confront him on any issue. "But I screamed at my parents years ago," he implored, refusing to go back in time and remember—and worse yet, feel—what it was like to be a child again. Yet he was feeling what it was like to be that child every time his wife suggested any sort of change for him. Out of desperation, Doug decided to launch himself into regular therapy to resolve his past.

Doug and I created an exercise for him to focus his anger where it properly belonged. Every time he began to get upset at a family member, he walked away and wrote in a journal that he carried with him at all times. In that journal he would write about the feeling he was experiencing and what it reminded him of about his childhood. In this way, he would be using the feeling he had at that moment as a catalyst to remember and be appropriately angry about his past. Instead of talking about his past as though he were writing some distanced book review, he could begin to genuinely feel the past and understand it from new adult eyes.

When Doug was a child and his father exploded into anger at him, he had no choice but to believe he was wrong and must have done something so bad that he deserved his father's wrath, since a young child personalizes the good and bad messages his parents send his way. Doug needed to go back and recognize—*while he was reexperiencing that same feeling in the moment*—that it wasn't his fault. He needed to see those feelings through the mind of an adult and realize how those childhood experiences made him angry at his father and at himself. He could now begin to understand his father's limitations and how his father had unfairly taken out his rage on Doug.

Doug's first journal entry occurred when his wife told him he had bad breath. It was a simple comment, one she had made often the last month since he had been battling a cold. Doug became immediately incensed. "But why? It's not as if I'm telling you about anything you did wrong. I'd want to know if I had bad breath so I could do something about it," Matty explained, but to no avail. Doug left the room and began writing in his journal:

What does this remind me of? It reminds me of my father telling me every day how I'm not standing up straight. He told me this every single day of my life from the time I was eight years old. He'd show me exactly how to stand, placing me up against the wall and sticking his hand sharply between my shoulder blades, forcing me painfully to straighten up. He sent me to bone doctors to learn exercises. To this day I have no idea how to stand up straight, and I've damaged my back trying to constantly compensate for what I've believed for years to be terrible posture.

~~~~~~

Doug was reminded of how pathetic he felt from his father's constant criticism of his posture. That was why Matty's "breath" comment made him so angry. But instead of displacing that anger onto Matty, as he would have done in the past, he was able to be angry at his father through his writing and thus begin to be angry at the source. This helped him realize there was nothing wrong with him. For example, until that day in my office, he had thought he had terrible posture. Yet Doug was a muscular man in his forties who worked out at the gym regularly and was in outstanding shape with absolutely no sign of any posture problem.

Over the next few months, Doug examined hundreds of memories like this one as he experienced hundreds of moments of feeling angry. After those few months, Doug's anger dissipated. He was able to make better choices for himself. He was able to listen to his own heart about himself and not his mistaken messages from childhood. Doug got his wish to be free of the constant pain of his past. He might always have to be on guard about his anger, but now he could take the time to understand his feelings before reacting, instead of becoming incensed so quickly that he couldn't think straight.

You may think that this step back into time caused Doug to hate his father even more. Indeed, Doug maintained a cool distance from his parents and during therapy did go through a time when he felt he hated them. But he never confronted them during this emotional period because he understood that his father never meant to hurt him, nor could his father do anything to correct the past. What Doug came to realize was that all that built-up anger that he was pretending away had caused him to have an extremely distant relationship from his father. It was Doug's responsibility to deal with his own emotions and relationships.

As Doug started to get a new, less angry lease on life, he began to get along better with his father. After all, as his childhood had less power over him, he had less resentment toward his parents. Whatever they did wrong, he'd corrected in the end. Their unintentional mistakes hadn't destroyed his life, and he no longer had to hold his problems against them, something he had done without knowing for all those years. Now when his father would be somewhat critical, Doug didn't cringe or vow never to see him again, something he'd done countless times before. He could let it pass without incident because it no longer had the power to hurt him deep inside. Now that he'd resolved his childhood anger, his father's criticisms were little more than the rantings of an angry, emotionally unhealthy man.

Don't think that because you don't face your feelings that your feelings don't already cause you to limit your relationship with your parents, or whoever else has hurt you.

Doug had another fascinating self-discovery. He identified that his anger was most fierce whenever Matty would stand up for the children when she felt Doug was wrongfully losing his temper with them. Doug could never understand why this made him angrier than anything else; he didn't think it tapped into his childhood issues because his mother never stood up for him as a child when his father was screaming at him. But Doug finally understood that every time his wife stood up for her kids, she was proving how much of a failure his own mother was when she hadn't stood up for him as a child. Doug would have rather continued to excuse his mother; after all, who could stand up to a hysterically outraged father? His anger at his mother for leaving him unprotected was yet another part of his journey to free himself from the pain of his childhood. His insight helped him reduce his anger about Matty and enjoy a better marriage.

Understanding Your Anger

Buy a small notebook to have handy at all times. Whenever you're angry with your spouse, walk away, open your notebook, and write the answers to the following questions:

1. What am I angry about?
2. On a scale of 1 to 10, how angry am I?
3. Would my spouse be as angry at me if I did the same thing (or didn't do the same thing) to him or her?
4. When did I feel this way in my childhood? (List at least one example.)
5. Is it possible I am more angry at my spouse than I should be because it reminds me of some difficult feelings from my childhood?

Share these answers with your spouse. They may be able to offer you some insight into how you may overreact under certain circumstances because of how they remind you of your past. Of course, not all anger springs from buried hurt. You may be angry at your spouse for a legitimate reason. What's important is that you take full responsibility for your feelings and act consciously on them.

Rehabilitating Your Parents

Sometimes we protect the image of our parents' relationship by recreating a similar scenario in our own marriage.

A week didn't pass when Harriet wasn't crying in bed while refusing to talk to her husband, Marc, about how sad he had made her. Marc tried to coax her into talking, but to no avail. He felt horrible for causing his wife such sadness, while Harriet felt more and more distant from her husband, whom she was convinced she could no longer trust with her feelings. Yet Harriet fell to pieces whenever any issue came up, and there was never any time when they could discuss it. Usually, Marc would simply apologize many times the next day until Harriet would forgive him.

Harriet's mother had been the same way. Harriet had grown up seeing her dad apologize to her mom while her mom took to her bed, unable to deal with anyone else, including Harriet. As an adult, Harriet mirrored her mother's behavior, the only model she had. One day, however, Harriet's mother, recognizing her daughter's behavior, intervened in a fight between Marc and Harriet. She talked to Harriet about how sorry she was for her behavior years ago and about how much she had tried to change over the years and learned to talk out her problems with Harriet's father.

In that conversation, Harriet suddenly realized that every time she went to bed weak and sad, she was legitimizing her mother's behavior from years ago, rationalizing it as normal. Once Harriet understood that she acted a certain way to protect her image of her mother, she could develop the strength to change her own behavior and discuss her hurt with her husband.

Men and Their Fathers

Since the dawn of humankind, there has always been competition between men. Unfortunately, most men live in a seesaw world. When one goes up, the other must go down. Someone else's rise must be connected to another's fall. This is a common theme in the relationship between fathers and sons. It's very subtle, and rarely ever recognized. I dare say most men would disagree with me, for we very much want to protect the image of our own fathers as well as our own personal image of fatherhood.

Competition doesn't preclude a father's wish for his son to grow and succeed. Rather, there is an unconscious struggle that can cause fathers to diminish their sons because of an unspoken fear of being knocked off the totem pole. This fear can lead to fathers being overly critical of their sons and dismissive of their accomplishments. For many men, it becomes clear around middle age that their fathers will never be able to see them as real adult men or recognize their true value.

Men, you can help yourself and your marriage by respecting this dynamic and remembering it the next time your spouse wants you to do something a different way or doesn't delight in your accomplishments the way you'd expect her to. Be aware that you might be displacing your own disappointment over your father's inability to approve of you onto your wife when she is somewhat disapproving. Recognize how this unconscious competition may lead you to compete with your male friends to the detriment of your family. You may spend less and less time with your wife and kids as you reach toward a fatter paycheck and higher status. You may never realize how true success falls on the men who are emotionally connected to their wife and children.

As the old story goes, there was never a man on his deathbed who lamented, "If only I had spent more time at the office . . ." Decide today to reexamine your priorities with the understanding that you may be unconsciously motivated by male competition.

The Basic Marriage Model: Your Parents' Marriage

I think most people have come to understand that we tend to copy our parents' marital style. It was the primary style we witnessed intimately, and thus we adopt it as normal (although some people who grew up with warring parents tend to enact the polar opposite of their parents' marital style). Your parents may have fought a great deal, or belittled each other. On the other hand, they may have been extremely sweet and kind to each other. In any case, you come to marriage with huge and powerful assumptions about marriage and you need to be open with your spouse about such expectations. That, of course, means recognizing them yourself first.

Esther told me how she cooked dinner for her husband, Saul, for the first year of her marriage and was amazed by how Saul was late on every single occasion. One of her fondest memories of childhood was seeing her parents eat together and how magical it was for them to spend that pleasant time together. It was a beautiful memory and one she thirsted for in her own marriage. However, Saul's father regularly traveled and was only home on weekends, when his parents would often eat out. He loved to eat out and didn't understand his wife's desire for him to be home for dinner. Both of them were operating from their parents' marital model. They needed to identify what they wanted to try together as a couple to create their own special moments. Finally, they were able to compromise and do a little of both.

Something as simple as whether to eat out or at home can become so complicated and cause such personal pain when we have assumptions we feel our spouse should understand without our even mentioning them. And your spouse's feeling that dinners at home are a waste of time may be just as intense as your feeling that eating dinner together at home is crucial. It can be difficult for you to see any way of marriage other than the one you grew up with. Be open with your expectations and ready to listen to your spouse's opinion, remembering that it, too, is likely to be based on childhood experience. Try to develop your own unique marital style and flair.

Research shows that if one or both lover's parents have an unhappy marriage, it is a forewarning of marital trouble.[4] Consider your parents' marriage. What roles did your mother and father play? How did they make decisions, deal with money, children, discussion of feelings? Start considering how your marriage may be similar. Your goal is to make conscious choices about your unique partnership.

Use your answers to the following questions to begin to recognize how your parents' marriage may be affecting your own.

Legacies from Your Parents' Marriage

1. My parents had a _____ marriage.
2. My father's role in their marriage was _____ .
3. My mother's role in their marriage was _____ .
4. When my parents disagreed, they _____ .
5. When it came to money matters, my parents _____ .
6. When I think of love, I think of _____ .
7. My parents showed affection for each other by _____ .
8. My parents felt very strongly about _____ .
9. My parents' marriage has changed over the years. Three examples are:

   a. _____ .

   b. _____ .

   c. _____ .

10. My beliefs in marriage are similar to my parents' in that _____ .
11. My beliefs in marriage are dissimilar to my parents' in that _____ .

Many spouses are aware of their parents' shortcomings as marital part-ners and vow to be different. These spouses may well be doing the insight-ful work they need to make healthy choices away from poor marital models. However, there are many spouses who are fooling themselves into thinking they are nothing like their parents when in truth, all they've done is to find different avenues to express some of the same problems.

Ted's father was a philanderer, and Ted swore he would never follow in his father's footsteps. He didn't, but he did. He never had any kind of affair with another woman, yet he had a different kind of affair—with his work. His work took him away from his wife, physically and emotionally, as much as his father's girlfriends took his father away from his mother. Ted would never see his behavior as resembling his dad's bad habits. Yet, he learned only too well from his dad, bringing with him the same discomfort with being close to his wife. Father and son shared the same fear of emotional connection. Ted simply found a different route to create that distance.

What You Learned from Your Opposite-Sex Parent

Where do you think you may have learned how to relate to your spouse? Many are surprised to hear the answer: from your relationship with your opposite-sex parent. After all, your first experience of an intense relationship with a member of the opposite sex is usually with your parent. And even if that parent wasn't around very much, it doesn't mean that you didn't have a relationship. In fact, it can mean that your first loving experience with the opposite sex was a sad, lonely, or confusing one.

If you are a woman, consider what it was like to love or be loved by your dad. What you came to expect from him will have a profound effect on what you expect from your husband. If your dad made you feel special and loved, you will expect this kind of behavior from your husband and unconsciously do things to bring this loving behavior out in your husband. If your dad belittled you or made you sad, you are more likely to expect this from your husband and unconsciously work toward this outcome. For example, you may continually bring up a subject that you know upsets your spouse and causes distance between the two of you, even though there is no imperative reason to do so.

Before you discount this theory, consider the last fight or disappointing event you had with your spouse. Be honest with yourself. How else could you have handled it? The point here is not to blame the victim. It's to help you realize that you have much more to do with your spouse's behavior (both good and bad) than you sometimes would like to admit. We usually have no problem taking credit when our spouse succeeds. We remember how loving and encouraging we've been. But we tend to shy away from our spouse's failures as if those failures occurred in a vacuum. This doesn't diminish your spouse's mistakes nor make them right or excusable. However, you have much more power over how your spouse approaches you and your marriage than you may think. You can bring out the best or worst in your spouse, and much of that will have to do with how your opposite-sex parent treated you.

If your mom was cold and uncaring to you as a little boy, you may unconsciously expect this from your wife. You may bring up issues that anger her and push her buttons in an unconscious attempt to cause her to be as cold toward you as you've come to expect from the women you love. You may do stupid little things that cause her to distrust you, or make sarcastic comments, never realizing that it's an unconscious way of creating a woman whose actions toward you will remind you of your mother's behavior.

⁓⁓⁓⁓⁓⁓⁓⁓⁓⁓⁓⁓⁓⁓⁓⁓⁓⁓⁓⁓⁓⁓⁓

Scott's mom was emotionally and physically abused by his dad. She was generally overwhelmed and unloving and offered little emotional support to Scott. When Scott came to me for help with his marriage, he complained that his wife was not loving or attentive. I asked him to consider his own ability to be loving and caring toward his wife. Scott felt his behavior had little to do with his wife's lack of affection toward him, but I asked him to turn on the love and charm for one week and see if his wife noticed or reacted any differently. Sure enough, he walked in beaming the next week. He had focused on loving his wife, and she couldn't get over it. He had had the best week of his life. She was a completely different person toward him.

Therapy over? Unfortunately not. The following week was a disaster. Scott simply couldn't keep up this level of love. The intimacy they had shared the previous week wouldn't have been unusual for the average couple, but it required a superhuman effort for Scott. He began to notice that whenever his wife did seem to be in a loving mood, he'd do something to ruin the moment. He'd ask her about the money she spent that day, or excuse himself to do work. He couldn't handle their relationship emotionally until he had a better understanding about his relationship with his mother and how it extended to his marriage.

⁓⁓⁓⁓⁓⁓⁓⁓⁓⁓⁓⁓⁓⁓⁓⁓⁓⁓⁓⁓⁓⁓⁓

Many people don't need years of psychotherapy to change their marital style. Rather, they need to be brutally honest with themselves about why they choose to act the way they do, and to choose to do things differently to enjoy the benefits of a happier marriage.

The Litmus Test

Generally, when a spouse has a complaint about his or her mate, the point is a valid one. But even if you have a right to be upset with your spouse, your reaction may still be based on messages you received from your childhood. People are often confused by this point. I've been asked, "Are you telling me I shouldn't be angry that he left me at the party for two hours and didn't even tell me he was going, let alone where he was and when he'd return?" You may have every right to be upset with your spouse, but it is generally the *intensity* of your reaction that tells you whether you've stepped into past feelings and issues. If you sense that you had a right to be upset with your spouse but that your reaction was far more extreme than warranted, it's the best indicator that you've borrowed anger or some other feeling from your past and plastered it all over this situation.

Yvonne wouldn't speak to her husband, Jamal, for two days because he'd given her two $100 bills for Mother's Day. She'd expected a present chosen especially for her; the money made her feel like Jamal was paying a utility bill. Granted that her husband may have needed some sensitivity training, but her reaction was extreme. Jamal's apologies fell on deaf ears, and Yvonne cried off and on for two full days. This Mother's Day reminded her of an earlier time when her parents shipped her off to boarding school and acknowledged her birthday with only a card and a check. They never gave her a present, even though she constantly told them what she would like. The intensity of her reaction told her she was confusing her husband's mild insensitivity with a painful insensitivity in her past.

When you have an intense reaction to something involving your spouse, ask yourself, "*When else have I felt this way? Where in my childhood have I experienced this feeling?*" Go to that time and discover what upset you then, how you felt, and how this interaction with your spouse has made you feel the same way. Your spouse doesn't have to do the exact same thing that your parent once did; the present situation just has to evoke the same feeling.

Perhaps your mom never spoke to you about your problems, and that made you feel terribly alone, but your spouse, unlike your mother, is always there to talk and understand. Yet when your spouse goes off and leaves you for hours at a party, you freak out because it gives you a homesick feeling, much the way you felt when you were little and were left out at parties, sensing that no one truly cared about you. You refuse to speak to your husband about it, or even sleep in the same bedroom with him, and have no idea when or how you will forgive him or get past this hurtful feeling.

Your mother's and spouse's ways of relating to you were different: Mom didn't listen well, whereas your spouse listened intently. But the feelings crept back in, and before you knew it, you were angered and forlorn over your husband's not keeping you informed about his whereabouts. The fact that he had a little too much to drink and ended up leaving the party with a friend he hadn't seen for years, the fact that he was grossly apologetic afterward, the fact that it was your best friend's party and you were quite busy with your friends anyway, and the fact that it took you a full hour before you even asked where he was didn't seem to squelch your anger and hysteria. Yes, he was wrong, but your reaction was too intense and therefore indicative of a deeper issue and hurt.

Stop yourself from fuming and think, "When else in my childhood did I feel this sad and lonely?" Don't be afraid to allow yourself to remember the parties that came and went as a child and your mother's lack of understanding of what a girl wears to be accepted at these parties, for example. Allow yourself to feel the loneliness of a mother who didn't seem interested in you. Go back to your husband and tell him why you had such a hurtful reaction and explain that although you still feel he was unkind, you can see how it could all happen. Share with him the details of your childhood experience so that he can know a little more about who you are and what makes you tick.

Your childhood can cause you not only to *overreact* but to *underreact* as well. For example, you should have been touched by your lover's gesture, but you're not; or you should've been upset by your spouse's behavior, but it doesn't bother you in the least. Don't hide from your reactions and excuse yourself by saying, "I don't know how a normal person should react." I've heard this from many of my patients and have found that they generally do have a clear sense of the appropriate reaction. You generally know how most of your friends would react. Stay in that moment and ask yourself if the situation or feeling reminds you of something in your childhood.

For every moment you take to consider your past and how it affects you will come countless benefits to your marriage and all those around you. Your reflection will allow you to make better choices—your own choices, which are firmly based on your personal beliefs of today. You will be able to be a true partner to your spouse, considering decisions solely on the basis of what is best for you and your mate, without confusing your marriage with unhealthy messages from your past.

It's Not Just You

Of course, how your past affects your marriage is further complicated by the fact that your spouse's past also affects the marriage.

Paolo and Maggie were always fighting bitterly over minor issues. Paolo complained that no matter what he said, Maggie had to disagree or take a strong, oppositional stand. Maggie, on the other hand, felt that Paolo had a criticism for every single thing she did, even boiling water, and that she had to fight back or else Paolo would never stop. What neither of them realized was that they both were being emotionally driven by the inner voices of childhood.

Paolo was raised by a critical dad who criticized Paolo, his firstborn son, for mistakes his whole life. Even in adulthood, Paolo was pained at how his father could find fault with everything he did, even though Paolo had become a successful businessman and proud father of two. Paolo criticized his wife the way he'd been criticized, and every time he heard Maggie disagree with him, he heard his father's voice all over again and fought back bitterly.

But it wasn't only Paolo who had come to the marriage with issues. Maggie had also been raised by a critical father, who was unkind to her mother. Maggie remembered her mom being harshly criticized; her mother took it and never answered back to her father. Maggie had sworn to herself as a child that when she grew up and married, she would never allow herself to be treated that way. So whenever Paolo began to comment on anything Maggie did, her fierce memory of her dad's negative behavior came to the forefront, and she instantly took a defiant stand against Paolo. Both Paolo and Maggie had past memories and pain that caused them to unconsciously react negatively in present situations that paralleled past trauma.

As much as you work to understand the dynamics of your marriage, you may never understand them all. Some of your ability to understand these dynamics is tied up in your spouse's ability to work on understanding them too. But every emotional riddle you unfold will make your marriage healthier and stronger.

The Ultimate Bond Builder

Discovering yourself in the context of how your past affects you as a marital partner is a powerful bond builder. It not only makes you better at being human, it allows you to share your deepest memories and feelings with your spouse, which in turn allows the two of you to feel closer. We can create meaningful bonds with those who are open about how they think and feel. The more we share about our essence, the more our spouse can love us; there is simply much more of who we truly are for him or her to love.

Lemonade from Lemons

Use this exercise to help yourself express some difficult moments and feelings of your past, consider how you can grow from it, and then learn to openly share these issues with your spouse.

1. Take ten minutes for each of you to write about some past difficulty with your own parents.
2. After sharing what you've written, write and discuss what good you can learn from the experience.
3. Write and discuss how you can continue to take positive steps toward a stronger marriage.
4. If you wrote about an experience that happened since you were married, write and share what you appreciated from your spouse during this period of time.

In doing the above exercise, one husband recounted how when he was a child, he hated to hear his father belittle his mother. He wrote about three different episodes. He then talked to his wife about how from this experience in his childhood he'd learned to see the good in people. His father was negative, choosing to focus on his mother's limitations. He felt he was learning to enjoy people more than the average person because of his resolve to see the strengths of others. There was one older person in his firm, however, whom he had difficulty doing this with, and he recognized that the coworker reminded him of his father. He decided to work toward preventing this resemblance from getting in the way of his seeing the good in this person.

His wife wrote of the many childhood moments when her mother would saddle her with her problems. Her mother was constantly using her as a sounding board, and usually it was the only time they had significant conversations. But through discussing it with her husband, she realized for the first time how careful she was not to impose her problems on others. In fact, she realized that her friends always told her how sensitive she was, and how well she listens. She talked to her husband about how she could become better at sharing her own problems with others instead of being limited because her mom had difficulty listening to others.

Every example of past difficulty doesn't hark back to childhood. You may discuss difficult times and what you can learn from them with your spouse that have little to do with any childhood theme. Your marriage will grow from the open sharing of feelings of hard times of the past. This honesty of self-communication and will to learn and grow from it will cause you and your spouse to feel more bonded, as though you're working as a team.

One couple had experienced three traumatic financial years that ended in an embarrassing bankruptcy and a plunge in their social status. They both wrote about what the bankruptcy meant to them. For him, it meant acknowledging the failure of a company he'd spent ten years developing. He got literally sick when he thought of having to start over and work as hard as he had for the last ten years. For her, it meant failing her children, forcing them to leave their private schools. It also meant losing friends who she thought loved her for who she was, not because of her philanthropy.

They then began to consider what positives could come from such difficulty. They found many. They learned what and who was really important in life. They both realized they needed each other more and had to stop finding outside activities to keep them occupied, most often separately. They definitely learned who were their true friends. They understood that their children meant more to them than all the money in the world and vowed never to neglect them the way they did when the business was being developed. Finally, they thanked each other for the support they offered each other. "I never heard you once say anything negative about my business skills or decisions, and it meant so much to me," the husband told his wife.

What If You Don't Remember?

Many people don't have many clear memories of their past. And when they do, they don't remember a clear feeling. Often they'll just recall events without the conscious thoughts or feelings they experienced as a child. The mind is our most powerful tool. When we suffer as children, we're able to do a host of things to cope. We push the memory away or forget about it—a coping mechanism commonly referred to as suppression or repression. We rewrite history, painting a new picture and meaning of what is going on. For example, if a parent is hurting a child, that child may feel "special" because the parent has singled him or her out to hurt. It may sound inconceivable, but when you are a small, vulnerable child and have nowhere to go for help, you have to be creative.

Revisiting your childhood may be complicated because you may have worked emotionally as a child to deny feeling pain or sadness. If your dad died when you were nine and you don't remember being sad at all, you should assume that any nine-year-old whose father died would have an emotional reaction that would at least include sadness. Allow yourself the freedom to make such obvious conclusions and logical deductions. Consider seeking a qualified therapist to help you. If you don't, you are "protecting" yourself from your past and will lock yourself out from a treasure trove of personal understanding and insight. Instead of burying and being rid of your feelings, you may have buried your feelings alive.

Useful tools for connecting to your past are old photos or videos of yourself and family, or a memory box from your childhood. Take out special elementary school projects, drawings, report cards, trophies, awards, and diplomas, using them to help you remember what daily life was like for you. Walk around a toy store and find some of the toys you used to love as a kid. Visit a candy store and buy the candy you loved as a kid. Listen to music and watch television shows from your childhood. If you wrote poetry or kept any kind of journal as a teen, review it. Look at any creation you made as a child to help yourself connect with your past.

Taking the Arms to Battle

Once you begin to connect to yourself through your past, you can begin the battle of making healthier choices. You can literally decide whether you should be getting so angry, disappointed, hurt or not. It may take some time, but eventually you will be able to reduce the unhealthy reactions you may have been comfortable with for years and find new ones that suit you better. Think of your personal growth as a four-rung ladder.

1. *Unconsciously Unskilled.* You don't recognize that deeper things from your childhood are affecting your behaviors and personal decisions. You react according to, and often repeat, the messages of your youth. You listen to that deeply imbedded inner voice without ever recognizing it or considering if those personal messages you accepted about yourself were accurate.

For example, Sally had always seen her mom as a weak woman who took verbal abuse from her dad. Therefore, whenever Sally's husband made the slightest corrective comment or got even slightly upset (even when it seemed valid), Sally would blow up and hit him with a barrage of angry comments, ensuring that she'd never turn into her mom, for whom she had serious disrespect.

2. *Consciously Unskilled.* You begin to realize that unconscious forces cause you to behave a certain way. You don't yet know what to do with that information or how to change, so you are still unskilled. But at least you now *see* that you are unskilled; that you have have illogical, intense reactions; and that you have work to do. Obviously, this is a great step, because you cannot begin to change until you are able to see you have a problem.

At this step, Sally began to notice that she was overreacting to her husband's words. Mostly she noticed it after she had already blown up. But she was apologizing for the first time in her marriage for her behavior.

3. *Consciously Skilled.* You have put great effort into changing your reactions and understanding the root of your behavior. You have great insight as to how your past affects you, and you're able to change your behavior because of these insights. You are healthier, happier, and constantly monitoring yourself to ensure that you are reacting in a healthy way that befits your personal adult choices. When issues arise, you stop yourself and consider your reaction and how much of it is being driven by your childhood messages.

Now Sally began to catch herself before she became inappropriately hostile. But it still took work. She had to have great focus to stop herself from exploding, walk away, and immediately talk herself through her reactions. She'd remind herself about her mother and how the present situation had nothing to do with those scenes of her youth. She'd recall her husband's kind and warm gestures as well, helping her remember that he wasn't the enemy.

4. *Unconsciously Skilled.* You no longer have to stop to consider whether your reactions are healthy choices or ones grounded in childhood confusion. You have worked consistently to change yourself and disallow the painful parts of your past from affecting your present decisions. Your healthy reactions are natural for you and don't require the mental energy they once did in the past.

Now that Sally had uprooted her memory of her mother, recognized how it affected her in the present, and practiced changing her own personal responses to her husband, she found herself not getting the least bit upset anymore when her husband corrected her. She didn't have to work anymore at changing her response. She no longer had those past memories welling up inside of her and causing her to struggle. Her natural reaction became to stay in the here and now and just deal with her husband's comments.

So, when it's two days after you had a big fight with your spouse and you realize you overreacted because of some childhood issue, welcome to the second rung of your personal growth. It's worlds away from the first rung. It entitles you to apologize, discuss the issues with your spouse, and continue important growth. Understanding how your childhood plays a role in everything you do and who you believe you are will allow you to battle your unhealthy self, the inner voice that restricts your ability to enjoy life. No one is perfect. No one's childhood is perfect. If someone tells you his or hers was, just shake your head pitifully and feel for them.

Everyone has a part of themselves that is emotionally unhealthy. When you recognize how your reactions are tied up in the past, your unhealthy reactions may spontaneously abate. In fact, you may need to exert little or no more energy toward helping yourself in situations that used to trigger these reactions. For example, when Paolo recognized he was hearing his father's critical voice whenever his wife disagreed with him, his reactions immediately softened, as did his criticisms. However, it's also common for many people to need to place a great deal of focused energy on monitoring their reactions and reminding themselves of their past.

Go to Battle

When you find yourself trying to overcome an unhealthy feeling, talk yourself through it.

Maggie had previously written down the memory of her father criticizing her mother and how sad and angry it made her feel. She then wrote down how she sometimes transferred this feeling onto Paolo whenever he suggested she do something a different way. Whenever she began to get mad, she'd excuse herself—even if it meant stepping into the ladies' room at a restaurant—and pull out her little notebook. It reminded her that her true battle was not with her husband. She forced herself to go back to her feelings of childhood and deal with the hurt while simultaneously not using the present as a convenient route to express some of this past anger.

Test yourself constantly during this period of self-analysis. Reconsider your reactions, and decide whether your past has come into play in an unhealthy manner. If you think it may have, talk it out with yourself.

Don't just look in the mirror and say, "I have to love my honey more today." Do the difficult but fulfilling emotional work of reminding yourself of the past: "I had a dad who wasn't there for me, but my husband isn't my dad, nor is he the one who truly makes me feel the sadness I felt as a child." With repetition, your reactions will soften, and you will find yourself acting without having to be so specific about the memory of your past.

There's Hope—Gotta Go

It's not uncommon: a wife who has suffered for years with a difficult, emotionally distant husband comes to me for help. After they attend a few sessions together, her husband for the first time "gets it." He admits his faults and commits to working hard at improving his marriage. This is the breakthrough the wife has wanted for years. She promptly returns to my office and tells me she just can't take the marriage anymore—she wants out.

Is it simply an unfortunate coincidence? Why now? After all, she stuck it out for all these years, but if her commitment to marriage in principle was the glue, why does she become unstuck now, just as her husband stops pulling away?

A deeper reason may be that, paradoxically, she is comfortable with the challenge of a difficult spouse. Not that she likes it, but she knows it. If this is you, think back to your childhood. If you grew up in a home more often than not rent with emotional strife, whether because of an unhappy marriage or a parent who was unkind or neglectful toward you, then you will quite naturally reenact such relationships as an adult. You haven't learned to do it any other way. *It's familiar*, and it's quite unconscious.

But now things are changing exactly as you had (consciously) hoped. As they do, though, you become overwhelmed and start finding all the reasons it'll never work: "He's just doing it now because he knows I'll divorce him. He'll return to the old person as soon as I take the pressure off. I've lost my desire. He's rejected me too much." Your brain isn't wired to do the hard yet loving work of a successful marriage if, in your childhood, you never saw genuine emotional sharing or the warmth or love you claim to desire. Yet understanding this is a step in the right direction. *Take a step back and force yourself to analyze your past so it doesn't ruin your future.* Only then can you take responsibility for your part in the marriage, for past problems, present change, and future happiness.

In addition, many spouses—husbands or wives—cut themselves off from their sad or angry feelings because of an unhappy marriage. You might have kept yourself busy for years in an unconscious attempt to distract yourself from the pain of your marriage. But now that you're paying attention to where your marriage has been and where it's heading, you may feel overcome by anger pent up for years. As uncomfortable as this is, don't stuff your feelings back in the safe and lock it. Work—and it is hard work—to express your whole range of feelings in healthy, constructive ways instead of allowing anger to dictate how you deal with your spouse. Again, you're doing the right thing even though it doesn't bring immediate bliss.

Tracing Your Reactions

When you have an intense emotional reaction to something your spouse has or has not done, ask yourself the following questions. Your answers will give you some insight into whether your past is influencing you in any unhealthy way. Share your answers with your spouse.

1. When else have I felt this way? List three instances.
2. Where in my childhood have I experienced this *feeling*? List three instances. For each instance, ask yourself, "What caused me to feel this way back then?"
3. Does this situation with my spouse remind me of any one of those times? How?
4. How can I change and react in a healthier way if this or similar situations happened again?
5. What have I learned about myself?

The Good Memories

I don't mean to imply that everyone has had a terrible past. Connecting with your past is extremely important in order to remember the good times as well. You want to learn about who you are and how you came to be, and you want to share that with your spouse as you continue this journey. You're not looking only for the bad but for anything that will give you insight into who you are, even if it only leads you to draw on the strength you received as a child.

Charlene grew up in a festive Italian home where food and family gatherings were crucial to family continuity. She loved seeing everyone laugh around the table almost nightly. When she married, she tapped into this memory and discussed it with her husband so he would give this kind of festive mealtime a try. She drew on her childhood memories to encourage herself to work hard at preparing lavish meals, inviting other happy couples and family members, and focusing on using a lot of humor to help these meals build a special sense in her new home. It worked. She made something special in her childhood come alive in her adult life.

Use your past to your advantage anyway you can.

Don't Take It So Personally

Just recognizing how powerful your past is can help you understand that whatever your spouse does that you deem inappropriate or unhealthy, you shouldn't always take it personally.

If your husband isn't loving toward you, it may have little to do with *you*. It may be more that he has issues with his mother in regard to giving and receiving love.

If you feel your wife is inconsiderate, it may have little to do with disrespecting *you* and much more to do with her resentment toward her father for his harshness.

If your spouse is depressed, don't see it as a personal failure. The more you can depersonalize such behavior, the less you'll be hurt, and the more energy you'll have to work on a healthier future with your spouse.

Most of our pain stems from the fact that we take things personally. If a drunk on the street came up to you and said, "You're stupid," you'd think nothing of it. But when your spouse criticizes you, it hurts. You may find out later that your spouse had a terrible day and didn't mean to lash out. At that point, you'd want to understand that your spouse was displacing his or her difficult feelings onto you. Don't take it personally. Discuss the situation, get your spouse's reassurance that it won't repeat itself, and let your hurt begin to dissolve.

When you're having any difficulty with your spouse, whether a disagreement, fight, or difference of opinion, remember that your mate's opinion or actions are influenced by his or her past. Much of the inappropriateness that comes your way has little to do with you and much more to do with your spouse's past. Whether your spouse realizes this is irrelevant to your reminding yourself not to be so hurt by taking your spouse's message so personally.

Your marriage deserves conscious daily effort toward the deep work of understanding your past. The secret to the healthiest marriages is dedication to becoming the healthiest you.

Sylvia and Al Rothfarb
MARRIED: 43 YEARS

How did your childhood affect your marriage?

Things weren't all great in my home as a kid. My mother passed away when I was five. I don't remember her. When my father remarried there was still tension in the home. When I met Sylvia and saw how close she was to her family, it comforted me. As we both grew together in our marriage we realized it was so important to us to focus a lot of energy on our kids and staying close to our siblings. Because of the tension in my home as a kid, I never wanted to bicker and fight in my marriage. We talked a lot and made sure that even through some tough times, we'd remain calm. We showed each other a lot of love and did whatever it took.

Al always would do whatever it took to help me. When I was in Mexico trying to finish a Masters degree, I had to study a book and there was only one copy. Back then there were no copying machines. Al spent days typing the book for me. Not only didn't he know how to type but the book was in Spanish and Al didn't know Spanish.

What's different for couples today?

Couples have too many distractions today. When we were first married we didn't have money or time to get a phone for the first year of our marriage. In retrospect it was wonderful to limit all of those intrusions that couples face today.

8

Great sex comes not from great sexual skill but from sharing your deepest, shyest self while trusting your partner.

We hadn't slept through the night for months. My wife finally stopped nursing, and we formulated our getaway plan. Our parents would stay at our place and watch our seven-month-old and two-year-old while we slept somewhere else, anywhere else, for one night. We landed a cheap summer rate at the Ritz Carlton in Naples, Florida, about a two-hour drive from our home. On my rabbinical student salary, the Ritz was quite extravagant, but for one night's sound sleep we'd spend anything.

For me, arriving at the Ritz was like arriving at the Oscars. People came to my car and greeted me as though I were someone important. I found this somewhat disquieting, since I wasn't used to such attention from uniformed staff. Upon entering, I instantly became completely uncomfortable. Perhaps I could handle the posh surroundings, huge bouquets of flowers, marble everything, chandeliers the size of my entire apartment. But when I saw the people, I just didn't know what to do with myself. They were all so beautiful. It was as though I'd been somehow transported into a fashion magazine. I think it was their clothing that did it for me; it all draped so smoothly and matched so well, with designer logos I didn't recognize. I looked down at myself: the most positive thing I could tell myself was that I was clean. My clothes didn't share the happy little emblems, and even my jacket buttons now paled compared with the shiny gold ones all around me. The man playing the grand piano was wearing a tuxedo. I hadn't worn one since my wedding. The tennis outfits seemed so crisp and white that I couldn't imagine anyone would wear them to actually play a sport. I'd brought my favorite pair of old sweats to wear for tennis, but after viewing the way everyone was dressed, I whispered to my wife that I thought I'd just hide in the room.

Greeting us in our room was a platter of strawberries the size of my hand, clad in white and dark chocolate tuxedos. Even the fruit was dressed better than I was. But a little while later, it all didn't matter because soon I would sleep a delicious slumber with no worries, cries, or diaper changes (our parents were given strict instructions not to call until ten the next morning). It was nine-thirty when my wife and I finally tucked ourselves in and practically shook with delight as the soft cotton sheets gently hugged and rocked us into our deep sleep.

The fire alarm sounded at three o'clock in the morning. I wasn't even surprised. I had already come to believe that there was a divine edict to keep my wife and me from ever sleeping through the night again. But after shouting my disbelief, I realized there was a severe problem. What does one wear to a fire alarm at the Ritz? There wasn't much time to consider. I surely wasn't going to show up downstairs in my ratty old sweats—I'd rather go naked. So we hurriedly grabbed those soft white terrycloth robes from the closet and began to follow the crowds down the ten flights of stairs to the grand lobby. As I scanned the countless heads in the lobby, I noticed that suddenly, they all looked like *me*. Everyone was in a white Ritz robe—a bathrobe in public, for shame. And suddenly they didn't look so good. No makeup, no emblems, no fancy shining smiles, just a bunch of people looking just like me. Everyone seemed a little smaller than they had the day before, as I, on the other hand, began to stand a little taller and straighter. It was my equalizing moment, the one that would allow me to spend the next day comfortably in my sweats, wherever my path took me.

I'd never realized the power of clothing until that moment. Our clothing says a great deal about us, and we use it to send whatever messages about ourselves we want to share with the world about who we are. You judge people before they open their mouths just because of how they are dressed. The power tie and killer suit (women tell me that for them, it's also the accessories) scream smart and controlled when they obviously could mean nothing more than a sales clerk's good taste. Some people dress in happy colors, others in black. Some keep a jacket open, offering a more inviting look, while others keep theirs buttoned up tightly, translating into an emotionally closed image. We cover ourselves up and put on a persona through our dress.

The Naked Truth

We are naked when we make love. This nakedness lies at the very heart of what making love means to a relationship. *Making love is about stripping down to our bare essence and giving and receiving this most private peek into our deepest selves.* Taking our clothes off serves as a metaphor for leaving behind the persona we attempt to show the world. We are going to our lovers with only ourselves, our imperfections on full view. We can be our most genuine selves, something we can hardly do most of the time. We don't have to worry about what we share or how private it may be. We don't have to hide our weaknesses.

Our spouse should take us and love us with all of our imperfections, from a flabby tummy to stretch marks. Lovemaking lies at the heart of our truest ability to be close to our mate because it is the most intimate and real moment we have to share. As we make love, we try to forget about who we are trying to be and just enjoy being who we are right now and who our lover is. No fanfare, no layers, just the two of us with no physical barriers.

You mustn't force sex to do the work of love or love to do the work of sex.

—Mary McCarthy

The Pleasure Is in the Love

Making love is not about sex. It isn't about how much physical pleasure you can get. You may not want to hear that, but let's face it, if it were just about pleasure, there are many people more skilled to give you pleasure than your spouse. We'd rather enjoy a good meal in the company of someone we have great fun dining with than sit down to an outstanding meal alone night after night; lovemaking is no different. Too often, people see lovemaking as just a tool for physical pleasure seeking. But lovemaking is so much more than getting to an orgasm. The real heightened pleasure is in the unity and partnership of the act. It is the giving and receiving, the sharing that makes love.

I recently read that one day a person will be able to swallow a computer chip that will house itself in a part of the brain to make the person think he or she is having wonderful sex. Will that be called lovemaking? It will yield wonderful pleasure, I imagine, but it will also prove how much love-making depends on partnership. The pleasure of making love far out-weighs that of having sex because during lovemaking, the pleasure brought to your body is significantly increased through the emotional experience of bonding. Biology drives us toward sexual experiences to force us to open ourselves up to another and connect. It is our greatest gift, the gift of giv-ing and receiving our truest selves. It is why children are born from this act. It is at that moment of truest connection between two people that we perpetuate our species, a species predicated on connecting and loving others.

There is no greater moment in humanity than when two people choose to bare themselves and offer each other a genuine look into each other's soul and psyche. I've spoken in previous chapters about building the connection between you and your spouse. Now we enter into the most fascinating phase of connec-tion: the connection between two bodies and souls.

Removing Layers

This concept of stripping down to our bare essence is a powerful tool for turning "sex" into "lovemaking." Focusing on the intimacy of sharing our naked selves offers each of us a great level of trust and respect. You have chosen only each other to receive that rare glimpse that no one else will ever see. How wonderful that you have someone who offers you such a gift. Making love is an intense emotional and physical journey into the heart of your spouse as well as your own.

Unfortunately, we seem to have lost the art of undressing. Hollywood's picture of sensuality lies in the passion of two people ripping off their clothes in haste because they can't wait to get down to it. Yet this could reduce the experience to sport, which is great some of the time, but it misses the crucial deeper message of what the two of you are offering each other.

The next time you are about to make love, consider the meaning of the act. Practice undressing each other slowly, and at times undressing yourself in front of your lover. *Undress slowly, taking the time for your mind to focus on how wonderful it is to let yourself go and be entrusted with your partner's deepest self.* Tell each other how wonderful it is going to feel to give over your whole self. This begins your time of intimacy with a meaningful statement of how much you love and trust each other.

Focus on your spouse's body. Forget about the bodies you may have seen elsewhere. See the beauty of your spouse. The phrase "beauty is only skin deep" misses the true point of beauty. Even the beauty of the skin depends on the inside warmth of a person. We carry our auras with us as well. Part of our beauty is our warmth, our smile, our shining eyes, the way we stand and carry ourselves. Allow yourself to see so much more than a naked body in front of you. See the love, the history you've shared, and the gifts you've given each other. Desire to do much more than have sex. Desire to become one with this person—to show him or her how deeply you feel with every touch, stroke, and word. Begin to make love by setting your mind straight on what it is you are offering and receiving: the naked truth of your spouse. Hold each other and take a huge, deep breath, simultaneously appreciating your ability to let go and not have to pretend as you each do the rest of your lives. Smell the sweetness of your spouse's love and desire to know you more than anyone else.

> *The greatest happiness of life is the connection that we are loved—loved for ourselves, or rather, in spite of ourselves.*
>
> —Victor Hugo

Lovemaking as a Marital Relationship Builder

"Sex is the least of our problems," piped in Deb when Stanley mentioned it as part of a long list of marital problems. After three years of marriage, they had asked for my help because life was stale for them. With the stress of Stanley building his own Internet company had come more fighting about "stupid stuff" and a general lack of "connecting." I was quite interested as to why Deb played down the sexual problems. After all, here were two young, healthy, attractive people. As a matter of fact, Deb had won a variety of beauty pageants in her youth and had even competed on an international level.

Every time I gently asked about their romantic lifestyle, I was subtly nudged in a different direction. It was only when I met with Stanley alone that I learned they had sex about once a week and it was okay, but Stanley felt it was missing something. He felt it was reflective of their general lack of togetherness and developing marital boredom.

Lovemaking is a marriage relationship builder. You don't wait to have a great marriage before you make love. Of course, certain factors like respect and emotional trust serve as a prerequisite for an outstanding lovemaking relationship; this is why I put this chapter in the second half of this book. But like every other part of marriage, it is an ever-developing part of the relationship that must be constantly nurtured. The fact that lovemaking holds the power to serve as a metaphor for opening ourselves and learning to give from our deepest beauty is the reason it is a crucial part of developing a great marriage from the very start.

Deb and Stanley each came to the bedroom with their emotional hang-ups. Deb's beauty pageant success had come at great personal cost. She had battled with weight issues and had developed an attitude that she was only as beautiful as she looked. As she explained, "In the beauty business, there's always someone more beautiful." She saw her body for what it was *not*, instead of for what it was. After three years of marriage, Stanley had never seen her completely naked, in full view. She met him under the covers and slept in pajamas. Stanley, on the other hand, had grown up as the class nerd, and girls had never been attracted to him. He almost died from shock when Deb became interested in him. He surely wasn't about to demand that she become more sexually involved with him, even after years of marriage. He was just grateful that Deb would have sex with him once a week. Sex for both of them was more biological than sensual.

Through therapy, Deb and Stanley realized that they had to connect. They both needed incredible reassurance about how wonderful and attractive each of them were to the other. They needed to help each other open up an area of themselves they had tucked away out of fear of rejection. Slowly, they could learn to finally undress and give something deeper than skin beauty to each other. It worked wonders for them.

Lovemaking became the metaphor for opening up and feeling unafraid to voice their inner thoughts and feelings to each other. Deb was able to recognize how attractive she was to Stanley, the only man who counted, and Stanley was able to voice this attraction without thinking he'd be seen as someone concerned only with appearances. Suddenly, they took sheer joy and delight in giving each other pleasure.

The sexual relationship extended itself into the rest of their lives as well. They became comfortable complimenting each other all the time. It even became a source of comic relief for them. Deb said that one day after Stanley had had a disastrous meeting with a potential investor, he came home devastated and feeling like a failure. All Deb had to say to him was, "I know one thing you do very very well," and it put a smile on Stanley's face. They both realized that what was most important was that they had each other, and as long as they could please and be there for each other, all would be right with the world.

Making Love All Day and All Night

When sex is elevated to making love, it also changes your entire approach to your sexual relationship. It's no longer just about jumping into bed and having intercourse. It's about sharing a deeper part of yourselves and becomes intertwined with every part of your relationship. You don't have to wait for "sex" to give over your deepest, truest self to your spouse. You don't have to wait to peel away your layers and just be yourself alone with your spouse. You don't have to wait to feel the sensuality pouring from your spouse. You can bring lovemaking to every part of your day.

Be actively involved in "undressing" yourself and your spouse throughout your day.

1. *Tell your spouse how wonderful he or she is and how much you appreciate his or her essence throughout the day.* Thank your mate for sharing this essence with you, and express how much it means to you to really know him or her. Build your desire to know your spouse by talking about how you can't wait to touch and be "one" together, how you long to just be yourself with your mate and relax together. Show your partner how much you see well beyond what others see, how you can look into your lover's heart and know its warmth and beauty.

2. *Touch each other more throughout the day.* Studies show that couples who touch more during the day have more intercourse. It's because those couples are elevating sex to lovemaking. After all, we can only have sex so many times

in a given period of time, but there is no limit to making love. When you hold your spouse's hand, kiss, hug, or rub each other's neck and shoulders, you are connecting. You are feeling each other's warmth and letting each other into your deeper self. When you let yourself be touched, you are allowing your spouse to feel you, smell you, see your every pore, waltz right into your inner, otherwise protected circle.

Touch is one of our most important relationship tools. In the late 1950s, researcher Harry Harlow conducted a famous study of newborn monkeys that revealed a powerful message about touch. Newborn monkeys were given two surrogate mothers. One model was made of wire that contained a steady supply of milk; the other was also made of wire but because it was wrapped in terry cloth, it was warm but lacked any source of nourishment. The infant monkeys tended to spend time with the soft yet foodless mother, even coming close to starvation as a result of their preference.

The study showed the world the importance of warm touch from mother to child. But it also told us something crucial about all of us. We yearn to touch and be touched. It is in our biological makeup. It not only is tied into our happiness but into our very core ability to survive. Touch your spouse more and let him or her know how good it feels to touch and be touched by someone so special. Let yourself enjoy the process of feeling the warmth of fingers, lips, another body.

3. *Create sensual touch.* There's touching and then there's "touching." You can give your spouse a peck on the cheek or you can plant the same kiss in the same spot for a second longer, with a tenderness that speaks romance.

When your spouse passes you the salt at breakfast, you can simply receive it as you would from your child. Or, you could take the same action and have your fingers linger for only a second longer—focusing on the touch instead of the salt shaker.

Learn to make touch sensual. For five minutes at night for three nights in a row, lie next to your spouse, close your eyes, and touch your spouse. Ever so gently, rub and feel the softness of your lover's skin and stroke his or her hair with great tenderness and sensuousness. Think how much you care for your spouse and how beautiful this person is as you touch. Learn to send intimacy through your touch so that there is a certain romance in your everyday connections. After five minutes of touch, keep your eyes closed and gently kiss your spouse repeatedly for one minute. Rub your lips softly above your spouse's skin and feel the intimacy, smell your spouse's sensual scent.

4. *Stand closer to your spouse.* The next time you are in a conversation with someone other than your spouse, move closer until you are only about a foot

away from this person. Notice his or her reaction. You'll never stay that physically close, because the other person will back away. We naturally feel uncomfortable allowing people to become too close to us, physically as well as emotionally. We are too concerned about revealing too much and letting each other be touched in a way that is reserved only for our mate. You can build a greater trust and intimacy with your spouse just by standing closer to each other, becoming "one" in your space while you cook, eat, or read together.

5. *Think about making love throughout the day.* Over 50 percent of men and 20 percent of women think about sex once or more during the day.[1] The more you think about making love with your spouse, the more excited you get. It creates desire and passion. Call and remind your spouse how sexy you find him or her. Think about how wonderful it will feel to relax in each other's arms and give yourselves to each other.

6. *Consider ways to open yourself to your spouse.* What would help you connect to your spouse today? How might your spouse answer that? Lunch, a rose, a card, a balloon, a CD? What would tell your spouse that you're thinking of him or her and that you want to connect even when you're not together? Extend your lovemaking to every part of your world, and you will build a greater passion than you have ever known.

The Power of Lovemaking

Making love is a kind of therapy for us all. We carry around internal concerns about who we are, and as a result we hide not only from others but from ourselves. I can't tell you how many times I've been told at parties, "Uh-oh, I'll bet you'll analyze that statement and know more about me than I do." One psychologist I know grew so tired of people not talking to him at public events for fear he'd reveal them for who they really were that now he tells people at parties that he works for Amtrak. We can't even stare too long at ourselves in the mirror because it is too intense to look deeply within ourselves.

But through lovemaking, we offer a part of ourselves that even *we* do not know. In general, it's not your spouse's job to *create* your positive self-esteem but rather to *boost* an already healthy one. Yet this isn't true when it comes to intimacy. There are parts of ourselves that lie so deep we never reveal them except to a spouse whom we trust implicitly. We offer our real selves during lovemaking and wait to see how our spouse will accept us. *It is our spouse's job to compliment us wildly and make us believe that the deepest, most intimate part of ourselves is our most beautiful part. It is our spouse's job to focus on the greatness and beauty of our body and soul and ignore our imperfections and weaknesses.* To do less would cause any healthy person to begin to close off that deeper part of him- or herself because none of us can find comfort if our essence is being rejected. We would have no choice but to bury that part of ourselves, perhaps never to be revealed again. None of us is strong enough or confident enough to be met with anything but extreme praise and love when our essence is revealed.

This is why lovemaking can be harmful to your deeper sense of who you are if you have sex with someone to whom you aren't emotionally committed, or who is not emotionally committed to you. Such people aren't worthy of your deepest trust, and the sexual experience could cause you to question or even dislike your essence when you're not met with the favorable, meaningful response you deserve. It becomes harder to recapture that experience of giving over your total self when you've been there, done that, and got burned from it in any way.

Lovemaking is the adult version of self-esteem building and can be as crucial to the human experience as hearing our parents' praise when we were little. Lovemaking will imprint on us a sense of who we are deep down, and we will continue to search through life for experiences that meet with our own expectations of what we deserve. When lovemaking reveals a good soul and warm heart, we are one more rung up on the ladder of feeling whole. Whether lovemaking makes us feel that our essence is beautiful depends largely, if not solely, on the response of our trusted spouse, who knows us more intimately with every touch. Be acutely aware of the power you and your spouse hold in this area of ever-developing self-esteem.

The Gift of Receiving

Lovemaking is therefore not only about you sharing yourself but about the gift you will offer your lover by receiving his or her deepest, most intimate self. Have the utmost respect for the powers you possess in helping your spouse formulate a positive self-image of his or her essence. Don't forget to tell your lover how wonderful he or she is. Describe your partner's beauty inside and out. You can't do it too much. Describe the beautiful parts of your lover's body, heart, mind, and spirit. Use lovemaking as an opportunity to take the time to describe what you love about your spouse's essence, his or her good deeds, kindness, strength, and warmth.

When your spouse bares him- or herself, be extremely complimentary. And I don't mean to simply tell white lies but rather to observe how truly beautiful your spouse is to you. You know so much more of that goodness than anyone else. Forget the weaknesses and the past arguments. You don't want your spouse holding onto every wrong or insensitive thing you've ever done. This is the time for finding only the best each of you has to offer. Focus only on the positive. *Never criticize, minimize, or jest in any derogatory way during lovemaking.*

Touch your spouse gently in a way that shows you thirst to know your mate more and more and appreciate being allowed a glimpse into his or her deeper self. Kiss your spouse warmly, letting him or her know how much you value your lover and how delicious he or she is to you. Smile a lot and show your spouse how happy you are to see him or her in this revealing way. When your spouse is met with your extreme approval of his or her innermost self, he or she will take such delight and strength in it that it can only lead to more intimacy and bonding. Your spouse will give back as much and more to you for the wonderful gift you have given.

The first time the Bible discusses sex, it does not use any Hebrew word that means sex. Instead it states, "Adam *knew* his wife Eve." Lovemaking is not about sex. It is about discovery, a knowledge of one's deepest, most intimate and vulnerable self.

Connection

It's no coincidence that the culmination of lovemaking is a physical bonding in which when our most private physical selves, our genitals, are intertwined, and we literally "connect" with each other. It is the exceptional crescendo of the loving talk and touch, the peeling of layers and offering of total self. To be literally within one another is another powerful metaphor as to how lovemaking creates a feeling of oneness. It is that feeling of unity, that we can never be truly alone ever again, that speaks to the power of love.

This feeling of "being as one" explains the research that faithful married couples have the most emotionally and physically satisfying sex.[2] Through a lifelong marital commitment, we can use lovemaking as a tool for reaching oneness.

The Delicateness of Vulnerability

Stripping and revealing ourselves puts each of us in a very unprotected state. The reason that so many have unsatisfying lovemaking relationships is because of the fear and reality of disgrace and humiliation when we're met with anything other than warm praise.

Richard and Denise felt they had a wonderful relationship, but they were unsatisfied sexually. Sex for them was like clockwork without any alarm bells. Each reached orgasm but didn't feel closer because of it. They were reduced to having sex now and then, and only if they both had the urge. Interestingly, their best sex was after a fight. Using sex to make up brought a certain intimacy to their sexual lifestyle that was missing otherwise. After fighting, they would try to give back to each other what they had taken away from each other during argument. They could only force open this deeper part of themselves through guilt. At other times, though, lovemaking was too intimate for them, so they reduced it to sex and held themselves back.

Another couple I knew hadn't had intercourse for many years. They pleased each other sexually in other ways. They had convinced themselves for years that if sex felt better other ways, why ever return to intercourse? But with all of the "pleasing" going on, both of them still felt something was missing from their "closeness" during sex and other parts of their life. They were limited in their ability to be emotionally open, and intercourse presented a certain intimacy that made both of them uncomfortable.

Our sexual selves are delicate. We are used to being closed and protected. We are used to hiding and rarely confronting our true inner selves. Lovemaking forces certain doors open that we are used to keeping shut tight.

Harold was a playboy. He was in his forties, wealthy, and uninterested in marriage. He had sex regularly with a variety of women. He called me when he began to have sexual dysfunction with one particular woman in whom he was interested for more than a "good time." He was perplexed that he could continue to perform with other women and yet have trouble whenever he attempted to have sex with this particular woman. When I asked him how sex was different when he was with her, he said, "We like to talk a lot, not nasty, but nice stuff, sweet stuff." Harold had no problems with "sex," but lovemaking presented him with a scenario he had avoided for years: opening up his real self to a woman.

You have to be so careful in your sexual relationship. Its delicateness makes it hard for us to open up. Focus intently on accepting and giving to your spouse.

The Great Trust

We crave control and work hard to maintain as much control over life as possible. Rarely do we ever allow someone else to take control over us. As much as some of us may look back longingly at the innocence of childhood, most of us are happier as adults because we can make our own decisions and not be under the control of others. We surely don't want anyone to control us physically.

Yet we make love. We tend to focus on the pleasure and release of orgasm, but we often fail to remember the moment immediately before orgasm, when we've allowed our spouse to take us to a point where we have no control over our body. From that moment on, we have no choice, no control but to have the surge, release, and uncontrollable pleasure of an orgasm. It is so unlike human beings to give away such control, and yet it is part and parcel of the lovemaking experience, because it's all about the connection.

Lovemaking is the metaphor for how much you need your soulmate in this life. And connecting and relating to your soulmate will demand loosening your sense of control over your world. It will demand at times putting your life in the hands of your spouse. But if lovemaking is done with love, you will experience *life orgasms*, moments of utter delight when you feel alive with emotion and a part of something far greater than you alone as an individual.

Lovemaking is about giving yourself away, your deepest, most personal and private self. During lovemaking, let your partner take you on a path you never knew. Give away that self-control and put yourself into the hands of your lover. Be revealing and trusting.

Can You Handle the Truth?

It all sounds so romantic, so simple, doesn't it? I don't mean to imply that great lovemaking comes easily. It happens not only in the bedroom but with every other part of our marital relationship. Lovemaking will largely reflect the rest of your relationship. So if you're feeling distant from each other, that will show up in the bedroom.

As discussed in Secret #7, much of our ability to be close to another lies within our development in childhood. Just as problems relating to each other show up in other parts of life, the same is true of our lovemaking relationship.

Bob knows his wife desires more foreplay and fun touching before intercourse, but he doesn't do it. And then he gets disappointed when his wife isn't "into" it. He may need to consider how his father complained bitterly about how his mom was not a happy person. Bob may unconsciously be trying to create a marriage in which his wife plays the sad role, one devoid of the light of romance and sexual energy. He'll help his marriage if he recognizes that because his mother was emotionally distant from him, he is avoiding a sexual relationship with his spouse that could bring them dramatically closer in all parts of their lives.

You must not only discover what "turns on" your spouse but also focus your attention on the details of those behaviors. When you see yourself skipping steps or behaviors that are important to your spouse, be honest with yourself so that you can make a warm effort to create a lovemaking relationship that will bring both of you much closer. Be willing to consider how your childhood might play a role in your difficulty in doing the things that would bring greater intimacy into your life.

Samantha saw her parents fight when she was young. Her entire family was never "touchy feely," and she had extreme difficulty offering her husband, Tom, the physical affection he so sorely needed. Tom's mother passed away when he was nine, and his fondest memory of her was when she stroked his cheek and rubbed his back every night before bed.

Tom and Samantha had a trying sex life. Tom demanded more love, and Samantha was tired of trying to make up for his loss of his mother. But once they understood how their past issues were affecting their present behavior, they became more aware of how to better their present-day relationship without allowing the past to taint it.

Samantha learned to focus on touching her husband and to make a conscious choice to become comfortable with touching and feeling. It took a great deal of time and energy for her to resist the urge to fall back into her past and see touching as "too much," but she learned to invite a new reality into her life, one in which being close and needy of her spouse was good and welcome.

At the same time, Tom needed to understand his wife. Her lack of touching was not her way of saying, "I don't care," but rather spoke to her own personal struggle against being (enmeshed) with her husband. As long as Tom in some way felt his mother's touch with every stroke of his wife's hand, he was giving that touch too much emotional power. When his wife wouldn't touch him, it meant too much to him because it represented his need to be connected to his mother, whom he still grieved for in some way. As Tom talked more about his mother and his personal loss as a child, he released his need for his wife to somehow fill that gap. He could be touched now for the sake of love today rather than for the love he was trying to recreate from his past.

Embarrassment and the fear of looking silly or ridiculous also hold us back from sexual pleasure. Many hide their groans, remain silent, and don't tell their partner what feels good. Too embarrassed to feel like their body is taking over and their spouse is in charge of them, many fall into a bland sexual style. Make it an open topic for discussion with your spouse. Make a pact that each of you can share what brings you pleasure without fear of rejection. Tell each other that no matter what is asked, neither of you will make fun in any way, scold, or criticize. This is so important. How can both of you be wonderfully close if you fear being belittled? On the other hand, each of you is equally allowed to say no to something that makes you feel uncomfortable. However, the answer doesn't need to be a flat-out no but rather an explanation of why you feel uncomfortable. Perhaps there is a compromise, something that will satisfy both of you.

Many couples opt to show each other what they like by guiding their partner with their hand or with words. Another option is to write down what brings you pleasure and have your partner read what you've written. It lessens the fear of being embarrassed, especially if you choose not to be present when your spouse reads what it is you desire.

Many people feel uncomfortable when their spouse focuses a great deal of sexual energy to bring them pleasure. As if they don't "deserve" it, they shy away from allowing their spouse to pleasure them and find excuses to avoid it. They figure it's okay because, after all, only *they* will miss out on this pleasure. False. It's important that you learn to receive pleasure from your spouse. Remind yourself that your spouse is so in love with you that he or she wants to give you such pleasure. It is equally as important that your spouse experience the delight of being able to bring you such pleasure. Your spouse wants to know that he or she can give you such a good feeling. There is great joy in giving to your spouse special pleasure that only you can offer. Let yourself be given to. Create the same partnership role in your bedroom as in the rest of your life. You should both feel that lovemaking is for both of you equally, even though, just as in the rest of your lives, it doesn't mean you will each receive the same pleasure every time you make love. But it does mean that both of you will be equally dedicated to making your lovemaking experience a wonderful one.

Focus on Receiving Pleasure

Create a list titled "What Builds My Desire." Include everything from kisses, loving words, flower petals, certain scents, music in the bedroom, thoughtful gestures (as my wife says, the greatest aphrodisiac is a man who does dishes—needless to say, we now have two dishwashers) to actual physical techniques during foreplay. (Avoid any item that might in any way make your spouse feel uncomfortable. For example, if you think your spouse dressing in a certain way will build your desire and you're unsure how comfortable your spouse would feel dressing that way, deal with that issue in a loving manner—either by avoiding the request completely because you wouldn't want to make your spouse do something uncomfortable, or by discussing it at a moment when both of you have each other's full attention. Don't throw in the suggestion as part of a "fun" exercise. At the same time, remember how good it is for us to get out of our comfort zone sometimes to try something new, something you may love.)

Trade lists and focus on what you can do to build your spouse's desire. It's not uncommon for women to have a more emotional slant in this list—loving words, soft touches—and for men to have a more sexual slant—having his wife dress a certain way or make sexual references. But don't be bound by stereotypes. Both of you should try to consider a fuller menu. Try to expand your horizons.

Write an Erotic, Romantic Story

In a separate notebook or journal, take turns writing a few lines about the two of you making great love. Remember, the story doesn't have to be a graphic sexual fantasy (unless both of you are *completely* comfortable with that. Remember, men, that a lot of women say okay even when they are greatly opposed to things, just because they want to please their husbands—you can tell if it's really something your wife is comfortable with or comfortable trying). Rather, your story is about making love—perhaps being in a faraway land, dancing the night away, or swimming in the ocean.

Create vignettes of the perfect lovemaking day and add to them together, taking turns writing as you lie next to each other. Better yet, leave this notebook in a private place and add to it secretly so your spouse is excited when he or she opens it next. Be sure to add or start a new vignette every week.

For the Fun of It

I certainly don't mean to imply that every time you make love, it has to be an intense, meaningful couple-bonding moment. We're not wired to bring such intensity to everything all the time. Often, it takes great time to learn about each other and become comfortable enough to give and receive more and more of this sexual pleasure. Every encounter doesn't have to be a deep, emotional sexual experience focused on opening yourselves up and trusting each other. Sometimes you just want to have fun, delighting in each other. Fun will bring you much closer, and I'm all for it, but do try to have a deeper emotional lovemaking session at least once a week—a time when both of you are fully focused on romance, each other's feelings, and the love you have for each other. This will enhance all the other times you make love, so that even without focusing on it, those other times will become more rich and special.

To get to know how to give pleasure to his or her body, focus each week on a different part of his or her body and spend at least three different intimate moments during the week focusing on that part. Try different strokes and movements with different parts of your body to find what makes your spouse squirm with pleasure. Break it down to as many body parts as you want, but take at least a week each for: head and face, neck-shoulders-back, chest-tummy, arms-hands, feet, legs–inner thighs, genitals. Each of you focuses on the same parts for each other during the same week.

Be sure to let your spouse know when he or she has hit on something wonderful, so your partner knows to do that more often. Be careful, however, not to constantly critique your spouse's performance. Everyone takes this very seriously. It's okay and necessary to say what feels good and what doesn't. Often, however, your spouse won't get it just right, but right enough. Focus more on your spouse's technique than on what you feel would be the ideal one. Don't search for the best pleasure at the expense of making your spouse feel belittled or a poor sex partner. Always be extremely appreciative and grateful for what your partner gives you; show the same enthusiasm you'd like to see when *you* give love to your spouse.

An active partner is a sexy partner. Learn to compliment your spouse by letting him or her know how good you're feeling. Allow yourself to make noises, moan (remember, never make any joke about your spouse's noises or bedroom behavior), and tell your spouse what you like.

One couple was unsatisfied with their "silent sex." But the wife felt that if she offered her husband direction, he would feel criticized. If this happens to you, sandwich your direction in between two positive comments: "This feels so good . . . could you _____ . . . that's wonderful."

Another way to develop each other's ability to receive direction is to practice during sensual massage. Give your spouse a massage for fifteen minutes. During that time, your spouse has to give you five different directions (no more, no less) using any of the following terms: "higher," "lower," "faster," "slower," "stay there."

The Opposite Sex

The term "opposite sex" holds no truer in any part of life than in the bedroom. Everyone jokes about how women "need" intimacy and men "need" intercourse. One study declared that a much larger percentage of men said they would use the services of a prostitute if prostitution were legalized compared to 57 percent of women.[3] But before you think women just aren't into it, another study showed that women were just as aroused physically as men when viewing erotic films, although when asked, many of these women denied (or were unaware of) their sexual responses.[4]

These stereotypes can be very constricting; they need not apply to you. However, even the stereotypical man who doesn't want the emotional buildup to sex can learn to open up his warmth and loving soul to his wife with her lead. Even the stereotypical woman can allow her husband to show her how to take extreme pleasure and delight without being ashamed or bashful. I am still often perplexed at how many couples don't focus on these differences.

Too many men can't understand why their wives can't just "do it," and too many women can't understand how their husbands can. Spouses can take it personally. I've counseled many men who felt their wives didn't want to give to them enough, that they were selfish and cold. I've also counseled many women who felt they were being asked to be sperm depositories so their husbands could relieve themselves.

The answer is in truly understanding how we are biologically wired. Husbands must understand that sex for many women is largely tied up in emotions. The wife who doesn't want to make love after an argument or when she's tired isn't rejecting her husband but honestly expressing an inability to have a pleasurable sexual experience. She requires much more mind work to help herself to achieve an orgasm. She needs to separate herself from her life stresses. She needs to feel respected and cared about. Wives need to understand that a husband who wants to have intercourse even if his wife isn't into it is looking to release the tension from his life stresses. No one is insulting the other.

Ideally, both spouses should opt for a sexual experience in which both feel the same level of desire. But, let's face it, life doesn't always offer us this equal opportunity, so we must be sensitive to our spouse's needs without taking it personally and creating negative feelings. A wife may sometimes make love to her husband even when she isn't up for it, simply because she understands his need to do so. Similarly, a husband may sometimes refrain from making love to his wife, simply because he is sensitive to her needs.

Sex isn't always about orgasm. Too many people focus on the orgasm as the purpose of sex. Having an orgasm is clearly wonderful, but giving pleasure without reaching orgasm is lovemaking as well. Sometimes only one of you will achieve orgasm. Other times, sex may just be about being close and feeling each other's bodies and warmth without orgasm. Being sensitive to your differences will allow each of you to have a satisfying sexual bond. Some couples neglect the fun of touching and petting because they feel that once they start, they have to work up to the grand finale of orgasm. Talk this out; why not enjoy sensual or erotic touch that has no other goal than making you both feel relaxed? Wouldn't it be wonderful if you could each feel free to touch the other without feeling that telltale body-stiffening response that signals "No, thanks"? You can say, "I just want some cuddling. We don't have to make love tonight."

Achieving orgasm is quite different for men and women. Couples must realize that men can reach orgasm in two minutes, whereas women can take twelve minutes or more. Foreplay is the key to getting to pleasure together. Use your lists for building desire as well as putting in the effort and focus to create a lovemaking environment throughout the day.

Lovers' Favorite Tips

Making love can become stale. Following are a few quick, creative ideas couples have found to spice things up.

1. *Read.* There are many tasteful books that discuss the physical techniques of making love. Enjoy the process of reading these books together and trying new ways of making love. Browse authors educated in their field, such as therapists, doctors, and nurses, or go with one whose voice moves you. There are books written for couples to explore together, ones to help one mate pleasure the other. Heat up that library card!

2. *Abstinence makes the heart grow fonder.* Go on an intercourse and orgasm fast for four days during which you must "fool around" every night but stop short of completely satisfying each other. If you really want to build desire, take the four days and abstain from touching each other in any genital area. Touch only those parts of your spouse's body that are comfortably exposed in public. This exercise is both a wonderful way to build desire and a way to get you both back into the mood of moving slowly with each other. It will get you out of the habit of falling into bed naked and tired and just "doing it" quickly. It will remind you of the fun of the "game," the buildup of desire and tension, and help you appreciate the moments of fully unleashing your sexuality when your period of abstinence is over. Using this four-day (more or less, as it suits you) period once a month is a great tool for keeping lovemaking exciting.

3. *Pick each other up.* As part of your date night (see Secret #6), plan to meet somewhere and pretend that you are meeting for the first time. Play a role, creating your own identity, and keep it up for an hour. "Picking each other up" reminds both of you how attractive you are and how much fun you can be.

4. *Make a romantic shopping list.* Create together a list of items reserved just for romance, and enjoy shopping for them together—for example, massage oils,

sensual foods, wine and two beautiful glasses, romantic CDs, matching silk pajamas.

5. *Make a romantic photo album.* Make an album with romantic pictures of the two of you. Include pictures you've taken or seen of beautiful or romantic places.

6. *Keep a sensual journal.* This is a special journal reserved for writing little loving messages to each other, such as poems, love notes, or reminders of little private jokes. Leave it out on your dresser, and be sure to leave a kind message for your spouse in it every day.

7. *Use all five senses.* When making love, consider bringing the pleasure of romance to every one of your and your spouse's senses. Try to make every sense—sight, hearing, touch, taste, and smell—overjoyed. All of our senses are connected, so it's more likely to feel even greater touch pleasure if we are simultaneously having great smell and hearing pleasure, and have just had wonderful taste pleasure as well. Plan your lovemaking to include full-bodied delight.

Only One Technique

I've suggested that you read books on sexual techniques because I'm not writing a lovemaking manual here. There are many wonderful techniques that couples should learn. But I will offer a simple one that you may likely know. This basic technique has helped many couples better understand each other sexually.

Different studies have reported varied statistics about what percentage of women achieve orgasm solely through vaginal stimulation by the penis. What every study does agree on is that it is a limited minority, and quite a feat. Women depend heavily on clitoral stimulation to achieve orgasm, so it's helpful to use positions for intercourse that will allow a man's penis to stimulate the woman's clitoris. The problem is that most women need, and enjoy lovemaking much more when there is, varied and focused attention on the clitoris—not just the clitoral stimulation the penis can offer during intercourse. Also, when I've read some of the descriptions of positions that allow for clitoral stimulation by the penis, I've often thought that you'd have to be double-jointed to accomplish them successfully.

Bottom line: The surest way for spouses to reach orgasm simultaneously is to use a position that allows the man or the woman to have free access to the clitoris so that it can be lovingly stimulated during intercourse. Take turns. Sometimes women want to get there faster and so want to stimulate themselves, while at the same time their husbands don't want to have to focus on anything else but their own pleasure. Other times, women want to be fully made love to, and husbands want to be fully responsible for bringing their wives to orgasm. There is no right or wrong. Just recognize that men and women climax differently, and it usually takes women far more time to do so than men. Wives, take control: tell him to slow it down because you're enjoying it so much. It will also serve to build his desire. Forget the unrealistic Hollywood messages of "perfect sex." Create a lovemaking relationship that is "perfect" for you through a great deal of sensitivity and understanding of reality.

These differences are what fuel our growth in marriage. Understanding how your spouse works sexually, both in mind and body, will offer you new sensitivity and perspective.

Bad Sex

While I advocate exploring the boundaries of your lovemaking relationship, there are things you should not do for sexual enjoyment. If your spouse feels humiliated or uncomfortable with a certain sexual technique or play, it's unhealthy for your relationship to insist on it.

You should be able to discuss ways to make lovemaking more exciting, fun, and intimate. If your spouse has asked you to do something you're uncomfortable with, consider whether your spouse's request is odd or normal. You may want to consult some books or seek a counselor's opinion. If you feel it's a normal request but something you "think" is gross or humiliating, consider why you feel that way. Perhaps you've simply accepted others' opinions that a certain sex act is "dirty" or that "nice people don't do that." What matters here is what the two of you think. Examine your prejudices. Perhaps they connect to your past. If you feel the request isn't reasonable, politely explain this to your spouse. Help your spouse understand that *you* feel uncomfortable ("It's me, not you") and that you're sorry, but you can't go along with this one. Try to find some compromise, such as a new technique you *are* willing to try.

More often, men are less bashful sexually and more open to trying new things. Husbands, remember that the pleasure is in the love. You may have tried or seen wild positions or fantasies that seemed to promise the greatest sex of your life. But your wife is also your soulmate, lover, and partner. Preserving your friendship with your spouse is more important than forcing the issue. Too often, wives agree to things because their husbands ask repeatedly and seemingly won't take no for an answer. These wives end up giving in but find it uncomfortable and resent their husbands for putting them in such a position. That can destroy a sexual relationship. Don't risk it when dealing with a relationship as important as lovemaking.

If either of you are feeling uncomfortable and unsure whether your reaction is "normal," seek the guidance of a licensed mental health professional for an educated, objective opinion.

Control

Sex can often involve control, whether being dominated or dominating. Be sensitive to this. Many women enjoy being made love to, and others find it far better to be more in control. Women who have had traumatizing sexual experiences in childhood are often helped by taking greater control of the sexual relationship, such as choosing positions where they don't feel pinned down, undressing their husbands, or choosing soothing background music. All of us come to lovemaking with our "baggage." Accept your spouse and help him or her to find the best and most comfortable ways to enjoy this very vulnerable and intimate relationship.

Keep Your Lovemaking Private

Because spouses let their most vulnerable, shy, and deepest selves be expressed through lovemaking, keep it private as the most personal precious gift your spouse has given you. Cherish your intimacy and don't betray your spouse's confidence. Only for therapeutic reasons, and with your spouse's permission, should you share your private lovemaking moments with a qualified professional.

Kids: Natural Birth Control

"So there we are in the bookstore on our 'date night' like you suggested," Henry began as he described a recent evening with his wife, Mia. "We're trying to stay out as late as our babysitter will stay, and it's getting hard because we're so tired with the kids and all. Anyway, as we're leaving, we pass the section dealing with the sex books, and Mia and I begin laughing because we realize that since the kids came along, not only are we too tired to do it, we're too tired to even read about it." Henry and Mia were raising two little ones, a sixteen-month-old girl and a three-year-old boy. They were overwhelmed. "Before we had kids, it was the first section of the book store we went to. Now *Winnie the Pooh* is as sexy as we can get."

So long for now to the days of spontaneity, the moments when you could look at each other and make an eye contact that said, "It's time." So long to the days of quiet peace when mood music served to fill the silence. When children arrive, life changes drastically forevermore, and huge adjustments are needed. But too many couples have an unrealistic expectation that things should fall into place naturally: "I expected that after some time, we'd be able to return to the way it was. If we'd just wait a while, we'd get back to it," Mia said wistfully. If you do nothing proactive to reclaim your sex life, you may as well put all your energy into saving for college, because that'll be the next time your sex life has any life at all. Sticking your head in the sand won't lead to romance, just a sandy head. You need to be assertive in your approach and find the ways to bring romance back into your marital lifestyle. However, returning to romance isn't about returning to where you once were.

Henry expected that after the kids stopped nursing, he and Mia could return to the solid and meaningful romantic relationship they had had before they had children. But there was no going back. They were tired, and the kids could wake up at any moment. The kids would get sick or be up all night. Reality set in, and Henry and Mia were forced to recognize that from this day forward, they would have to create a new romantic relationship that took their children into account.

Lovemaking Appointments

Schedule a time when the two of you can be most at peace with each other. This may be late at night after the children are sleeping, although never discount the daytime. Perhaps your child takes a nap or is in school, or a you can arrange a babysitter to take your children for a walk to the park. Create a situation in which both of you can enjoy some privacy.

Henry and Mia didn't like the sound of this. "Spontaneity is everything," they both felt. But spontaneity is the Hollywood way, where steamy sex can't wait another moment. Yet in real life, it can and will, and it will be delightful in an hour or day, perhaps even sweeter as the desire is allowed to build. Don't be taken in by what others see as romance. If you want romance, if you want to make love, make it happen. Remember, if you want a vacation or a party, you have to plan them. It's the same with lovemaking.

Henry and Mia took a lunch break from work as a lovemaking rendezvous. Their three-year-old was in preschool, and they arranged for someone to take their little one out to a nearby park for an hour. When Henry and Mia stood in their now-quiet house, it dawned on them that they hadn't been in their home alone since the birth of their oldest child. The silence and the knowledge that they were completely alone were intoxicating. "It was like rediscovering each other," Henry summed up. "Yes, it was planned, but it was meaningful," Henry continued, as he and Mia exchanged a private glance.

Perhaps you'll make love less once you start your family, but not necessarily. Don't give in to the idea that once you have children, your focus must be totally absorbed by them. The love you make can be ever so powerful and should become even more meaningful as life goes on. You are now much more than lovers: you are parent partners, a lifelong bond that can never be broken. Because lovemaking is so much more than sex, the more history and life you and your spouse live together, the better it all becomes. You want to bring that new identity into the bedroom, the identity that says, "Look what we've done together—we've created life."

Lovemaking appointments can be just as romantic as the spontaneous moments because you have the added benefit of anticipation. Work to build the desire on the day of the appointment with touches, loving messages, and comments that say, "I can't wait to love you so closely."

When You Aren't into It

There are times when you don't want to make love. A pregnant woman and her husband may be preoccupied with the baby. After the birth, a woman experiences hormonal changes that can play tricks with her desire. A man reaches his sexual peak in his late teens, whereas a woman reaches her peak in her late thirties and early forties. Both men and women will have their sexual peaks and valleys. If you don't want to make love, continue to push yourself to stay open to the idea. Naturally, no one wants a person to make love when there is pain after childbirth or other trauma. But it isn't healthy to conclude, "It's not a good time, so I'll just wait until my desire returns." Don't wait. Create the desire. Find out where it went and call it back. Go away for a day or two with your spouse if that will kick-start it. Be creative. Work on it, and find some creative way of returning to lovemaking. It's just too important to your relationship. It's fuel to the rest of your marriage.

It Takes Time

When most of us think of passionate lovemaking, we picture youth. Once again, we've allowed Hollywood to dictate what is sexy. Lovemaking gets much better with time in a marriage. As we grow together as husband and wife, we gain greater trust and comfort. As the years go on, we are more comfortable revealing our inner selves. We can share more about what we like without embarrassment because we've grown into a strong, trusting friendship. Even letting yourself fully enjoy your orgasm may be something you only feel comfortable with after being married for some time. We're often embarrassed to allow ourselves to enjoy such lack of control. And, of course, practice makes perfect. As the years progress, we simply get better at what we do for our spouse. Drop the unrealistic notion that sex should be magical from the start. Recognize how much better it is going to get as you put proper focus on making it meaningful.

The message is clear. Lovemaking is crucial to your marriage and deserves as much attention as any other part of your relationship. Whatever the obstacles, find creative ways around them, and keep making the effort to give your deepest, most private self to your spouse and to receive the same.

Fred & Chavie Cohen
MARRIED: 43 YEARS

How We Met
We met in Williamsburg, Brooklyn, at a dance party. It was good, clean fun. My father put my friends and me in a taxi to go to this function. Fred was very busy helping at this party, taking pictures. A whole van of the young people were going to get ice cream and he jumped in and came along. I was fifteen years old at the time and I said to my friends, "You see that tall good looking boy who was busy taking pictures? I'm going to marry him." Well he got my phone number and called. We got married when I turned eighteen.

What Made It Work?
My mother always told me, "Whatever you do in the privacy of your bedroom, as long as it's beautiful to you, you keep doing it and making it beautiful." My husband says, "Don't let them go looking for it somewhere else." Kiss, hold hands, a kind word, caressing, this is all a part of the physical relationship. It's a big problem when there's guilt or shame over the physical part of a marriage.

What Challenges Face Couples Today?
Couples need to realize it's not all peaches and cream. That doesn't mean the marriage isn't good if you go through hard times. You may want out a certain times, but you think of the marriage, the kids, and the damage that could be done by divorce. Give yourself a cool-down period and look at the consequences.

Advice to Young Couples
Things generally get to be much more fun as you mature. The kids grow older, things get easier, and if you like each other, life keeps getting better.

9

Your marriage comes before your child. But your child is one of your best tools for creating a great marriage.

"**B**ottom line: the kids come first, then me." Harold gave voice to a most common feeling of married fathers. "Well, he's the adult. If it's a choice between him and our kids, I'd think he'd want his children to be cared for first," was his wife Cindy's response.

Many couples do great on vacation when they're alone and have the time to offer each other their full attention, but they lose miserably at love when living in the daily grind of life. When children enter the picture, the greatest marital challenge often begins. Our children are our own flesh and blood, totally dependent on us. It's easy to fall into the trap of putting every other part of life on hold and focusing all of our energy, physical and emotional, on caring for and supporting them. Too many couples can even pinpoint the moment of childbirth as the time when their marital problems intensified.

Unfortunately, there is much more talk about how you can be a better parent than about how you can have a great marriage. Advice abounds when it comes to caring for your kids, but not so when it comes to caring for kids, as a couple, or to considering how children can significantly enhance your marriage. In fact, so as not to alienate single parents, experts will often avoid the topic of childrearing as a couple. Having written a book about helping children through divorce, I understand the plight of raising a child as a single parent. Yet, because I feel both parents are so crucial to the upbringing of children, I strongly encouraged parental togetherness even in my divorce book. Our children need us desperately, more than most of us may ever recognize.

The Meaning of Your Marriage to Your Children

"Look, I'm the kids' mother," Cindy said with frustration. "My kids need me now." Cindy was right, of course. Her two-year-old, for example, needed her attention and often couldn't wait. If he was hungry, dirty, or ill, Cindy couldn't put his needs on hold while she gave Harold the attention he wanted. Cindy was understandably consumed with her child, unwilling to leave him with anyone else until he was older. She felt a constant need to nurture him, reading to him every chance she got, researching the most advanced toys to develop his mind and body. It was the same way with her six-year-old daughter, Katie, who was involved in a different extracurricular activity almost every day of the week. After caring for her two kids, Cindy had little left over for Harold.

Cindy was doing so many things right. But there was one area in which she was sadly mistaken: she needed to realize how important her marriage was to her children. And I don't only mean that her kids would be devastated if their parents divorced. Rather, the amount of strength and love that children draw on a daily basis from their parents' loving marriage is enormous. If you want to put a huge smile on your young child's face, give your spouse a big hug and kiss right in front of her. She'll explode with delight and then try to squeeze her way in to be a part of the loving gesture. Even older kids who make a big show of gagging or saying, "Ew! Gross!" when you kiss aren't good at hiding the fact that they also are glad you're doing it. Kids need to be surrounded by their parents' love. After all, it was that love that brought them into existence. I remember a wise twelve-year-old who, while struggling with his parents' divorce, told me, "I feel I was created from my parents because of their love for each other. Now that they don't love each other, I feel as though I don't exist on some level." This young man taught me how deeply children identify their own creation and existence with the love between their parents.

Children need to feel secure, and nothing offers stability as much as your loving marriage. Children can deal with any number of changes when they feel that their core family is unquestionably intact and full of love. It's not enough to stay together for the sake of the kids. *Your children deserve to be cloaked in love.*

Marriage Does Come First

Of course, this doesn't mean that when your four-year-old child comes home hungry from preschool that you say, "Sorry, honey, I'll be with you in an hour, after Dad and I make love." It means that you take your marital relationship extremely seriously because it is crucial to your children. *Cindy and so many parents like her were trading their marital passion for childcare without recognizing that kids gain much more from having parents who are in love than from all of the music lessons and advanced computer technology in the world.*

Of course, parenting is a full-time job, but too many parents decide that they don't need to focus on their marriage because their kids need them. There is the big mistake. I'm not implying that you need to spend the same amount of time alone with your spouse as you do with your kids, but your marriage is far more important than so many things you do for your children, even though you are expending the energy only because you think it benefits them. So, if you just spent three hours making sure your kid was placed on just the right team for Little League, think about the last time you spent three hours focused on your marriage. If you haven't, you are placing your marriage and children in danger.

Believe me, I wanted my son to learn violin and took him for lessons. My daughter takes ice skating lessons. But at some point, all parents must realize they can't do it all without it coming at the expense of something else that is equally or more important (which means they haven't done it all anyway). The focus on children's extracurricular activities often comes at the expense of your marriage, either directly or by zapping energy that could later be used for your marriage. I had to face the fact long ago that my child was not going to be a violin prodigy (even though my grand-father was and I figured it's in our blood). But more important, he'll be surrounded by parents who really love each other.

Many Extracurricular Activities Are Extremely Extra

As I continue, please remember that my wife and I have five wonderfully active children. I may find their activities far more time-consuming than a couple who has one child. I only wish to highlight potential pitfalls of using important marital energy for children's *extra*curricular activities. Stop and think before you sign your kid up for everything in sight. Consider creative ways to have your child experience these activities without it taking too much energy from you. Following are some suggestions that will help you keep things from getting out of hand.

1. *Carpool.* Get involved in activities in which you can be a part of a carpool so you don't have to drive both ways all the time.

2. *Set the standard at the start.* Make it clear to your child before he or she decides to sign up for an activity that you won't be able to see every game/performance. Explain that you will be there for the huge events, but that your time doesn't allow you to be there all the time. If you have a younger child who may feel hurt when you are absent from the sidelines nonetheless, find out the number of performances or games before you sign your child up. Your child may have to choose a different activity that has fewer performances if he or she wants you to attend every one.

   So many parents think they have to be there every time their kid is going to sneeze (and, yes, I am probably at my kid's school plays more than most fathers), but when it comes to extracurricular activities, help your child understand that you can't be there all the time. If this is disturbing to your child, be very understanding and explain that he or she can choose not to be involved in this activity. Learn to drop your child off at the activity instead of hanging around. You don't need to be there the whole time. That time would be better spent in a way that will give you more energy for your marriage.

3. *Choose wisely.* Before you sign on any dotted line, map out what your week would look like if you indulged each kid's requests for activities. Is your stomach going to be in knots as you career through traffic from one pick up to the next drop-off? Will there be tense negotiations about which spouse can work late while the other races from the commuter train to the recreation center? Is all this fun leaving everyone exhausted and cranky? Are the expenses going to lead to money fights? Look down the road and check out the speed bumps.

   One of your kids may want to be involved in Little League while the other wants to play ice hockey. And they can do that and more when they can drive and have their own cars. But for now, they will need to agree on one activity, or switch off every year, if it will be a huge burden for you to have different children involved in different activities in different parts of town (unless, of course, all the activities are at the same time at one youth center . . .). Kids don't have to get what they want because they want it. They can understand that your time and money are limited and that they will have to choose wisely.

4. *Limit birthday parties.* I have five children, and each has approximately twenty-five kids in his or her class, which means that my kids have a potential of 100 invitation-wielding classmates (my youngest two are twins and in the same class for now). There are fifty-two weekends per year. You do the math. Weekend is family time around my home, which it cannot be if each child has a different party to attend. Our kids are given their choice of three to four parties to attend each year (yes, we're flexible and have no problem going to an extra party here or there if the family isn't together anyway for some reason). It's not that we are limiting our kids' fun but rather that we are teaching them the importance of family time. We want most of our children's fun to come from the sense of family togetherness, not Chuck E. Cheese.

Kids First, Marriage Second: The Guilty Answer

As parents, we feel obligated to give our kids the most life has to offer. If we give less, we feel guilty. Often that guilt is a strong motivator for parents to place their children ahead of their marriage. When this guilt overwhelms you, remind yourself of the young child who receives the fabulous new high-tech toy and is far more interested in the box than the toy. It's a metaphor for your child's outlook on life. Sometimes as parents we're searching for the new incredible gadget that will offer our children great hope while forgetting that the most important things to children are the old standbys: a loving family and parents who have a great marriage. You can be a great parent on paper while not offering your child the most you have to offer. Your marriage is the basis for love in your child's life. Make life simple and great by protecting and putting great effort into your loving marriage.

It is the cavalier attitude of parents about their marriage that can use improvement. Don't think your marriage can wait. It can't. Sure, you can coast for a period of time, spending less time together . . . but without attention and focus, your marriage will die. If you want to get away alone and have a nursing baby, you'll have to wait. But you'll want to talk about how much you look forward to getting away, how you can take that newborn out with you on a date, and what little extra time you can squeeze out today to connect even amidst a newborn's needs. Don't let your marriage slip to a distant second on your priority list. Being in love with your spouse will bring great joy and peace to your child, from newborn to adulthood.

Redefining Your Marriage

Marriage isn't only about the moments when you and your spouse are alone and focused on each other. It encompasses every part of your life, including employment and parenting. I've discussed the importance of sharing what happens at work with your spouse so that your work becomes part of your marital communication and connection. It is even more important to establish your children as part of your marriage. Your kids will be your marriage's greatest project.

Children can assist you in developing a wonderful marriage. Usually, we hear advice on how to make a great marriage in spite of having children. But it's our children who hold a special ability to bring a powerful love into our marriage far beyond what we could ever have developed without them. Our children become a symbolic part of the love we've created in our marriage instead of something outside of our private love. Consider the following ways to help make your kids a vital part of your marital life.

1. *Experience life together.* Find activities that offer togetherness. Take time regularly to read together with your children. More often than not, parents feel this is a chore that should be split; sometimes Mom and sometimes Dad reads with the children. But why not have everyone lie in the same bed and hear the same story? If Dad is reading, Mom can cuddle in just as well, and vice versa. Try taking a tag team approach in which you begin to tell a story (perhaps a familiar fairy tale or one you're making up as you go along) and your spouse continues it when you give the signal. As your kids get older, they can become part of the creative fun. These are the moments that make us a family, the times that we work together with our loving spouse on something so special we can't help but feel closer because of it.

   Consider other creative activities like dancing together, singing together, or teaching the kids a favorite song (perhaps your old love song). Have your own special family song. Kids love to see their parents dancing and love to join in. My wife and I often break into dance in our kitchen around mealtime. I can't dance for more than ten seconds without our kids dancing around us and often trying to wedge their way in. Teach your kids the dances you know. You and your spouse together can teach your kids to swim and bicycle. Family bicycling is a wonderful way to spend time together. Try to do as much with your kids together as possible. It produces the rich history every marriage needs.

2. *Compliment each other in front of your kids.* Say to your children things like, "Isn't your mother/father the most beautiful/handsome woman/man in the world, inside and out?" Show your children how in love you are with your

spouse. Your kids will smile and giggle, practically bursting with delight. It's heartwarming for children to see their parents in love and willing to show it.

3. *Cook together.* Cooking is a very sensual experience and one that is grossly undervalued in today's rush to get it over with. Cook with your spouse and kids once a week. Create a special theme. We create a dinner once a week that revolves around a different country. Each of us does different things to prepare, from cooking to getting information about the country from the encyclopedia to drawing its flag to finding music from that country that we can play at dinner.

   You'd be surprised at how much kids love to do anything, even chores, when it's done as a family. Kids as young as four love to wash dishes as long as there is other loving activity going on simultaneously. Bake cakes together, roll dough, taste and stir together with your spouse and kids, and you'll find fun and romance about it all. The kitchen always seems to be the place our family ends up (all of us absolutely love to eat), and we've discovered how much fun and love can fill that room.

4. *Have dinner together.* A consistent dinner together as a family focuses attention on our family, and on the importance of knowing what's going on with each family member. It's during dinner that we talk, share, and wonder about what will be tomorrow. Dinner won't necessarily be a quiet, peaceful time. My youngest two talk so loudly at dinner that the veins in their neck bulge. Being the youngest, I guess they've learned to speak loudly or else they won't be heard. When we recently replaced the sheetrock in our dining room, we added an inch of soundproof board to the walls so that dinner chatter will be more peaceful.

   As your kids get older, they can sit longer and learn to wait to be excused. But make dinner time more about family than about nightly lessons in manners. Make it the time that the kids look forward to because they'll get attention and hear everything that's going on in their family. You and your spouse should make sure to catch each other's eye often during dinner as if to say, "Look how special we made it. Look what we've done together."

5. *Plant a garden together.* It's a miraculous activity to make things grow and create actual life. Caring for a garden is microcosm of caring for your own family and teaches everyone to work together to keep living things healthy and happy.

6. *Cuddle together.* Cuddling as a family offers genuine family intimacy. While reading or watching a video, take the opportunity to touch your children and your spouse. Cuddling creates a warm bond that transcends words of love. It sends the message that we want to be united with our family. Despite any differences we may share, when it comes right down to it, our cuddling shows that we know how important it is to always feel close to each other.

7. *Find activities that everyone likes, including the adults.* Granted, there will be plenty of times when most of the fun will be seeing your kids smiling. But don't underestimate how many places and activities there are that the entire family can enjoy. Check out the beach, bookstores, libraries, bowling, ballgames, and so many other places that offer fun for adults as well as for children. The idea is to find a place where you can have adult fun and keep the kids happy.

Plan ahead to keep the kids occupied and contented. Keep your backyard stocked with bubbles, bikes, sandwiches, and drinks so you and your spouse can sit down and relax with your children instead of jumping up every ten seconds to help a little one. On family trips, be prepared. Take along enough food and books, perhaps a goodie bag for young kids with a little toy.

Keep family trips fun. Taking your kids to Home Depot while you're trying to make decisions about your new kitchen ain't fun. Shopping for adult clothes rarely lights up a kid's face. Here are two words that for me as a father of five rarely ever go together: *mall* and *children*. Stay away from those experiences that add stress to your marriage. Yes, there are errands to run, and sometimes the kids will have to tag along. But you can also use your ingenuity to find ways to get them done alone or in a more comfortable manner.

Before I wised up about Home Depot, we'd take the kids. I'll never forget my son saying to me, "Please, just pick one—they're all beautiful," as I obsessed over drawer pulls. But then we said, "Enough is enough," and did what we should have done a long time ago. We paid our handyman to go for us. Yes, he couldn't pick out just the right thing, but I didn't care, because I was in the pool with my kids on Sunday, while he was combing the aisles. Let errands take a back seat to family time.

8. *Laugh together.* Tell jokes together, make funny faces, tickle each other. Do whatever it takes to keep your family smiling.

9. *Use your children to be a child again.* Reconnect with your inner child by playing with your children and spouse. When we are more like innocent children, we bring out a very special, fun-loving, imaginative, and curious part of our spirit and can give that part of ourselves to our spouse. As your children grow, remember what it was like to be a kid at every stage. Get into your teen's music with your spouse and remember the romance of adolescence.

∽⅋

Cindy understood that she was neglecting her marriage because of the attention she gave the children. But she wasn't about to neglect her children either. She made an effort to find activities that all of them could be involved in.

Cindy used to read to the children because she felt it was her job, and Harold felt he wasn't welcome to be a part of the reading time. They decided to read to the kids together and began to do more activities as a family. This added to an intimacy they were missing before and, most of all, allowed them to spend much more time together, even if it wasn't time alone. Instead of Harold overhearing his wife with the children while anxiously waiting for her to spend time with him, he joined his wife and kids and extended his marriage into a loving family setting.

The Privacy of Marriage

As much as I've discussed including your children in your marriage, there is an equally crucial need for couples to have private time. We need consistent time to relate to each other solely as lovers and adults without any interruption.

Parents often worry that their children will feel left out if they spend private time together. Naturally, your children want your attention every second of every day. But as long as they receive healthy love and attention from you, they will not suffer because you choose to spend time alone. In fact, it is a healthy message to send: you are in love and need time alone to work on your marriage.

Every person needs time off, time to relax and regenerate, to think and to feel. Running through the details of life makes us tired, and eventually we have to stop and take a break. If you run too long without a drink, you'll dehydrate and put your entire system in jeopardy. Your marriage needs the same respect. Taking those moments to be alone with your spouse is the nutritious drink your marriage needs. You are not sending the message to your children that they are "excluded" from your private time with your spouse. Rather you can help your children (and yourself) understand that parents need time to be able to focus on each other. Most children can understand this by a simple example about their own friendships. How would their friendships be if they could never be with a friend without Mom or Dad always there involved in the conversation?

We yearn to have adult conversation, flirt, be sensual, and just touch each other as spouses without having the interruption of a child. We need it. Unfortunately, too many of us know the feeling of finally sitting with our spouse for a private moment, then staring at each other blankly, feeling out of practice in the art of romance, love, and simple chitchat. Your marriage can't afford to be "out of practice." You need time to bond and just "be" with each other, to remind each other what you love about each other, to smell the pleasant aura of your soulmate. Your kids will understand—if not now, then when they are older. They will appreciate what you've done for them: given them parents who dearly love each other and offered their kids a feeling of stability and a model for a strong marriage. By putting your marriage first, you've developed an intense love with your spouse that will overflow and extend into the loving relationship between parent and child and the entire family.

Consider the following ideas to help you find the peaceful, private times together:

1. *Hire a regular babysitter.* Anyone who knows me will tell you I am a hands-on parent. I've changed thousands of diapers, read countless stories, and given an ocean of baths. But I need a break, and that break comes when the babysitter walks through the door. Some parents are apprehensive about leaving their kids with a sitter and may be more comfortable having a relative stay.

   The cost of proper childcare limits some couples from being able to be alone without their children. Be creative. Swap weeknights with a friend so that you watch each other's children for one evening a week while you go on your date night. Hire babysitters for short periods of time, even just an hour if that will give you and your spouse time to grab a bite, make love, or just cuddle together. I've hired babysitters just to entertain our kids in our home while my wife and I spend some quality time in our room.

   Avoid thinking of babysitting as a huge event that happens only on "special occasions." I've seen too many babysitters hired so that the parent can go to divorce court. A mother's helper (perhaps today this person should be called the parents' helper) is a younger person who can give you an extra pair of hands to care for your child. Having someone help at those difficult childcare times, like dinner and bathing hour (I know, I have five, so maybe it's not as hectic for smaller families) can create a less frenzied atmosphere at home. It can leave you and your spouse with more energy and allow both of you some extra time alone.

   Obviously, as your kids get older, you don't need the same help now that they can tend to certain needs themselves. When you do have a child who is old enough and responsible enough to babysit for younger siblings, create this as a responsibility. Don't pay him or her for babysitting. You can offer an allowance that includes babysitting responsibilities. Give your older child the consistent responsibility to babysit so that you and your spouse can comfortably go out or be alone. Once you give your child the idea that he or she is doing you a *favor* by babysitting, you will lose the quiet comfort of going out with your spouse.

Couples have shared with me that they cannot go out because their older child is too busy to babysit. Don't fall for that one. Luckily you weren't too busy for the lovemaking that created him or her. All children, young and old, need a healthy respect for their parents' marriage. Helping make that marriage great is a family affair, one every child should be proud of.

2. *Create private time every single night.* By the time your children are four, you should be able to take them through their bedtime ritual, then let them fall asleep by themselves. They can read, play, or do whatever you find appropriate, in their own room. When nine o'clock rolls around, you and your spouse should declare private time to unwind together. This is your shining moment to cook together, have a marital meeting, do the dishes, lie side by side and read, watch a show, make love, or all of the above. Realistically, this will not happen every night. With five children, chances are that one of my kids will be sick, for example, and need extra care or be in my bedroom for some of the night. But for the most part, our bedroom door closes, and our children find it calming knowing the evening activity is over.

If your children are regularly wired at 9 P.M. and just won't leave you alone, you should consider why they have so much energy at that time. Not to turn this into a "getting your child to sleep" section, but it is so important to marriages that I must say one thing: *the key to sleeping children is tired children.* When we were looking for a home to purchase, my wife and I didn't look at any house that did not have one item: a pool. Everything else was negotiable. While living here in south Florida, we learned that if you put a kid in a pool for a while (every day), that kid is begging for sleep at night. Many kids have enormous energy and need a lot of exercise so they're tired at a decent hour.

Close your bedroom door at a decent hour, and let your children know that their parents are spending private time together while resting. After a while, it will become the norm and your kids will be used to and comfortable with your private time. Most of the time, your children will be sleeping during your private moments. As they grow, they can entertain themselves and not interrupt your private marital time, even if they stay up later than you.

3. *Lock your bedroom door.* Some parents feel uncomfortable locking their bedroom door for fear that their children will feel shut out or be unable to come into the room in the middle of the night if they need to. Guess what? They don't *need* to. What they need are parents who still have a great lovemaking relationship that overflows into everyday loving gestures. By the time they're

old enough to sneak into your room, they're able to understand your need for privacy. This does not mean you should abandon your children in the early evening. All it means is that your children will have to knock on your door before entering, which makes all of us a little more comfortable while making love. It will also teach your children that their parents need and deserve private time.

Consider what you might be losing if you don't lock your door. You'll always feel anxious that your children could interrupt you at any time. You might not sleep naked holding each other, you might not "fool around" well before you plan to make love, you might not let yourself truly relax with your spouse because at any moment your child might "need" something. Creating a private time and place for your marriage is necessary, and making that time after you have cared for your children for the day is appropriate and healthy.

Sometimes, younger children (perhaps three and under) need a compromise, such as keeping your bedroom door open until they fall asleep. Then you can close your door while you spend quiet time with your spouse. You can teach your children to disturb you only under serious circumstances, such as nightmares or illness—not just because they want to snuggle at five-thirty in the morning. Teach them to play in their room, and to fetch a prepared juice or milk cup from the fridge on their own. Leave a cup of water next to their bed at night if that will help them go back to sleep or let you sleep. Don't trade in your sex life to be on call for your children.

The older your children get, the more disciplined you need to be in closing your bedroom door at a decent hour. By the time nine o'clock rolls around, you should have time with your spouse in the privacy of your room. Don't do it just on the night you are going to make love (unless you want your teenagers to know every time you make love). When making love, turn on the music if you have kids in the house, even if you think they're sleeping. You may be trying to keep it pretty quiet, but you never know. One couple told me that they found their five-year-old crying in bed in the middle of the night because he was so scared. After regaining his composure, he explained that he had heard cat noises in his parents' bedroom and was terrified (they obviously didn't own any cats). Music adds mood, plus gives you the extra comfort of knowing your children cannot hear your intimate moments.

4. *Make it a vacation for everyone.* Go places that your children and you will all enjoy. Take along a babysitter or mother's helper when you have small kids. If you're planning an extended vacation, remember that taking someone along (or preparing a responsible babysitter at the vacation site) will give you and your spouse a grown-up loving vacation time as well. You can go out to dinner

alone after you've enjoyed dinner with your children, or take walks while your children are napping (if you have younger children). It will allow you and your spouse a little more vacation on your vacation.

Learning Not to Take It All So Seriously

Being happily married around your children will take proper perspective. All the skills you've learned in regard to listening and respecting each other will meet their greatest challenge when you have to deal with child-related issues. "After all, what's more important?" you may think. "If we're going to fight about something important, what's more important than our own children?" Realize, however, that when you fight about your children, you make your kids feel guilty and desperate. Even though you may perceive the fight as helping your children, the marital love lost in the process is damaging to them. They need you to love each other. No matter what decisions you make concerning your children, they'll still be forced on the same unexpected journey that each of us must take in this life. Don't get bogged down in decisions. Do your best while putting your marital love first.

As much as we obsess about raising our children the "right" way, our kids will surprise us endlessly, and as responsible as we attempt to be, they will foil us at every turn. Remember that most decisions aren't as important as you think. If your kid learns to read now or next year, is potty trained now or in two months, gets an A or a B, it's still not worth the personal stress that often translates into marital stress. Try to take the intensity out of your conversations and decision making regarding your children. When you find yourself getting more intense than the situation should require, look deeper into yourself. If your childhood issues are going to rear their ugly head anywhere, it'll be when dealing with your own children. Be very aware of how this intensity may affect your marriage and learn to reduce the tension.

If you want your kids to feel comfortable coming to you with their issues, let them see that their disclosures won't lead to marital conflict and fighting. Show them how much you love them by working together as a couple for their sake.

Everyone needs help with their parenting. Unfortunately, some spouses find it acceptable to offer harsh criticism in this area because, after all, "It's our children we're talking about." Use the same rules of offering criticism discussed in previous chapters. On the other hand, open yourself to hear-

Barbara & Ben Harvey

MARRIED: 44 YEARS

How We Met

We met at college in the spring of '56. We were both attending, and my big brother was one of his frat brothers. My brother introduced us, and I liked him right away. He had a car, and that was a big thing at the time. About seven months later we were serious, and a year later we were married.

What Was the Biggest Challenge in Your Marriage?

Well, we were poor. My mom left me when I was a baby, and I was raised by my grandmother. Ben's parents were separated, and Ben grew up away from his siblings too. So that was hard. But we were determined to make it work because, I think, we'd both grown up so alone.

What Made It Work?

We spent a lot of our time together and with the kids. There were little trips and projects that brought us together. Our short alone times as a couple were good for us too. We wanted to make sure we had some fun time together, some time as a family.

We talked and talked and disagreed and kept talking until we'd work out a problem.

I had to change my personal style of being angry. I used to get quiet and distant when something bothered me. When I worked to change that, our marriage improved a lot.

What Challenges Face Couples Today?

It seems like these days couples don't concentrate a lot on being a unit. They go to their separate places, and cut down on actual time together.

The media also gives us unrealistic sexual expectations. He's not going to be Prince Charming day in and day out.

ing constructive, loving criticism when it comes to your children. They need you so much, and the better parent you become, the better their lives will be forever. Avoid the differences in your opinions and instead learn to listen to each other's point of view. Take time to discuss if your children are getting the best you have to offer. Read parenting books, and share the ideas. Attend parenting seminars. Remind yourself regularly that part of being a great parent is offering your kids a great marriage. Make your children a marital project, and grow together as you make your project flourish.

10

Time is on your side. A great marriage has many stages and takes years to develop properly.

Perhaps the single most damaging myth regarding marriage is that the wedding ceremony marks the moment dreams have come true.

⌘⌘⌘⌘⌘⌘⌘⌘⌘⌘⌘⌘⌘⌘

"I worry that if we're not feeling so together and like 'one' at this point, we just aren't meant to be," Merrill told me in frustration. Married for four years, she expected to be feeling a stronger "connection" with her spouse. But Merrill failed to take into account that she had just given birth to her second child, her father-in-law had passed away suddenly within the last year, and she and her husband had recently begun new jobs that demanded a great deal of their energy and attention. It was simply unreasonable for Merrill to question her marriage, to wonder whether her husband was indeed her soulmate just because she didn't feel "one" with him during a period of intense stress.

⌘⌘⌘⌘⌘⌘⌘⌘⌘⌘⌘⌘⌘⌘

You want your marriage to be easy. We've been duped into believing that the greatest intensity, friendship, and romance of our marriage should materialize the moment we marry. It doesn't, nor is it supposed to. Like any important relationship, it takes time, experience, and history. It takes many years to develop the easygoing, carefree marriage most dream of. To be rid of the tension that comes with working toward compromise, understanding each other's weaknesses and learning to accept them and not take it all so personally, and learning to control your desire to have it all your way takes years of marital love and positive experiences. Too many couples think that after two to four years, they should have worked out all the kinks and confirmed that they were made for each other, that nothing will ever come between them. Welcome to Fantasy Island. I don't mean you can't feel intense love and warmth at any stage of marriage. This book is dedicated to making that happen. But great relationships must have time.

Can you compare the love and trust you have for the dear friend you met within the last two years with how you feel about someone who's been your best friend since childhood? No matter how close your more recent friend is, your friendship lacks the history of life, the ongoing experiences that make us feel comfortable and tranquil in a relationship. Consider your own children. Although you feel a biological love for them from the very start, you love and bond with them more and more as they grow and you get to know them more and more. In fact, part of the love for a child is the fascination of never knowing exactly how things will turn out (albeit this is nerve-racking at times), what kind of person he or she will be, and what kind of experiences you will bring to love each other more.

It is an understandable pressure that we place on our marriage to become everything we expect it to be as soon as we marry. After all, we've made a huge commitment, a lifetime promise to each other. But this promise is only the beginning, the necessary foundation for the development of a great marriage. It is not the entire definition of marriage in and of itself.

Every marriage follows its own path. Yours will as well. The problem is that you probably won't see much of the path until you're past it. Only after the children arrive will you realize you've passed the romantic, carefree stage when sex was spontaneous and life was relatively stress-free. You may kick yourself for not taking greater advantage of those easier times. Only when your kids are older will you realize that you've now passed the stage of childrearing when you could have created indelible memories of love and warmth. You may pine away for those young family times and wish you'd taken more family vacations, pictures, or private getaways with your spouse. And so it goes for every stage of your marriage.

It's easy to look back and see what you've been through and recognize how you could have taken better advantage of it—hindsight is 20/20. But it's far better to focus on looking at the present and recognizing the stage you and your spouse are experiencing *right now*. With every stage of life come new possibilities for your marriage as well as new struggles. By understanding the reality of the present, you can develop an attitude that allows your marriage to grow at every stage while avoiding unrealistic expectations—for example, that romance and sexual passion will remain unchanged when you're raising small children. To spend time being dismayed that you don't feel as connected to your spouse because you don't have much time together while you (or your spouse) are nursing an infant is a waste of time and focuses you on the glass being half empty. Instead, focus on what you can do at that stage to make yourself and your spouse feel closer, and take advantage of your stage of marriage.

Even though having little children may put a damper on your sex life and spontaneity, it will also offer profound moments of togetherness that can make you and your spouse feel incredibly bonded, moments that will never again be offered in the same way. Each stage of life is crucial to our development as human beings and spouses. The rest of this chapter outlines the six common stages of marriage. They may not all apply to you. For example, you may never have children or experience financial stress; or you may have severe financial stress and end up with your grandchildren living with you later in life. My purpose is to make you aware that as different life events occur, they offer advantages as well as limitations. It's your job to be aware that each stage can give you the power to create a system and focus that will make your marriage grow.

There is one more extremely important advantage to understanding your marriage in terms of stages. As I explained to Merrill, "This too shall pass." Sometimes no matter how fulfilling a stage is, it is still hard, and we often begin to tire of it and, unfortunately, begin to define our marriage through it. Merrill needed to be reminded that there would be a time when life wouldn't revolve around diapers and the stress of a new job. Knowing that life will get easier in certain ways helps us to take greater advantage of a certain stage. Once Merrill appreciated that life would be drastically different one day, albeit a long time in the future, it reduced her marital frustration and allowed her to find new resolve to make her marriage work among the complexities of her daily life.

Look for answers. Talk with your spouse about what isn't working in your stage of marriage and find creative ways to improve it. For example,

Merrill felt like a stranger to her husband during this time of life. But after discussing it with her husband, she realized that *both* of them missed each other. When they talked about it, they realized that they never went out on a date anymore because they felt uncomfortable leaving the baby with a sitter. Once they focused on how to get more private time, they decided to hire a sitter for their older child and take the baby on the date. It wasn't quite being alone, but they found they could still spend private time even when the baby was with them. Discussing the problems leads to answers.

The Six Stages of Marriage

Stage 1: Acquaintanceship

This is where it all begins. Too many couples think this stage began well before they were married. True, but only to some extent. Once you marry, you begin to learn a lot more about who your spouse is in the context of marriage. Things that didn't matter when you were dating, or even living together, make a difference today; your actions now have an instant effect on your spouse. You can no longer just decide to work late, go away for the weekend, have drinks or dinner with friends, or make most plans without consulting with your spouse. Suddenly, you find yourself noticing your spouse's personal hygiene, how many times he or she calls Mom or talks with friends, his or her eating habits, how much television he or she watches. You are acutely aware of your spouse's moods on waking and on coming home after a stressful day. You may have had a clue about some of these things while you were dating, but now they're the fabric of your new life together.

One spouse told me how delighted he was to learn how calm his wife was under pressure. He felt so much more relaxed because of her easy-going attitude. Yet another spouse shared how on his honeymoon he mentioned to his wife nicely (his perspective) that maybe she shouldn't have another scoop of ice cream because she was on a diet—and was met with a scoop of ice cream in his face. Even if you were living together before the wedding, you'll find a host of new things to learn because your commitment of marriage changes your sense of responsibility to each other. Before, you may have felt it wasn't your place to ask your fiancé to stay home that evening because you were a bit down and out. Now you do ask and will learn what your spouse's reaction is.

The key to the acquaintanceship stage is to consider how you'd treat a new acquaintance that you are really interested in. Acquaintances spend plenty of time learning about each other without a lot of demands. Newly married couples mistakenly equate the term *marriage* with "Now you are mine." Love and respect still need to develop; making hosts of demands is not an endearing quality. You do want to create new ground rules for marriage, but remember to choose your battles wisely. You need loads of time, but remember, you do have the time. You have made a lifetime commitment before creating a lifetime of love. You need to allow your relationship to catch up a little to your commitment. You do that by spending time together, going out on dates, reading the paper together, cooking, discussing your past and present, finding new experiences, learning what turns you on sexually with lots of practice—anything that brings the two of you together.

There is a biblical injunction against sending a man to war if he is in the first year of his new marriage. This reference illustrates how absolutely crucial it is for newly married couples to spend time together. This time of relationship building is not to be disturbed, even when it might compromise a nation's security. The first year of marriage is not when the two of you take jobs that keep you in different cities except for weekends (not to say that there is any good time for that). It is not the year when one of your younger siblings comes to live with you so he can attend a school in your neighborhood. It is not even the time to have guests (including in-laws) who will stay more than a few days. Some of these instances may be unavoidable, but under any circumstances, make creating an atmosphere that lets the two of you learn about each other in a relaxed way a top priority.

Jewish tradition offers a supportive view to making this first year as easygoing as possible. Newly married couples are often invited out to other homes for dinners and are not expected to reciprocate. Respect how complicated the move to marry is in the first place and avoid unnecessary pressures. You'll have plenty of pressures and demands in life. Now is the time to allow the foundation of your union to establish healthy roots. The psychological adjustments of marriage are significant. Couples who consider themselves worldly and sophisticated are surprised by how lost they may feel in their new roles as husband and wife.

Don't be surprised by what you did not know about your spouse before marriage. You may disapprove of some of the traits you discover. But if you don't like your spouse's eating habits, or the way he or she treats Mom, avoid pressuring your mate to change. Focus only on the areas that involve you personally.

I recall the first time my wife and I had guests over, a few months after we were married. I had a long history of making sarcastic remarks and personal put-downs (I had four brothers and went to all-male schools). This was considered funny among my many male friends. But when I began to make jokes at my wife's expense, she was suddenly taken aback at my behavior. She asked me to join her in the kitchen, where she corrected my insensitivity in the kindest and cleverest of ways. She told me that I had a wonderful and witty sense of humor. I surely didn't have to stoop to such a low level as to make jokes at her expense to be funny, did I? I got the message.

You may be unpleasantly surprised as much as you are pleasantly surprised at what you will learn during the acquaintanceship stage. It is a stage of adjustment, a time to gather information, talk about life, and learn to compromise. Take it slow, and only make corrections when they are absolutely necessary.

Stage 2: Marital Identity

This stage is when you begin to define your unique marriage. It begins when you marry. After about six months to a year, your marriage will begin to fall into its rhythm. This is the time you will be developing your roles in the marriage. Are you a fun couple or an intense one? Are you going to be a frugal couple or conspicuous consumers? How will you make joint decisions? Will you find compromise or argue? What personal roles will each of you adopt in the marriage (see Secret #4)? What are your dreams for your marriage: children, travel, money, a large house? What goals are you going to work toward as a couple?

This is the stage to discuss your marital goals, as outlined in Secret #3. Discuss everything you ever dreamed about marriage. Talk about what you liked and disliked about your parents' marriage and what parts you'd like to infuse into your own. Talk about money. Don't wait for it to cause stress in your marriage. Decide how you will deal with money in your relationship. Create a budget, and update it every three months.

One friend of mine changed dramatically from the first year of his marriage to the next. The first year, he was like a stand-up comic. By the second year of marriage, he was much more serious and far less humorous. He'd learned what he had to be responsible for, and how to plan to reach his goals. He wasn't as much fun to be around, but clearly he'd fallen into a role that worked for their marriage.

Stage 3: Pregnancy

This stage can happen at any moment but often will occur one to three years after your marriage begins. How you handle pregnancy says a lot about your marriage. It's a time requiring extreme sensitivity. The wife will experience dramatic physical and hormonal changes that will test her ability to give to and focus on her husband. The husband will struggle to adjust to the upcoming expected changes, including possibly embracing the role of the spouse who is depended on.

Your family begins with pregnancy, not birth. It is during the pregnancy that you as a couple make important decisions about family. Make your decision as a couple to be kind to each other and to cut each other a great deal of slack.

Expect less from your wife, as her life is changing the most. Understand if your husband is nervous about money, or just the idea of becoming a father. Remember that the first baby brings up unconscious feelings from our own childhood as well as reminding us of the strengths and weaknesses of our parents.

Pregnancy changes life immediately. One month ago you may have been going out to dinner regularly, dancing, enjoying the greatest sex of your life, and reveling in enormous reserves of energy. This month might be full of vomiting, weakness, exhaustion, and anxiety. Quite a change for such a wonderful event.

Decide what kind of pregnancy you want. Make it one that brings you closer together. Read *What to Expect When You're Expecting* and other pregnancy books *together*. Visit the doctor *together*. Make pregnancy an experience that makes you both feel closer because you are sharing the experience. Create a realistic sex life. Talk to your obstetrician about lovemaking during pregnancy so that both of you can make informed decisions and relax if the doctor gives you the go-ahead. Recognize that many pregnant women have a marked decrease in sexual desire whereas others find a heightened sex drive during certain trimesters.

It's all about sharing your feelings and respecting each other. Use this stage as a way to learn how to work through the difficult times you'll share into the future. This is the time for each of you to realize that even if you're thrilled by the pregnancy, it comes loaded with so much pressure that each of you may not be at your best. Yet you will get through it. You made the decision to start a family, and with that decision comes certain realities. This is the best time to show each other that you can be depended on.

Stage 4: Raising Young Children

Without a doubt, this is the most difficult of the marital stages. I believe the "seven-year-itch" concept—the notion that we're most susceptible to temptation outside marriage at the seven-year mark—developed because it's often the time when your little ones leave toddlerhood. Too many well-meaning couples lose sight of their marriage during this stage and are very distant when they come out of it.

There is little more complicated than caring for infants. They *need* so much. It isn't the work of caring for them as much as caring for them *on their terms.* Your baby can't wait to be fed, changed, or burped. You have to do it *now*—all else in life becomes second priority. Only when your children enter the late-three- to five-year-old stage can they literally wait a few minutes for food or even grab a juice box from the pantry themselves.

You'll spend most of this stage completely sleep-deprived. Don't underestimate what this means. If you "slept" seven hours, but little people woke you up three times, you didn't get seven hours of sleep. And let's face it, the younger your children, the less sleep you're likely to get. When you have an infant, one of you will have to awaken every two to four hours and feed, diaper, and burp this completely dependent child. Lack of sleep makes us much more than tired. It makes us irritable, anxious, and depressed. It's hard to keep a positive perspective when you haven't slept well for weeks or months. The first lesson in brainwashing and forcing information out of prisoners of war is to disturb their sleep. Lack of consistent sleep could even cause you to hallucinate. You and your spouse must recognize that neither of you will be at your best during this stage. You will be anxious. You will be grouchy. Your child will get sick, and her vulnerability will scare you. This is the time to structure your marriage.

1. *Decide your roles (see Secret #4).* Try to do as much together as possible. You can share feedings, even if the baby is nursing (the husband burps and changes the baby's diaper). Who will care for what in the house and in the family? Who's cleaning, paying the bills, and cooking meals? Always try to get some form of help during this stage, whether for chores or the baby, either hired help or supportive friends and family. If you have other kids, how will their needs be met and by whom?

2. *Create as many family together times as possible.* Have the whole family go to the park. Spend time with your spouse pushing your kids on the swings and

sharing as many family moments as possible. Take family trips to the beach and places that you enjoy as well.

3. *Reduce your expectations.* Lovemaking will likely not be as spontaneous as it was. The family trip may be tiring. If it's supposed to be a vacation for you and your spouse, make that happen by getting extra help or going alone. Don't allow yourself to be frustrated when you're on vacation and your kids aren't sleeping well. Recognize how each of you is going to feel pulled in too many directions and that the marriage will be at its greatest test.

4. *Make time for your marriage exclusively.* Every minute counts. Grab half-hour or one-hour blocks of time for a walk (even while pushing a sleeping baby), one-night getaways when you can leave your children with a family member, or planned sexual rendezvous. Keep touching and saying, "I love you" as much as you can to keep your focus on each other. Be sure to remind each other constantly how much you appreciate all that the other does. Tell your spouse what a great parent he or she is. Create personal space for yourselves to exercise, read, take a bath. Play soothing music in your home to create peaceful surroundings. Know that there will come a stage of life when demands won't be so immediate and stress will be significantly reduced. Some day you will sleep through the night, enjoy romantic dinners and wonderful lovemaking, and go away with your spouse for nights at a time.

This stage is often full of stress regarding money as well. This is often time when you're building a career and choosing a financial path. Everything from worrying if you'll climb the corporate (or whatever) ladder to how much you'll be able to afford for your family's future to coping with the ups and downs of difficult bosses can cause even the sweetest of individuals to become irritable. Talk about that stress together. Just discussing it will help both of you feel closer and reduce the anxiety.

As much as this stage will seem like a blur when you're past it and don't know how you got through it all, it will attest to your marriage's ability to weather any storm, and it will use the love generated between the two of you to bring love into the life of another, your child. The tiring yet meaningful stage of raising young children can offer your marriage a closeness and bond that goes well beyond what you ever expected.

Stage 5: Parents, Yet Individuals

Now your children are older, anywhere from six and up. They are in school much of the day, and your physical work to sustain them has dropped off dramatically. The challenge of this stage is learning a whole new lifestyle for your marriage. Now you'll have the time to go out more, enjoy hours together at night, and with the help of family or babysitter, vacation alone with your spouse for many nights.

But will you do it? The danger of this stage is taking your newfound time and energy and quickly placing it outside of your marriage. Because you haven't enjoyed spontaneity in your marriage for so long, you may not bring it back when you can. So many couples tell me they don't have the time. The problem is that they still think as if they're parents of toddlers. They never switched out of the mode of caring for little ones. They never returned to their marriage and developed a new part of it, the one that had the time for much love, friendship, and romance.

Use this stage to spend regular time together alone. Go out on dates, focus on lovemaking, spend time talking and relating to each other. This is the stage in which many couples grow apart. They find all kinds of new things to do that exclude their spouse because, in part, they haven't seen their spouse as free enough to be with them for so many years. Instead, find new interests together and grow as a couple.

This stage also requires a great deal more conversation about the children. As kids grow, the decisions you must make in relation to them become far more complicated. Schools, friends, religious beliefs, puberty, sex and drugs, emotional health, and so much more require your intense concentration. You'll have to learn to speak as one to your children even though you will often not completely agree with each other. But, as always, these deliberations should be about love, your marriage, and willingness to continue to grow as a couple as you continue to grow your own unique family.

Take private vacations. I can't stress this enough. Those vacations alone do so much for a marriage. They allow you to connect again. You need the time away because it often takes a couple of days to really slow down and begin to talk comfortably about life again with your partner. And when you know you have a private marital vacation coming up, it helps you get through the stress of your day. If you can, try to spend three nights away every three months in addition to whatever other vacations you may plan. This focuses your marriage on connecting with each other in a big way.

Now that you have the time, build your love and friendship with enriching experiences and a history of loving time spent together.

Stage 6: Left to Yourselves

Your kids are leaving the house. If you haven't reached this stage yet, you may think you're going to shout hooray. Yet for most couples, the empty nest poses a whole new issue—your changing identity. Your kids leave for work, college, and marriage and find other people to relate to and listen to. They may call often, but they don't take the regular place in your life that you've been used to for the last eighteen or more years. Parenting is such a vital part of our life experience that we often lose our vitality when it's gone. If you took time to focus on your marriage during the years of stage 5, weathering the empty nest is far easier because you've begun to develop a private marital relationship again and have redefined yourself through your marriage. But let's face it, young kids or old, a large portion of your time and definition revolved around parenthood. Now that has to change.

I counsel many people who don't know how to reconnect to their spouses. Unfortunately, they've spent years developing private interests and worlds exclusive of their marriage and in large part only related to their spouse as the other parent of their children. Now that the children are gone, they have very little to talk about or to share.

This stage is about dating again. About knowing that even the best of marriages are starting a new relationship. About relating that you are far different than you were years ago when you first married. Yes, you have a rich history together, but now a new world has opened up to you and you want to find it together. It's time to woo again. Date each other and learn about each other all over again. Discuss your new dreams and aspirations for the rest of your lives, and talk about how each of you can help the other achieve these goals. It is at this stage that we realize there is more to life than our children and begin to wonder what we want to do with the rest of the time we have. Make this life decision together and together develop a plan to create this meaningful life.

It is also common at this stage to experience the passing of a parent. Being able to discuss it and consider it with a spouse who is your best friend is a crucial component of coming to healthy terms with death and personal loss.

What Marital Stage Are You In?

Discuss with your spouse where you think the two of you are in the six stages of marriage.

Discuss whether you as a couple have fallen into any of the pitfalls discussed for each stage. What have you done to avoid or cure these pitfalls?

Make a list (each spouse does this separately) of ways to feel closer during your specific stage of life and marriage. Each of your lists should have at least five suggestions.

See what suggestions appear on both of your lists, and then start acting on them.

Beverly & Sydney Olesky
MARRIED: 46 YEARS

What Made It Work?

The hanging in makes it work. There will be times when both spouses just have to hold on, when you don't really understand each other. I lost my mom and dad in the same year. Nobody could understand my grief. It took me two years to come out of the pain. But my husband was patient. He didn't take it personally. He knew I'd be back and gave me time. What makes it work is hanging in there during the rough times.

What Challenge Couples Face Today?

You go through stages. The relationship goes through stages, and things do change. You are different in many ways when you are raising a family, and then the kids leave home. Getting to know each other as real individuals takes a long time.

Many couples will live through combinations of these stages. For example, their children will leave home, but they'll need to start a new business for financial reasons. Or a spouse will experience the birth of a child and the passing of a parent during the same year. Whatever your unique situation, these stages help you understand that your marriage will largely follow a general path. Knowing your marital focus during each stage is the difference between wonderful marital growth and incredible frustration.

11

Focus energy on creating a healthy relationship with your spouse's parents.

Early in the last century, there were two young rabbinical students who were matched to be wed to two young women. The two men had never met or seen their prospective brides and had to travel three days by horse and wagon to meet and marry them. Sadly, robbers attacked their wagon along the way, and one of the students was seriously harmed and unable to continue the journey. The one young man who was able to make the trip finally appeared in the city. The two mothers of the brides were quite taken aback when only one gentleman exited the wagon. On hearing the unfortunate story, the two women began to argue, each claiming that their daughter should be the one to wed this healthy young man. As their fight became more pronounced, the townspeople suggested they visit the rabbi of the community to discuss the matter.

After listening carefully to each woman's claim, the rabbi shrugged and said, "Unfortunately, neither of you has a stronger case than the other. I have only one suggestion. Like the wise King Solomon suggested with the baby that two women brought to him, we can cut this boy in half and give each half of him to each of your daughters." Immediately, one woman said that such an idea was preposterous: "Killing the boy would serve no purpose for either of us." At the same time, the other woman strongly agreed with the suggestion: "Yes, what a wonderful idea. Let's rip him in half immediately, and I'm willing to personally participate in the procedure." The wise rabbi stopped both women, stood by the woman who was in favor of his suggestion, and declared, "It's settled then. She's the mother-in-law."

Our families of origin can become one of the most complicated issues in a marriage. Our parents, siblings, and other relatives can be a wonderful asset or a destructive force. And, unlike others in our lives, such as our children, our extended family is not in our lives because of our own choice. The problem is that too many couples consider their families as "independent" forces. They develop a complacent attitude about their inability to "control" their family.

"What can I do? That's who my parents are," was what Luke told his wife, Anna. They had been married sixteen years, and the only problem they felt they had was Luke's parents.

"The straw that broke the camel's back was when I miscarried two weeks ago," explained Anna. "I have no family in this country, and when my mother-in-law went through chemo, I was there for her more than her own daughters. But they never are there for me. Not a visit, not a phone call until one full day after they knew."

Luke interrupted, "They tried, they tried, but they couldn't get through. Be reasonable. I told them everything was okay."

This reaction made Anna furious. "I hate it when you stick up for them even when they're wrong. For sixteen years, you've found excuses for them. I'm tired of them and your excuses. I'm tired of you not standing up to them and telling them what they did was wrong."

Every family comes complete with its own set of issues. Unfortunately, these issues can wreak havoc with our ability to develop a wonderful marital relationship. *But it is the power we give our families that causes marital problems, not our family.*

⸻⸻⸻⸻⸻⸻⸻⸻⸻⸻⸻⸻⸻⸻⸻⸻

What Anna wanted was a husband she felt was on her side. She later admitted that even if her husband had never told his parents how upset she was, if he would have just agreed and sympathized with her, it would have gone a long way. But Luke never criticized his parents. His nature was to respect them for who they were, no matter what. To disrespect them by criticizing them would be a sign of weakness to him. He felt as though he was being forced by Anna to choose her over his parents.

⸻⸻⸻⸻⸻⸻⸻⸻⸻⸻⸻⸻⸻⸻⸻⸻

On closer examination, I found there were a host of issues other than Luke's parents that were deeply affecting Luke and Anna's marriage. When you feel family is somehow intruding in your marital life, focus away from the single event that is upsetting you and consider some deeper issues (yours and your spouse's) that may be affecting your marriage.

The Power of Childhood

As I've discussed in these pages, much of who we are is tied up in our parents and their response to us (see Secret #7). To judge or stand up to our parents is no easy task for most. After all, when you come right down to it, most of us never want to hurt our parents. In fact, part of our self-esteem as adults is still tied up in trying to make our parents proud of who we are. For example, when we hand them their first grandchild, we have a feeling of "Look what I've done for you, Mom and Dad." Because having a grandchild means so much to our parents as they age, we take pride in making them happy. We avoid confrontations with our parents, and even if they weren't good parents in our estimation, we usually soften our positions as adults and tell ourselves that they tried their best. And as they age, even the most tyrannical parents look more vulnerable. Most of us don't want to rock the boat.

This is where the problem begins. Many people have difficulty developing a healthy adult relationship with their parents. It could be the fault of the parent, the child, or both. As children, we tend to have difficulty growing out of the need for a pat on the back from our parents. On their end, parents sometimes find it hard to view the child they potty-trained as an adult who may be even smarter, stronger, and more accomplished than they. This difficulty in sharing an adult relationship is often the cause of tension in a marriage.

Luke, a prominent attorney, had taken over his father's practice. Luke felt a serious responsibility to ensure that the practice his father had begun wouldn't falter under Luke's direction. Luke spoke to his father daily about business matters, and even though Luke was in charge at work, psychologically his father still maintained a huge significance in Luke's workplace.

Luke's need to please his father and make him proud was one reason that Luke always defended his parents to Anna. He never wanted it to get to the point where he had to correct his dad in some way. So he played down anything Anna would complain about whenever it concerned his parents. Luke's defensive reaction to Anna was tied in to many different issues, and it was crucial for both of them to understand how they had come to this point.

Following are the most common reasons these family issues get out of hand. Consider how these issues may apply to you and affect your relationship with your parents and spouse. Being honest with yourself will help you in your effort to grow and be a healthier partner in your marriage.

1. *"I want to make my parents proud."* The first issue to consider is the struggle we all have to be accepted by our parents. How important is it to you or your spouse to hear encouraging words from your parents, and how does it make you feel inside? You may be allowing your parents to mistreat your spouse because you fear losing their regard.

2. *"I'm used to being treated this way."* Every parent has shortcomings. Children become used to their parents' imperfections and often learn to accept them. Luke's parents were never very supportive during illnesses. He remembered being in the hospital as a boy for three days, with his parents only visiting occasionally. As an adult, even though he understood cognitively that he was deeply hurt by their neglectful nature, he emotionally accepted them. He told me it "wasn't a big deal" that his parents didn't stay with him at the hospital. But after he spoke these words and I pressed him (particularly when I asked if

he'd ever treat his own children in the same manner), he began to understand how deeply such an experience could hurt a child.

Luke coped with his parents' lack of support by explaining it away: "My dad was real busy building a law firm. My mom had three other kids at home." In doing so, he protected himself from feeling anger at his parents for failing him in a time of need. When Anna was mad at her in-laws for not being supportive of her after her recent miscarriage, Luke didn't share her angry reaction because he had worked for years to quell that anger and explain his parents' behavior away.

The fact that your parents treated you in a certain negative way does not give them the right to treat your spouse in the same manner. As your spouse's partner, you are responsible for protecting your mate.

If your mom likes to make belittling remarks at your expense, perhaps you have found a psychological mechanism to cope with it. But that doesn't mean your spouse has to be belittled. You can surely try to explain to your spouse that he or she shouldn't take those comments personally because your mother acts that way toward everyone. But this remark should never *excuse* inappropriate behavior.

3. **"I depend on them."** Sometimes, you may ignore your parents' hurtful or inappropriate behavior if you are financially dependent on them, whether they are presently helping you out with financial gifts or loans or plan to leave a sum of money to you upon their demise. This becomes a personal decision between each couple as to whether it's worth confronting parents if you fear they'll change their financial arrangements with you because of the confrontation.

4. **"I owe them."** Here the issue is the incredible emotional debt you feel to your parents. This was another part of Luke's problem in confronting his parents. His dad graciously gave him a thriving practice, which he could have sold for huge earnings. Anything his parents did "wrong" to Anna was significantly outweighed in Luke's mind by the good they had done for both him and Anna.

5. **"I don't want to turn on my parents."** When we approach our parents about an issue regarding our spouse, we feel as though we're saying to them, "I've chosen him/her over you." This is especially true when we don't fully agree with our spouse.

These issues can cause you to ignore problems in your marriage caused by your parents. It is usually uncomfortable to confront our parents. We worry they'll take it the wrong way, and feel betrayed and hurt. Perhaps their reaction will cause us to wish we would have said or done nothing in the first place.

Change Your Perspective

Many people, when they think of confronting their parents, picture fighting and arguing that will go nowhere. However, with diplomacy, adult children can usually get across any message without it turning into a world war. Many people are worried that they're deeply hurting their parents just by offering them some insight and asking for some change. Yet, how can you expect to grow in any relationship unless you voice your opinions, concerns, and desires?

Avoid seeing yourself as a child who is mustering the courage to knock down your parents. Instead, see the situation for what it really is: a discussion among adults who want to learn to get along better. You don't have to agree with your spouse's perspective to discuss with your parents that you'd like them to babysit more often, call before they come over, or call more to inquire how your spouse is. You're only trying to help everyone get along better. It makes no difference that if you had married a different spouse, this wouldn't be an issue. It only matters that you married this specific person, that you were brought into this world and raised by certain people, and that all of you must learn to cope and deal with each other in a unique way.

Luke didn't need to chastise his parents or even make them feel judged. He merely needed to point out to them how his wife felt and that, for everyone to have a better relationship, they needed to be more sensitive to this kind of issue. He also had to recognize that Anna was deeply hurt and, like it or not, he needed to be sensitive to her pain. He needed to approach his parents not only because Anna was hurt but because he felt some of her pain and wanted to do what he could to ensure she wouldn't have to suffer similar pain in the future.

If you are even mildly uncomfortable with discussing these kinds of sensitive matters with your parents, plan ahead. Think about the best words to use, and avoid charged and attacking language like, "You always/ never . . ." "How dare you . . ." Consider what your parents may say and how you can best have them understand what you need.

Developing a Healthy Relationship Between Your Spouse and Your Parents

You can prevent friction between your spouse and your parents by making smart choices from the very start of your marriage.

1. *Let your spouse know that he or she is the most important person in your life.* Recognize that for many spouses, in-laws can represent competition. No one can ever cook like your mom or give you the same sense of calm and love. No one can ever give you the feeling of being taken care of like your dad. For most of us, this is true simply because our parents cared for us when we were far more vulnerable than we are now. Thus, we may ascribe to them a certain level of warmth and ability to care for us that no one else, not even our spouse, will ever attain.

   But we're not looking to be taken care of now in the way we were when we were five. Our spouse isn't set up to carry on such a role. We marry because we are, or hope to be, the most special human being in our spouse's life. If you are constantly singing your parents' praises, it may make your spouse feel that he or she can't measure up. There's nothing wrong about saying nice things about your parents. Just make sure your spouse is getting the message that he or she is tops in your life.

2. *When your spouse has a complaint or issue with your parents, try to understand how your spouse is feeling.* If your first impulse is to defend your parents, your spouse may interpret your message as though you feel your parents are more important to you and can do no wrong. In a way, it is *you* who may be causing the strife between your spouse and your parents. As spouses, we often are calmed just by being heard and understood. Your spouse will probably understand if you don't want to interact with your parents over a touchy issue, as long as you don't create the appearance of choosing one over the other. Accept the fact that your parents did something that annoyed or hurt your spouse. Let your spouse know that you are on his or her side in this manner.

   This doesn't mean you have to say or do what your spouse requests. The war between Anna and Luke really began because Luke couldn't empathize with Anna when she vented about his parents. Had he agreed with her and helped her understand how sad he felt for her, she would never have taken her in-laws' actions so seriously. Instead, she felt that not only were these people unkind but that her husband felt it was her fault for taking it all to heart. He made her feel that he had chosen them over her. All Anna needed was to have her feelings understood. This would have made her feel loved, and she could then have coped by feeling the strength of having her husband on her side.

3. *Keep your problems private.* When you call your mom or dad and complain to them about your spouse, you are placing your parents in an incredibly difficult position. A large part of your parents' hopes and dreams is tied up in your happiness. When they get wind of the fact that your spouse isn't making you happy or, worse yet, is making you sad, it arouses a protective instinct that is not easily calmed. So if you tell them about the argument you just had and how your spouse called you horrible names, four hours later you and your spouse may apologize to each other, go out to dinner, and make love. You've gotten over it. But your parents are left with their angry, concerned feelings. And you expect everybody to be loving and happy tomorrow night when they come over for dinner?

Unless you really need to reach out to your parents (to be rescued from an abusive spouse, for example), keep the specifics of your arguments to yourself. If you are concerned about your marriage, seek the help of an objective, impartial therapist. I don't mean you can't mull things over, or ask your parents questions about what they did when they had fights. But watch exposing the details. It's the details of what happens between you and your spouse that rope your parents into feeling upset on your behalf.

4. *Keep your private issues private as well.* If you're very close to your parents, you might be tempted to share intimate sexual or romantic details of your marriage. Don't. These are your private secrets. Furthermore, keep whatever your spouse shares with you about him- or herself private. Do it just because it was asked of you. One husband couldn't understand why his wife got so terribly angry at him after he called her parents to tell them that she was upset with them. He thought he was helping open up the lines of communication between his wife and her parents. But he still needed to respect his wife's wishes as they related to her family and not try to second-guess her reasoning.

5. *Speak highly of your spouse in front of your parents and your spouse.* Your parents want you to be happy and ultimately will come around to your spouse if he or she makes you happy. Let your parents know how thoughtful your spouse was the other day. You get extra bonus points from your spouse when you share these positive attributes, and it creates a positive feeling between your spouse and your parents.

6. *Don't ever throw up something your spouse said about his or her parents in your spouse's face.* When your spouse shares issues about his or her parents, be extremely sensitive and understanding. But never use that information as a weapon, even in your angriest moments. Because our childhood is so powerful, using information about parents in a mean way even once could destroy a trust it took you and your spouse years to develop. It wouldn't be right for

Anna to put down Luke's parents in the middle of a fight by saying, "Your parents couldn't even visit their own son in the hospital." We have to feel safe in opening up old wounds to our spouse.

7. *Choose your spouse over your parents.* It should go without saying, but you have to create a marital atmosphere separate from your parents and family of origin. The date night I spoke of in Secret #6 should not be a weekly trip to your parents' house for the family dinner. You need to create a private marriage with your spouse, a unique bond that your parents will never share and which will lessen any sense of competition between your spouse and parents.

8. *Plan for success.* Plan for get-togethers between your spouse and parents that allow everyone to feel comfortable. If your parents think your spouse is a spendthrift, don't suggest they shop together. If you have questions about how they are getting along, keep visits short. If your spouse isn't at his or her best at the end of the workday, choose a different time to get together with your parents. If your spouse wants the house to look its best when your parents visit, discourage those spontaneous drop-ins.

9. *Be in charge of your relationship with your parents.* When your parents hurt your spouse and you think your parents should be made privy to it, be strong enough to approach them diplomatically and help them and your spouse create a closer relationship. In many instances, this will take time, because much of our trust and love for others develops through shared history.

You have a great deal more to do with whether your spouse and parents will get along or be close than you may think. I've focused on parents because this relationship is often more difficult than other family ties. Because of our bond to our parents, it is much more difficult to deal with issues surrounding them than with those we may have with a sibling, for example. You would likely find it easier to support your spouse when the issue is between your spouse and your sister than if the problem were between your spouse and your mother. However, the suggestions remain the same. The more you help your spouse feel special to you, the more able your spouse will be to deal with family issues.

When You Are Having Problems with Your In-laws

The burden of making the relationship between you and your in-laws work is by no means the sole responsibility of your spouse. Consider your own responsibilities in making this a healthy relationship.

1. *Recognize that your spouse had a relationship with his or her parents full of issues long before you came on the scene.* Don't take it all so personally! Your spouse's lack of support may have absolutely nothing to do with how much he or she loves or cares for you. When you feel your spouse isn't supporting or hearing you as you are discussing your dismay with your in-laws, remind yourself how difficult it may be for your spouse (like so many) to focus on his or her parents' mistakes. In fact, consider how much deeper it may go.

Luke discovered that he didn't want to hear his wife's complaints about his parents because if he let himself understand her pain, it might open his own Pandora's box of pain for the many years he suffered because of his parents' lack of support. He had worked for years (without his ever knowing it) to reduce his anger and disappointment with his parents' behavior. But deep down, he was extremely mad and never wanted to go there. Anna was forcing him to visit that abyss of anger. He thought he was angry at Anna for being too "sensitive," but his angry reaction was far too intense for the situation. He projected his reaction onto Anna because he didn't want to face his own anger that his parents had treated him so poorly when he was younger. His lack of support had nothing to do with his feelings or love of Anna.

2. *Broach any criticism of your in-laws extremely carefully with your spouse.* You (and often your spouse) have no idea what might be tied up in the criticism you're about to make, just as Anna and Luke had no clue that her reaction would probe a deep psychological scar for Luke. If your spouse isn't reacting like his or her usual self, recognize it for what it is, an illogical reaction that points to something deeper that you don't have enough information to understand. Your spouse makes love to you, lives with you, wants to make a family with your, shares everything with you. That should speak far louder than anything else about where your spouse's allegiance lies. Be careful not to come on too strong about your in-laws or else your spouse is likely to take an instinctual protective stance.

Anna would often scream at Luke about how terrible she felt his parents were. She painted them in such a negative light that it made it particularly difficult for Luke to agree with her. He would have felt like he was betraying his parents to agree with her.

When you discuss anything about your in-laws, remember to use diplomacy. There is a great deal of emotional energy tied up in your spouse's relationship with his or her parents. Discuss the subject delicately. Limit the discussion to *your* feelings instead of judging your in-laws as wrong. Anna needed to say something like, "For me, it hurts not to hear from them. I really love them, and their support means a great deal to me." That would have a been a diplomatic yet honest and clear message that Luke could have agreed with and comfortably discussed.

3. *Keep in mind the limitations of your relationship with your in-laws.* I'm always taken aback when a divorced person is angry at his or her ex-in-laws because they haven't offered him or her enough emotional support. Let's face it: they are *your spouse's* parents. As much as their child will do wrong and be imperfect, they are ultimately going to side with and support their flesh and blood. Usually it's a sign of good mental health to be in your child's corner. Sometimes as a son/daughter-in-law you're looking for too much out of this relationship and are angered when it doesn't live up to your expectations.

Your in-laws are not your parents. It's not their responsibility to treat you as if they were your parents. Of course they should be loving and warm and only want to enhance your relationship with your spouse, but this may or may not be.

Anna admitted that she wanted to feel like the true daughter of her in-laws. Because her family lived in a different country, she made the mistake of assuming she could develop this surrogate relationship with her in-laws. It didn't work. And she became extremely frustrated and hurt when she felt her in-laws weren't treating her the way her parents would have under the same circumstances.

Once again, your in-laws aren't your parents. It's not fair to expect them to fulfill that role.

All along, I've been discussing how it may be complicated for your spouse to see the truth about his or her parents. *It may be hard for you to see the truth about your in-laws.* Your in-laws may be better parents to your spouse than your parents are to you. Unconsciously, you may be looking to rag on your in-laws as a way to protect your own parents' inadequacies. You may be overreacting.

4. *Choose your battles wisely.* Because family issues tap into deeper emotional challenges, do your best to reserve any criticisms or suggestions regarding your in-laws for very important issues. If you feel you've been humiliated by your in-laws, discuss it. But if your in-laws didn't call you back when they said they would, deal with it without burdening your spouse with it. Try to overlook as much as you can.

5. *When it's between your in-laws and your spouse, stay out of it.* If you feel your in-laws aren't treating your spouse properly, try not to offer suggestions. It would be better for you to convince your spouse to speak to an objective party like a therapist. When you get involved, you are treading on deep psychological issues. You don't want to be around for the day your spouse takes your advice and it backfires and damages the relationship with his or her parents forever. Respect family ties and neuroses. Help your spouse by listening and being supportive of his or her family frustrations, but when it comes to what to do about it, find other objective help (unless of course, you feel your spouse is being abused in some way).

6. *Don't draw the line in the sand.* Don't request that your spouse never speak to his or her parents ever again because of how your in-laws treated you. Of course, again, I'm not referring to a situation where your in-laws were abusive toward you. But you'd be surprised how may people demand that their spouse show how much they love them by cutting off ties with parents. Don't be the one to come between your spouse and his or her family. If it's even a faint thought in your head, go directly to a therapist.

7. *Remember that your spouse doesn't control his or her family.* Even if your spouse does discuss a matter with his or her parents, it doesn't mean the issue will be resolved to your satisfaction.

When Luke did discuss the matter with his parents, they didn't fully agree with Anna. Anna then blamed Luke for not being forceful enough in pointing out her pain to his parents. Anna had to consider the fact that no matter how forceful Luke might be, his parents would choose how to interpret his remarks. Luke couldn't make them do anything.

8. *Understand the web of financial dependence.* One couple complained to me that the wife's parents demanded to see where every dime was being spent as a condition to the financial gift the couple had requested of them. This upset the husband, who felt his in-laws distrusted his ability to spend wisely. Yet this man had to understand that he had a choice other than being upset with his in-laws. His in-laws surely didn't owe him the money—they were giving it out of the graciousness of their hearts. If the husband felt they weren't being gracious enough, he didn't have to accept the gift.

I don't mean to imply that this son-in-law had no right to discuss the matter with his wife or in-laws. In fact, I thought it was a good idea for him to do so, hear what they were nervous about, and try to find a creative solution. It was the son-in-law's angry feelings that seemed out of line. If you are taking money from your in-laws or are somehow dependent on your in-laws and there's something you don't like about the situation, by all means discuss it diplomatically—if it's worth the battle, as discussed earlier. But if you plan to get mad about it, don't. Instead, don't take the money or whatever it is that's causing you to feel dominated.

9. *Accept what is.* Your in-laws may never change nor want to. You may have to learn to accept them, or to create a relationship in which you feel emotionally protected while still allowing your spouse to enjoy his or her parents. Don't take it personally if your spouse still enjoys a warm and respectful relationship with his or her parents when you have chosen otherwise. Your spouse isn't choosing them over you but is rather holding onto an important psychological family bond.

Anna and Luke are still happily married. Anna has gained realistic expectations, and Luke has gained perspective on his parents. They both found a way to feel together on an issue that had previously torn them apart. The change didn't come from Luke's parents; it came from Luke and Anna.

Parents can offer much encouragement, support, and love to a marriage. Work at developing a satisfying relationship with your in-laws for the sake of your marriage.

Hilda & Robert Stark

MARRIED: 54 YEARS

What Made It Work?

We are very different people, but we expect those differences and compromise around them. We pick and choose the battles.

Family was always a big part of our lives. We never made an important decision without considering how it would affect our family and even the in-laws.

Challenges Facing Couples Today

There needs to be a common goal that both people feel is worthwhile. Dealing with that, as equals, makes the marriage strong.

There isn't as much emphasis today on showing consideration. The two people must be polite and considerate with each other as much as possible. That kindness is worth a great deal.

As I come to the end of this book, I wonder what you will take from it. Will you follow the program weekly, or only read an individual chapter? Will you commit or recommit yourself to making a great marriage? I hope you take away this one point if nothing else: *Believe in your marriage. Only you can make it work.* Don't listen to the skeptics or the statisticians. Make the decision that you will want a great marriage; and do the time-consuming, loving work to create it. It's worth it.

Secret #1

1. University of Chicago survey, as quoted by Jabeen Bhatti in "Infidelity Still Scorned: Cheating Goes On But Remains Frowned Upon"; www.infidelity.com/channels/infidelity.html.
2. Knox, 1984: 50% of men and 20–40% of women. Michael et al.: 1994, 25% of men and 15% of women. Maggie Scarf, *Intimate Partners* (New York: Ballantine, 1996): by age 40, about 50–65% of husbands and 45–55% of wives. Shere Hite, *Women and Love* (New York: Alfred Knopf, 1987): 70% of married women.
3. CTV/Angus Reid Group Poll, September 14, 1997.
4. *The Guardian*, May 2, 1998: Marriage, Cohabitation and Divorce Statistics.
5. Kerby Anderson, www.probe.org/docs/adultery.html.
6. Frank Pittman, *Private Lies: Infidelity and the Betrayal of Intimacy* (New York: Norton, 1989).
7. "Immunized Against Infidelity," *Chicago Tribune*, August 8, 1998.
8. Susan McRae, Oxford Brookes University, research on 300 women.
9. Blumstein, P. W., and Schwartz, P. (New York: Morrow, 1983).
10. Glass, as reported in *Chicago Tribune*, August 8, 1999.
11. Infidelity survey, *New Woman*, October–November, 1986.
12. Stanley, Thomas J., Ph.D., and Danko, William D., Ph.D. *The Millionaire Next Door* (Longstreet Press, 1996).
13. Williams, Virginia, Ph.D., and Williams, Redford, Ph.D. *Life-Skills* (New York: Times Books, 1998).
14. Frank Pittman, *Private Lies: Infidelity and the Betrayal of Intimacy* (New York: Norton, 1989).

Secret #2

1. http://mentalhelp.net/psyhelp/chap10/chap10b.htm.

Secret #4

1. "Shift in Family Lifestyles," *Daily Telegraph*, October 31, 1996.

2. Keicolt-Glaser, J. K., et al., "Negative Behavior During Marital Conflict Is Associated with Immunological Down-Regulation," *Psychosomatic Medicine* 66 (1993): 395–409.
3. National Opinion Poll survey, as reported in *Daily News*, June 10, 1998.
4. Blumstein, P. W., and Schwartz, P. (1983). New York: Morrow.

Secret #5

1. *Harper's*, 1985.
2. Brehm, 1985.

Secret #6

1. http://mentalhelp.not/psyhelp/chap10/chap10i.htm.
2. Michael Medved.
3. *Harper's*, February 1985.

Secret #7

1. Weiten, 1986, p. 386.

Secret #8

1. Doskoch, 1995.
2. Laumann et al., 1994.
3. Easter, 1975.
4. Heiman et al., 1976.

M. Gary Neuman is a Florida-state licensed mental health counselor, a Florida Supreme Court–certified family mediator, a rabbi, creator of the internationally recognized Sandcastles Program® for children of divorce, and author of *Helping Your Kids Cope with Divorce the Sandcastles Way*. His work has received national media coverage including multiple appearances on *The Oprah Show, Today, The View*, and National Public Radio's *Talk of the Nation* as well as appearances on *Dateline, NBC Nightly News, CBS Weekend News*, and *Good Morning America*. He has been written about in numerous publications including *People, Time, Washington Post, Chicago Tribune, Baltimore Sun*, and *Miami Herald*. He has won various awards including the Gold Excellence Award from Parents Publications of America for his syndicated column, "Changing Families," and the Significant Contributions to Families & Children award from the Florida Association for Marriage & Family Therapy.

Gary tours the country, speaking about marital and family issues as well as motivational seminars. He maintains a private practice in Miami, Florida, where he sees adults, children, and families. He lives with his wife and five children in Miami Beach, Florida.

If you would like information on *Emotional Infidelity* seminars or the Sandcastles Program® please write to:

M. Gary Neuman, LMHC
Post Office Box 402691
Miami Beach, Florida 33140-0691
or visit
www.emotionalinfidelity.com
www.sandcastlesprogram.com